LAW AND ORDER IN AMERICAN HISTORY

Kennikat Press
National University Publications
Multi-disciplinary Studies in the Law

General Editor
Rudolph J. Gerber

LAW AND ORDER
IN
AMERICAN HISTORY

edited by

JOSEPH M. HAWES

National University Publications
KENNIKAT PRESS // 1979
Port Washington, N. Y. // London

81-1180

Manufactured in the United States of America

Published by
Kennikat Press Corp.
Port Washington, N.Y. / London

Library of Congress Cataloging in Publication Data

Main entry under title:

Law and order in American history.

(National university publications)
Bibliography: p.

   1. Criminal justice, Administration of—United
States—History—Addresses, essays, lectures.
I. Hawes, Joseph M.
HV8138.L317   364'.973   79-469
ISBN 0-8046-9238-6

CONTENTS

INTRODUCTION
   Joseph M. Hawes   3

1. THE DEVELOPMENT OF AMERICAN CRIMINAL LAW
   Lawrence Friedman   6

2. POVERTY, PAUPERISM, AND SOCIAL ORDER IN THE PREINDUSTRIAL AMERICAN CITY, 1780–1840
   Raymond A. Mohl   25

3. PRISONS IN EARLY NINETEENTH-CENTURY AMERICA: THE PROCESS OF CONVICT REFORMATION
   Joseph M. Hawes   37

4. THE TRIUMPH OF BENEVOLENCE: THE ORIGINS OF THE JUVENILE JUSTICE SYSTEM IN THE UNITED STATES
   Anthony Platt   53

5. COMPLAINANTS AND KIDS: THE ROLE OF CITIZEN COMPLAINANTS IN THE SOCIAL PRODUCTION OF JUVENILE CASES
   Richard M. Brede   77

6. THE RISE AND FALL OF THE POLICEWOMEN'S MOVEMENT, 1905–1975
   Samuel Walker   101

7. REFORMING THE POLICE: ORGANIZATIONAL STRATEGIES FOR THE URBAN CRISIS
   Dennis Smith   112

8. THE KEFAUVER COMMITTEE AND ORGANIZED CRIME
   William Howard Moore   136

9. CRIMINAL JUSTICE HISTORY AS A FIELD OF RESEARCH: A REVIEW OF THE LITERATURE, 1960–1975
   John A. Conley   148

NOTES   162

ACKNOWLEDGMENTS

For their assistance in the development of this project, I wish to thank Richard Brede, John Conley, Lawrence Friedman, Raymond A. Mohl, William H. Moore, Anthony M. Platt, Dennis Smith, and Samuel Walker. My thanks also to Pergamon Press, D. C. Heath and Company, the Kansas Trial Lawyers Association, the University of Texas Press, and Simon and Schuster for permission to reprint some of the selections which follow.

LAW AND ORDER IN
AMERICAN HISTORY

ABOUT THE EDITOR

Joseph M. Hawes is Associate Professor of History at Kansas State University in Manhattan, Kansas. He is the author of *Children in Urban Society* (1971) and several articles.

CONTRIBUTORS

Richard Brede
Department of Sociology
Kansas State University

John Conley
Department of Criminal Justice
University of Wisconsin–Milwaukee

Lawrence Friedman
Marion Rice Kirkwood Professor of Law
Stanford University

Joseph M. Hawes
Department of History
Kansas State University

Raymond A. Mohl
Department of History
Florida Atlantic University

William Moore
Department of History
University of Wyoming

Anthony M. Platt
Berkeley, California

Dennis Smith
School of Public Administration
New York University

Samuel Walker
Department of Criminal Justice
University of Nebraska at Omaha

INTRODUCTION

In a modern and increasingly troubled world, the importance of the history and development of the American criminal justice system may be difficult to see. The problems of our age—particularly those that confront our police, our courts, and our prisons—seem to be too immediate. The study of these problems as academic subjects in a classroom appears to be a decided contrast to the world of day-by-day action. But there is a clear relationship between the classroom and the "real" world. Everything that goes on inside the criminal justice system, for example, depends on a tradition that is older than this country. The purpose of this reader is to demonstrate some of the areas in which the worlds of tradition and contemporary society come together.

Only by understanding the workings of this system—the police, the courts, and the prisons—and how they developed, can a modern student fully appreciate the complexities and interrelationships of the system. Typically the three parts of our criminal justice system have not viewed each other in a favorable light. Courts complain about police disregard for the law, the police complain about court leniency and insistence on technical interpretations of the law; police, courts, and society join in condemning prisons for their failure to reform, and the prisons complain that no one understands their role. This list could go on, but the point is made: the system itself suffers from a lack of perspective. Not that this slim volume purports to provide the necessary perspective. My hope is much more modest. I believe that by reading this book and thinking about some of the issues the selections raise, the reader will come to an appreciation of the growth and development of the complexities and interrelationships of the criminal justice system.

The American criminal jurisprudence system is older than the country itself and has seen a number of changes and modifications. But the basic assumptions on which it operates are rooted in the Anglo-Saxon legal tradition and date from the period before laws were written. Americans and their ancestors have always believed that crime should not pay, that criminals should be punished, and that punishment should serve both as a deterrent to future criminals and as a means of retribution (at least for society) for the wrong done. The Anglo-American legal tradition has also long insisted on a formal process to determine guilt and a public proclamation of both the findings of the process and the punishment meted out.

Since the founding of the English colonies in North America, there have been a number of important developments in the criminal justice system. Probably the most important changes took place during the Enlightenment. The major thrust of Enlightenment philosophy concerning the system of jurisprudence of western Europe was to emphasize both rationality and equality. All men were supposed to be equal before the law; the law was not the whim of any particular man; and punishments were to fit crimes and not the men who committed them. Another assumption which gained wide acceptance during the eighteenth century was the view that criminals could be reformed and restored to society.

The logic of these new assumptions led to the creation of a new (and presumably rational) system of criminal jurisprudence. In the middle of the eighteenth century, Blackstone's *Commentaries* codified the common law for the Anglo-American legal tradition. Criminal courts had gradually come to rely on elaborate rules for the presentation of evidence, an adversary system that gave several advantages to the defendant.

What follows is a set of readings—with brief introductory notes—designed to examine historically and analytically some of the parts and processes of the American criminal justice system. The collection is not comprehensive. No easily portable collection could hope to achieve such a goal. But it presents a number of different methodological perspectives, and provides long-range views of some of the pressing difficulties in the criminal justice system of modern America.

The selections that follow address themselves to the question of how our criminal justice system and society as a whole have interacted. They show how American institutions reflect American social values, and how efforts to understand such institutions as the police, the courts, and prisons must take the larger social context into consideration. One cannot understand the police—let alone reform them—without first realizing that the role the police play and the basis for their existence are rooted in American tradition. The American criminal justice system does not function apart from the society it serves; rather, it mirrors that society—and reflects images from the darker shadows.

The selections are chosen with particular care. The aim is not comprehensive coverage; it is to provide points of view—to provide perspective and a climate for debate rather than final explanations. Consequently, the selections attempt to look at the several parts of the American criminal justice system—courts, police, prisons, criminal law—over time—from the colonial period to the present—through a variety of approaches—the contributors include a sociologist, a criminologist, a political scientist, and several different kinds of historians.

LAWRENCE FRIEDMAN

1

THE DEVELOPMENT OF AMERICAN CRIMINAL LAW

In a selection from his History of American Law, *Lawrence Friedman traces the growth and development of American criminal law. He outlines some of the major changes in criminal statutes and describes the application of the law, noting, for example, that nineteenth-century governors used their pardoning powers frequently. He argues that "in criminal justice . . . the system of checks and balances worked,* par excellence. Judge was played off against jury, state against citizen, county against state; state against federal government." Periodic outbursts of vigilantes testified to the failures and inconsistencies of this system. Friedman devotes a section to these irregular "helpers" of the law and to other "self-help" groups. The major trend in criminal law was the growth of the number of statutes. "Criminal codes, like the dollar," Friedman remarks, "became markedly inflated." Most of Friedman's work details that inflation.*

The American Revolution, whatever else was at issue, fed on resentment against English oppression. Like all revolutions, it was a struggle for control of the reins of power. The criminal law is one of the levers through which governments bring power to bear on the individual citizen. The Revolutionary leaders, quite naturally, identified oppression with abuse of criminal law, and identified the rights of man with basic rights to fair criminal trial. The Bill of Rights, as we have seen, contained a minicode

From *A History of American Law* (New York, Simon and Schuster, 1973), pp. 248–258, 502–517.

of criminal procedure. The late 18th century, moreover, was a period in which intellectuals began to rethink the premises on which criminal law rested. Great reformers—men like Cesare Beccaria, whose *Treatise on Crime and Punishment* was written in Italy in 1764—suggested that the premises were wrong, and argued for a more enlightened criminal law.[1]

Reform ideas left an imprint on the early state constitutions. Section 38 of the liberal Pennsylvania constitution of 1776 stated that "the future legislature" had the duty to "reform" the "penal laws." Punishment must be made "in some cases less sanguinary, and in general more proportionate to the crimes." Enlightened opinion was revolted by the severity of criminal codes. The Bill of Rights outlawed cruel and unusual punishment. "No wise legislature," said the New Hampshire constitution of 1784, "will affix the same punishment to the crimes of theft, forgery and the like, which they do to those of murder and treason.... [A] multitude of sanguinary laws is both impolitic and unjust. The true design of all punishments being to reform, not to exterminate, mankind" (art. 1, sec. 18).

Of course, these were mere exhortations. Real penal reform was not easy to achieve. Pennsylvania's 1776 constitution was not implemented for ten years. In 1786, the death penalty was abolished for robbery, burglary, and sodomy. In 1790, a new, more conservative constitution omitted the clause on penal reform, and the act of 1786 was repealed. But in 1794, Pennsylvania enacted an important, innovative law about murder. The statute stated that the "several offenses, which are included under the general denomination of murder, differ ... greatly from each other in the degree of their atrociousness." The statute then proceeded to distinguish between two different "degrees" of murder. Murder "in the first degree" was murder "perpetrated by means of poison, or by lying in wait, or by any other kind of wilful, deliberate, or premeditated killing, or which shall be committed in the perpetration, or attempt to perpetrate, any arson, rape, robbery, or burglary." All other murder was murder in the second degree. Only murder in the first degree was punishable by death.[2] This idea of degrees was borrowed, first in Virginia, then in Ohio (1824), New York (1827), and Missouri (1835). Some states (for example, Missouri), also divided manslaughter into degrees.

The agitation in Pennsylvania was part of a wider movement, which wanted to do away with the death penalty altogether.[3] In the new penology, the proper goal of criminal law was deterrence of crime and rehabilitation of the criminal. Death was dubious as a general deterrent, and as an agent of rehabilitation, impossible. It had no place, then, in a rational system of law. These propositions were put forward with great vigor, but they probably never commanded a majority of articulate people. Many, then as now, put the case strongly on the other side—people like the "citizens of Albany," who, by petition in 1842, asked the New York legislature not to do away with the death penalty for murder:

The Penalties inflicted by human law, having their foundation in the intrinsic ill-desert of crime, are in their nature vindictive as well as corrective.... Beyond all question the murderer deserves to die.... Death is the fitting penalty for murder; fitting because, in addition to its correspondence with the enormity of the crime, it must needs be more efficacious than any other, in preventing its repetition . . . God has revealed to us His will, both through the laws of reason and conscience, and in His written word, that the murderer should be put to death.[4]

Judging by the results, neither side carried the day. The penal codes changed (quite dramatically in some instances), but the death penalty was not fully abolished in the majority of the states. In 1800, Kentucky restricted it to murder. Edward Livingston had no provision for capital punishment in the penal code he wrote for Louisiana; but the code was never enacted. In 1837, Maine passed a statute which *almost* went the whole distance. A man under sentence of death would be placed in the state prison, in "solitary imprisonment and hard labor." He could not be executed for one year. The whole record of his case had to be certified to the governor; and the death sentence would be carried out only if the governor issued a warrant, under the great seal of the state, "directed to the Sheriff of the County wherein the State Prison shall or may be situated, commanding the said Sheriff to cause execution to be done."[5] In 1845, Michigan became the first state to abolish capital punishment completely, followed by Wisconsin. All other states kept the death penalty; but they drastically shortened their list of capital crimes. In South Carolina, 165 crimes carried the death penalty in 1813. By 1825, only fifty-one, by 1838, only thirty-two, and by 1850, only twenty-two crimes remained in this group.[6]

In these states, the death penalty was not an everyday matter; yet men and women continued to be hanged—and hanged publicly, before morbid or festive crowds. A hanging was an occasion, a spectacle. People eagerly watched the trip to the gallows, eagerly listened to the last speech of the condemned man, when, as sometimes occurred, he spoke from the shadow of the gallows.

Liberal reformers and humanitarians had led the movement to abolish the death penalty; but a strong practical argument could be made for taking the blood out of criminal law. Severe penalties were not terribly effective, because they were not consistently applied. And their very severity distorted the working of criminal justice. A jury, squeezed between two distasteful choices, death or acquittal, often acquitted the guilty. The New Hampshire constitution of 1784, criticizing "sanguinary laws," voiced a fear that "where the same undistinguishing severity is exerted against all offences; the people are led to forget the real distinction in the crimes themselves, and to commit the most flagrant with as little compunction as they do those of the lightest dye" (part 1, art. 18). In South Carolina, the typical defendant in a homicide case was either acquitted or found guilty only of manslaughter. In one district, thirty-three men were tried on murder indictments between 1844 and 1858. Eighteen were acquitted, ten found guilty of manslaughter; only five were convicted of murder. . . . [7]

A system of criminal justice is more than rules on paper. It is also a plan for distribution of power among judges, jurors, legislators, and others. In American legal theory, jury power was enormous, and subject to few controls. There was a maxim of law that the jury was judge both of law and of fact in criminal cases. This idea was particularly strong in the first, Revolutionary generation, when memories of royal justice were fresh. In some states the rule lasted a long time, and in Maryland, the slogan was actually imbedded in the constitution. [8] But the rule came under savage attack from some judges and other authorities. There was fear that the rule, if taken seriously, would destroy the "chances of uniformity of adjudication." It also threatened the *power* of judges. By the end of the period, many states, by statute or decision, had repudiated the doctrine. [9] In any event, the maxim probably meant very little in practice. Juries did not divide their verdicts into separate bundles of fact and of law. The maxim did recognize explicitly that the jury held ultimate power to make decisions about crime and criminal law. Juries were not afraid to exercise this power. In South Carolina, according to Jack K. Williams, "the same jury which would change a murderer's indictment to manslaughter would condemn a common thief to the gallows without hesitation," if so inclined. [10] On the other hand, the jury could be quite cavalier about the letter of the law, not to mention the facts of the world. In *State* v. *Bennet* (1815), a South Carolina jury found as fact that the goods John Bennet had stolen were worth "less . . . than twelve pence," even though all the witnesses had sworn they were "of much greater value." This "pious perjury" let the jury find Bennet guilty of petty larceny, rather than grand larceny, which would have sent him to the gallows. The appeal court affirmed the jury's right to do as it pleased. [11] This same process had made England's long list of capital crimes random and toothless in operation. This type of behavior has been called jury lawlessness; but there is something strange in calling lawless a power so carefully built into law. Jury power meant that a measure of penal "reform" could take place without formal change in legal institutions. Jerome Hall has suggested that as social attitudes toward criminals and crime begin to change, the changes first appear in the administration of criminal justice; penal "reform"—enacted laws and new rules—follows as a "ratification of practices" already developed.[12]

The South Carolina experience, studied by Jack Williams, shows that few people were convicted in the 19th century, compared to the number indicted. Even fewer men were actually punished, because the governor used his pardoning power lavishly. Today, indictment usually leads to conviction, and pardons are relatively rare. Police and prosecutors filter out the weakest cases; most of these never get to court. Most of those accused plead guilty to the charge brought against them, or to some lesser crime. Judge and jury played *more* of a role in the screening process in the 19th century, partly because police and prosecutor staffs were weak. They were at best on the brink of professionalism. Cities did not even have police forces until late in the period, if at all—in Boston not until 1838, under Mayor Samuel Eliot; before that, the watchmen and constables of Boston did not and could not hope to cope with "the incendiary, burglar, and the lawlessly violent."[13] In rural areas, there was no professional enforcement at all.

The jury system had its faults. Outcomes were unprofessional and unpredictable. The rules of evidence were one way the law attempted to keep the jury under control. . . . A system of checks and balances, in the trial process, grew almost cancerously. It was in criminal justice that the system of checks and balances worked, *par excellence*. Judge was played off against jury, state against citizen, county against state, state against federal government. Every master had to submit to another master. Whatever its benefits, such a system, from the standpoint of any particular group, had the defect that one could never be sure that policies, however well formulated, would be actually carried out. This was one reason for the periodic outbursts of lynching and vigilantes. These cracks in law and order were no accidents. The degeneracy (or overvigor) of judge, jury, state, or national authority sometimes reached the point where justice (as defined by the vigilantes) demanded that "the public" take the law into its hands. Vigilantes and lynch mobs, in other words, were pathologies of a system with too many checks and balances for public opinion. Vigilantes flourished in the South. Here the legal culture nurtured them. Lawlessness was a way of life; violent crime was common; men habitually walked the streets carrying guns. Vigilantes were the logical negative of the governor's power to pardon. The pardoning power was itself one kind of check and balance; the mob was another. In Montgomery, Alabama, for example, a vigilante group called the Regulating Horn sprang up in the 1820's. The men blew horns to summon the rest of the group. They gave suspects a hearing on the spot. If they found a man "guilty," they tarred and feathered him, and rode him out of town on a rail. Violence can be an addictive habit; with success came excess: the Regulating Horn lost legitimacy, and community tolerance evaporated. After that, they were doomed to fail. . . .[14]

The strength of the idea of checks and balances was also one of the factors that impelled penal law toward codification. To build up the power of citizen against state, rules of criminal law had to be open and knowable. The criminal law therefore tended to become highly codified. Codification, as the Puritan magistrates found, can be looked at as a means of controlling authorities. The same theory was behind codification of penal law in Europe, after the shock waves of the French Revolution.

The common law was supposed to rest on the community's moral consensus, refined by the collective mind of the judges. Courts had invented and elaborated doctrines of crime at common law, just as they had elaborated other sorts of doctrine. But the common-law decisions were in a sense retroactive; and judges were less subject to public control than legislators. Statutory rules, on the other hand, were prospective only; and they were enacted by the people's representatives. The way the king's judges had behaved, in England and in the colonies, made it easy to disapprove of the power of judges to invent and define new crimes. There were instances on record where the concept was used in this country, too. In *Kanavan*'s case (Maine, 1821), the defendant dropped the dead body of a child into the Kennebec River.[15] No statute covered the case explicitly; but the highest court of Maine affirmed the man's conviction. An appeal court in Tennessee sustained an indictment for "eavesdropping" in 1808.[16] But the concept of the common-law crime was in retreat during the whole of the 19th century.

There were special reasons to object to the idea of a *federal* common-law crime. The concept was completely and early exploded. The case was *United States* v. *Hudson and Goodwin* (1812),[17] defendants were indicted for "a libel on the President and Congress of the United States, contained in the Connecticut Courant of the 7th of May, 1806, charging them with having in secret voted $2,000,000 as a present to Bonaparte, for leave to make a treaty with Spain." No statute covered such an "offense" against the federal government. The Supreme Court held that no federal court was "vested with jurisdiction over any particular act done by an individual in supposed violation of the peace and dignity of the sovereign power. The legislative authority of the Union must first make an act a crime, affix a punishment to it, and declare the court that shall have jursidiction of the offense." If federal prosecutors and judges could define crimes for themselves and punish them, enormous (and in this instance, unwelcome) power would accrue to the central government.

Codification was only a partial curb on the power of the judges. Judges lost power to invent new crimes; but the common law still *defined* the precise meaning and application of old crimes, like rape or theft. The strong, sometimes freewheeling power of judges to interpret the laws remained. The judges developed and used *canons of construction*—rules of interpretation—that maximized their discretion and authority. One such canon declared that penal statutes had to be narrowly construed, that is, limited to the smallest possible compass their language would bear. The canon made some sense; otherwise, retroactive, judge-made criminal law could be brought in through the back door, so to speak. Only those acts ought to be crimes which were plainly so labeled. Courts should not widen the coverage of a penal law beyond the unvarnished meaning of its words. Criminal law had to be known and knowable, without subtlety and artifice:

The law to bind [the prisoner] should first be *prescribed;* that is, not only willed by the legislature, but should also be announced, and clearly and plainly published, that every citizen, if he would, could learn its meaning and know the measure of its punishment.

This was said by counsel at the trial of one Timothy Heely of New York, charged with stealing a lottery ticket. The statute made it a crime to steal a "public security." The court agreed with counsel that a state lottery ticket was not a public security, and let Heely go.[18] The canon of strict construction, in theory, expressed the humble role of judges, subordinate to the people and their elected representatives. But there was no short-run control over whether courts used the canon or avoided it. Hence its application was in fact if not theory a matter of discretion. And what was or was not a strict or narrow construction was itself a difficult question, which gave still more discretion to the courts.

In English law, treason had been a complex, protean concept, used to suppress all sorts of persons or groups defined as enemies of state. It was treason to levy war on the kingdom; it was treason, too, to violate the king's (unmarried) eldest daughter. It was treason to alter or clip coins; or to color "any silver current coin . . . to make it resemble a gold one."[19] When war broke out, the colonists seized this terrible weapon for themselves. New York, for example, passed a fire-breathing law in 1781; anyone who preached, taught, spoke, wrote, or printed that the king had or ought to have dominion over New York thereby committed a "Felony without Benefit of Clergy," punishable by death or by banishment.[20] When the war ended passions cooled. Maryland, Massachusetts, New York,

Pennsylvania and Vermont all provided, in their early constitutions, that the legislatures had no power to attaint any person of treason.[21] The federal Constitution radically restricted this king of crimes: it defined its content, once and for all, and hedged treason trials about with procedural safeguards. Treason against the United States "shall consist only in levying War against them, or in adhering to their Enemies, giving them Aid and Comfort. No Person shall be convicted of Treason unless on the testimony of two Witnesses to the same overt Act, or on Confession in open Court."[22]

Treason was a special crime, with unusual political significance. The shrinking law of treason mirrored a prevailing theory of criminal law. A total state, even a semitotal state, has trouble distinguishing between treason and ordinary crime. In the Soviet Union, for example, it is a crime against the state, severely punished, to deal in currency, or to steal factory property (which is all state-owned). The United States took a strikingly different path. It shrank the concept of state crime to an almost irreducible minimum. The men who drafted penal codes were willing to accept a lot of slippage in enforcement, to protect the innocent, and (even more) to keep the government in check. No doubt much of this liberality was only on paper. The Sedition Law of 1798, passed by a nervous, partisan federal government, showed that historical fears were not groundless.[23] But the theory helped determine how government was structured, and what resources government was given to do its job.

Not that the criminal law was not important in the United States. By any measure, the *number* of acts defined as criminal grew steadily from 1776 to 1847, despite the decline in the use of the common-law crime. The classic crimes (theft, murder, rape, arson) remained on the books. There were great numbers of economic crimes, and laws defining public morality; and new ones were constantly added. The revised statutes of Indiana of 1831—a fair sample—made it a crime to allow epsom salts "to remain unenclosed and exposed to the stock, cattle or horses of the neighborhood." It was a crime in Indiana to "alter the mark or brand" of domestic animals; to sell retail liquor without a license; to ferry a person across a creek or river for money, within two miles of any licensed ferry. It was a crime, too, to keep "either of the gaming tables called A.B.C., or E.O. Tables, billiard table, roulette, spanish needle, shuffle board, [and] faro bank." It was an offense, punishable by fine, to "vend any merchandize which may not be the product of the United States, without having a license." Profane swearing was a crime; so was "open and notorious adultery or fornication." Major statutes often included, as a final clause, a provision punishing violation or frustration of the policy expressed.

One usually thinks of a crime as an act which offends some deep-seated moral sense. But crime can also be neutrally defined, as any behavior punished at public expense and through criminal process. An unpaid seller, or a person who slips on the ice, sues the buyer or landowner at his own expense, and on his own initiative. The costs of punishing a murderer are socialized, partly because violence is thought to be a danger to everyone, not only the victim's little circle of family and friends. Murder was once privately enforced. But private justice was not always effective, and when it was, it escalated the letting of blood. Regulatory and economic crimes are enforced at public expense and initiative, but for rather different reasons. If a man sells ten baskets of defective strawberries to ten different people, it would not pay any one buyer to sue the seller. The lawsuit would eat up far more money than could possibly be recovered. If the sheriff and district attorney—public servants, paid by the state—had the power to enforce the rules, they might deter the seller's behavior far more effectively. This is quite apart from whether or not selling spoiled strawberries is considered especially immoral or not. Criminal process, then, can act as a king of crude, undifferentiated administrative agency. This (largely inarticulate) conception was one of the reasons for the flowering of the regulatory crime. Economic crimes never gave trial courts much work. They never captured the imagination of the public. Criminal provisions of regulatory laws were not always even *meant* to be rigorously enforced. They were meant more as a last resort, as a threat to persistent and flagrant violators. When administrative justice developed in later generations, some of these "crimes" actually disappeared from the books.

The *relative* rise of the economic crime, on the statute books, was probably an external sign of a real change in the center of gravity of the criminal law. If crime was sin—fornication, blasphemy—before the Revolution, it gradually shifted to concern for protection of private property and furtherance of the community's economic business. William E. Nelson's research, in Massachusetts, supports this notion. Nelson found that prosecutions for fornication, Sunday violation, and the like declined after 1780; prosecutions for theft, on the other hand, rose. By 1800, more than forty per cent of all prosecutions in seven counties studied were for theft; only seven per cent for offenses against morality. The criminal "was no longer envisioned as a sinner against God, but rather as one who preyed upon the property of his fellow citizens."[24] From this attitude, however, it was a short step to the instrumental use of criminal law, the use of criminal law, in other words, as a means of fostering economic growth. . . .

At one time, most lawyers were generalists, and handled criminal matters along with civil suits. Even so prestigious and prominent a business lawyer as Alexander Hamilton did criminal work. In the West, and in small towns generally, criminal law remained a staple of the practice. Later in the century, the bar in major cities became more specialized. There developed both professional criminals and a professional criminal bar. It was not necessarily a dignified bar; and it lacked the prestige of the bar that served big business. Some small-scale lawyers eked out a living by gathering crumbs of practice in the lower criminal courts. A few big-city lawyers made a more handsome, and sometimes less honorable, living. In New York, the "magnificent shyster," William F. Howe, flourished between 1875 and 1900. He was a member of the infamous firm of Howe and Hummel; he defended hundreds of madams, pickpockets, forgers, as well as the most notorious murderers of his day. Howe's specialty was gilded courtroom oratory, judiciously backed up by perjury, bribery, and blackmail.[25]

The leaders and money-makers of the criminal bar were always flamboyant, though not always unscrupulous. Howe and Hummel were not afraid to advertise their wares. Over their "shabby but conspicuous offices . . . hung not the modest shingle of a firm of counsellors-at-law but a sign thirty or forty feet long and three or four feet high . . . illuminated at night."[26] The organized bar gradually stamped out the practice of openly asking for business through advertisements and illuminated signs. A criminal lawyer had no retainer business, and few repeats. This left word of mouth one of the few ways he could build a practice. This fact made the criminal bar, if anything, more flamboyant than otherwise, since it had to have publicity or die.

The criminal law itself, quite naturally, underwent considerable change in the later 19th century. It became and remained by and large a matter of statute. The concept of the common-law crime, as we have seen, had been wiped out in federal law. The common-law crime decayed on the state level, too. As of 1900, most states still *technically* recognized the possibility of a common-law crime. But some states had statutes that specifically abolished the concept. These statutes stated bluntly that all crimes were listed in the penal code, and nothing else was a crime. In some states, the courts *construed* their penal codes as (silently) abolishing common-law crime. Where the concept survived, it was hardly ever used; the penal codes were in fact complete and exclusive.

The living law was somewhat more complicated. The New York penal code (passed in 1881) provided that "no act . . . shall be deemed criminal or punishable, except as prescribed or authorized by this Code, or by some statute of this state not repealed by it." This was plain abolition. Yet the penal code had a sweeping catchall clause: "A person, who willfully and wrongly commits any act, which seriously injures the person or property of another, or which disturbs or endangers the public peace or health, or which openly outrages public decency or is injurious to public morals . . . is guilty of a misdemeanor."[27] Obviously, prosecutors and courts could have almost as much power under this language as under the reign of common-law crime. In fact, the section was probably little used, as little as the concept of common-law crime, in those states which retained it.

In *Hackney* v. *State* (1856),[28] an Indiana case, Hackney, the defendant, had been arrested for maintaining a "public nuisance"; this consisted of "keeping a ten-pin alley, and procuring for gain certain disorderly persons to meet there, rolling balls night and day, cursing, quarreling, drinking, and making great noises." Indiana had abolished the common-law crime. There was no statute on the books which said anything specific about ten-pin alleys, but maintaining a public nuisance was a statutory misdemeanor. The question was, what was a nuisance? There was a body of common-law decisions, defining nuisance; the court explicitly denied that these cases were relevant. The common law was not to be used, even as a source of interpretation. Instead, the court turned to an Indiana statute, which defined "nuisance" as anything "injurious to health, or indecent, or offensive to the senses." This, said the court, could cover Hackney's conduct; they affirmed his conviction by the lower court.

The New York statute, and the *Hackney* case, raise the suspicion that there was more to the death of the common-law crime than meets the eye. What died was the overt, unabashed power of courts to pull out new crimes from the folkways. It was killed by that pervasive feature in American legal culture, horror of uncontrolled power. Lawmakers believed that courts should be guided—ruled—by the words of objective law, enacted by the peoples' representatives; nothing else should be a crime. But at the same time, the courts found covert substitutes for their lost jurisdiction. First, they benefited from vague general clauses, like the one in the New York Penal Code. Indeed, a camouflaged power was more suitable to the courts, more soothing, more protective, than a naked power at common law. Second, they allowed themselves more amplitude in interpreting the law. They rejected the extremist language of *Hackney*, about common-law interpretation. But they retained the flair for "interpretation of statutes" that *Hackney* signified. There was an old maxim that courts had a duty to construe penal statutes narrowly. Courts constantly referred to this maxim; yet even this helped judges elbow their way into power. It was the judges who decided, after all, what was narrow and what was wide.

As we have seen, countervailing power, one of the great themes of American history, was particularly strong in criminal justice. Trial judge, appellate judge, jury, legislature stood in uneasy balance. The Constitution, the Bill of Rights, and the 14th Amendment struck some sort of balance between federal and state power. At least in legal theory, criminal trials were hedged about by many safeguards. A stern law of evidence, juries, and meticulous attention to procedure were thought to be essential, to protect the life and liberty of the citizen. And the "hypertrophy" of procedure was, as we saw, at its most extreme in appeals from criminal trials.

The picture that emerged was one of precision, rigidity, care. Crimes were only those acts clearly engraved in the statute books. Laws were to be strictly construed. There was no margin for error at the trial. Probably no field of law, however, was quite so two-faced. The ideal picture of criminal justice must be contrasted with the real criminal law, parts of which were blunt, merciless, and swift, other parts of which simply ignored whole kingdoms of crime. It was true that most appeals from criminal cases succeeded; but few were appealed—one half of one per cent of total prosecutions in Chippewa County, Wisconsin; only five per cent of the cases before the Wisconsin supreme court were criminal appeals.[29] It was an aspect of living law that the safeguards did not safeguard everybody; it was also an aspect of living law that many more were arrested than convicted, and that in the view of some the law was too soft, rather than too hard. The regular criminal law had many irregular helpers. The Ku Klux Klan rode in the South, from 1867 to the early 1870's; it burned and pillaged, and punished blacks and whites who transgressed against the Klan's concept of a proper social order. In the slums and tenderloins of big cities, street gangs, prostitutes, and thieves were mostly left to run their own underworld, enforce their own rules, govern their own society. Force was the only kind of law that ever penetrated this jungle. Alexander S. Williams, of the New York police force, became famous in the 1870's, because he "invoked the gospel of the nightstick," and organized "a strong arm squad." Patrolling the Gas House District, Williams "clubbed the thugs with or without provocation." Charges were preferred against Williams no less than eighteen times; but the board of police commissioners "invariably acquitted" him. He justified his "furious clubbing" by the observation that "there is more law in the end of a policeman's nightstick than in a decision of the Supreme Court."[30]

The vigilantes of the West, those self-help groups, were in some ways following an old American tradition. The first American vigilantes, the South Carolina regulators, appeared in 1767.[31] But the movement really flourished after 1850. As we have seen, the most famous, and the models for the rest, were the two Vigilance Committees of San Francisco (1851 and 1856). Vigilante justice cropped up throughout California; in Colorado, Nevada, Oregon, Texas, and Montana; and generally in the West. "Swift and terrible retribution is the only preventive of crime, while society is organizing in the far West," wrote Thomas J. Dimsdale, chronicler of the Montana vigilantes, in 1865.[32] All told, there were hundreds of vigilante movements. One hundred and forty-one of them took at least one human life. The total death toll has been put at 729. Virtually all of these were in the West, and before 1900. Texas was the bloodiest vigilante state; and the peak decade was the 1860's.[33]

The vigilantes were not the only groups that engaged in private criminal justice. Claims clubs in the Middle West, and miners' courts in the sparse, bleak reaches of the Far West, constructed their own version of property law and punished offenders. Later in the century, "Judge Lynch" presided at an all too frequent court in the South and the border states. Mobs, in the 1890's, tortured, hanged, and sometimes burned alive black men accused of assault, murder, or rape. They sometimes snatched their victims from jail, furious at delay. Lynch mobs and vigilantes had their own sense of mission. Some of them, hungry for legitimacy, parodied the regular written law; they had their own "judges" and "juries," their own quick and summary trials. They punished crimes without names or without remedies, and enforced public policy as they saw it. They were responses to the absence of law and order (as in Montana), the disorganization as a defeated society (as in the South), or the feebleness or venality of regular government. They also were a much cheaper form of punishment than tax-fed trials and long prison sentences. A newspaper writer, after a vigilante lynching in Golden, Colorado, in 1879, reported that "the popular verdict seemed to be that the hanging was not only well merited, but a positive gain for the county, saving at least five or six thousand dollars."[34]

The Southern lynch mobs were the most savage and the least excusable of all the self-help groups. Their law and order was naked racism, no more. Their real complaint against law was that the courts were too careful and too slow; that some guilty prisoners went free; and that the lesson for the rest of the blacks was not sharp enough. The Western vigilantes, on the other hand, have become almost folk heroes; it is usual to regard them with sympathy, or as a necessary evil, or even as a form of popular democracy. The historian Hubert H. Bancroft praised the vigilance committees lavishly. Indeed, he loved all forms of Western justice. Vigilance, he wrote, is an "expression of power on the part of the people in the absence or impotence of law." It is "the exercise informally of their rightful power by a people wholly in sympathy with existing forms of law." It is "the keen knife in the hands of a skillful surgeon, removing the putrefaction with the least possible injury to the body politic." The San Francisco Committee of 1856, for example, was just such a surgeon: "Never before in the history of human progress have we seen, under a popular form of government, a city-full rise as one man, summoned by almighty conscience, attend at the bedside of sick law . . . and perform a speedy and almost bloodless cure."[35] It was certainly true that public opinion was not overly severe on the "beloved rough-necks"; many who joined the vigilantes were leaders of their communities, or became prominent in later life; they found that a vigilante past was no disgrace, no impediment.

Under some conditions, self-help law can make a persuasive case. The Donner party, in 1846, tried, convicted, and banished a man named James Reed, who had killed John Snyder in a fight. The travelers were months away from Missouri—in Mexican territory, in fact—and hundreds of miles from any court, or judge, or arm of any state.[36] The ideology of self-help was strong, too, in the 19th century; and government was stingy. It is no surprise, then, that a Wisconsin law of 1861 authorized the "organization of societies for mutual protection against larcenies of live stock." The societies were given power to choose "riders" who might "exercise all the powers of constables in the arrest and detention of criminals."[37] A similar law in Pennsylvania in 1869 incorporated the "Spring Valley Police Company of Crawford County," a "company for the recovery of stolen horses or other property." Its members were to have the same power of arrest and detention as policemen of Philadelphia.[38] The anti-horsethief movement arose "spontaneously" after the Revolutionary War. From the 1850's on, the societies sought, and got, legislative authorization. They lasted until better public police and the automobile put them out of business. In their heyday, they had more than 100,000 members.[39]

Private law enforcement was an attractive idea. A statute of 1865, in Pennsylvania, gave railroads the power to employ their own police. An act of 1866 extended this law to any "colliery, furnance or rolling-mill," thus creating the "coal and iron police." The state here authorized "a veritable private army," at the request of "powerful interests." These private police—they existed in other states, as well—became anathema to the unions. They were "toughs," strikebreakers, "necessarily the enemy of organized labor."[40] But it was not until the 1930's that they were finally abolished in Pennsylvania.

Over the years, the criminal codes, like the dollar, became markedly inflated. Traditional crimes—treason, murder, burglary, arson, and rape—stayed on the books; and new crimes, some of which seem quite unnecessary, were added. Roscoe Pound found fifty crimes in 1822 in the Rhode Island penal code. The number had grown to 128 crimes by 1872....[41]

The steady growth of statutory crimes continued. Few were ever repealed; fresh ones were constantly added. In 1891 it became a misdemeanor in Indiana to "willfully wear the badges or buttonaire [sic] of the Grand Army of the Republic" or other veterans groups, unless one was "entitled to use or wear the same" under the rules and regulations of the organization. Another law required road supervisors or "Gravel Road Superintendents" to cut hedges along the highways; failure to do so was an offense, and was punishable by fine. It became a felony in that year for officers of public institutions to "purchase, sell, barter or give away to any other officer ... or to appropriate to his or their own use any of the slops or offal of any of the said public institutions." Railroads had to employ flagmen at railroad crossings; for failure to comply, money penalties were prescribed.[42] About a dozen more distinct items of behavior became criminal, in 1891, and other, older crime laws were amended.

In every state, every extension of governmental power, every new form of regulation brought in a new batch of criminal law. Every important statute, governing railroads, banks, and corporations, or the marketing of milk, cheese, fruit, or coal; or concerning taxation, or elections and voting, or licensing an occupation, trailed along with it at the end a sentence or two imposing criminal sanctions on violators. No doubt many of these stern laws were not criminally enforced at all; violators were rarely or never tried; appeals and reported cases practically did not exist. The full discussion of these statutes belongs more to the story of government regulation of business than to criminal justice.

These regulatory crimes should not, however, be written off completely. The multiplication of economic crimes did not mean, necessarily, that people looked on sharp business behavior with more and more sense of moral outrage. It meant, rather, a decision to socialize responsibility for enforcing certain parts of the law. This process began long before the Civil War. Crimes are, among other things, wrongful acts punished wholly at the expense of the state, and largely on the state's initiative. The states, and the federal government, were invoking criminal law in one of its historic functions—a low-level, low-paid administrative aid. In New York, in 1898 an amendment to the penal code made it a misdemeanor to sell articles as "sterling silver," unless they consisted of 925/1000ths of pure silver.[43] If a silver merchant sold a coffee pot or creamer to a housewife, and cheated her, it had long been true that she had the right to bring an action against him. But nine times out of ten, the cost of the lawsuit, compared to the dollars at stake, hardly merited the trouble. In a criminal action, enforcement and punishment were entirely at public expense. The enforcing officials, of course, were only the usual array of policemen, district attorneys, and judges. They were not specialists in regulatory crimes, and rarely bothered with them. Criminality was often only a halfway stage on the road to administrative law—to professional, specialized policing of some area of economic life.

The Indiana statutes, as we have seen, retained the letter of the law on many old crimes against morality and public decency. In most states, some of these were only fitfully enforced; others were dead letters. But aspects of public morality remained controversial, and engendered new outbursts of law. Liquor control was a constant fountain of law. In 1887, six states were legally dry: Iowa, Kansas, Maine, New Hampshire, Rhode Island, and Vermont.[44] The temperance movement fought hard, had many triumphs, endured many defeats, before its last and most famous victory, national prohibition, in 1920. Joseph Gusfield has argued that the point of the liquor laws lay less in their real effect—less in whether or not people drank—than in whether the law, the official norm, allowed them to drink. The struggle, in short, was symbolic, not instrumental. The issue was: whose norms were dominant, whose should be labeled right and true: those of old-line, middle-class, rural Protestant America, or those of Catholics, immigrants, the working class, dwellers in cities, who drank without shame? Whether these newcomers drank more or less than old Americans mattered less than their attitude toward drink. . . .[45]

The criminal law, legitimate and illegitimate, assumes that there is a reality, called crime, on which law operates. Obviously, in one sense, a society chooses for itself how much crime it wants. When an act is declared criminal, all its actors are committing crime. In 1900, there was vastly more criminal law on the books than in 1850 or 1800, hence in this sense probably vastly more crime. But those who worry about the crime rate are usually concerned, not with economic crime, but with the classic crimes of violence and social disruption, murder, robbery, assault. These are enforced much more systematically and with greater use of public resources than other kinds of crime. The definitions of these crimes remained more or less constant during the century; or at least constant enough for meaningful comparisons, if only the figures were at hand.

Some facts are known about crime in the real world in the 19th century. What evidence there is suggests that the crime rate for serious crimes, at least since 1860, gradually declined.[46] There was proportionately *less* violence, murder, assault in the 1970's than a century before. Roger Lane's research, for 19th-century Massachusetts, saw a marked falling-off in jail commitments, from 333 per 100,000 population to 163, between 1860 and 1960. The social investment in crime-fighting increased; so, too, did the worry and the tumult. The basic reason may be that violent crime, particularly in the cities, becomes less tolerable the more society is one and interconnected. The city is the heart of modern society; society is governed from the city; the economy depends on city life. The city is the place where people are most interdependent; where they are most confronted with strangers, and where their lives, property, and health are most at hazard. The more a society is urban, industrial, and interdependent, the more there is division of labor in the economy, the less the society can tolerate violent crime. Crime is bad for business, and bad for the social order. The city civilizes and tames, to a certain extent; for this reason violence has diminished. But by the same token crime has not gone down fast enough; the public demand for law and order more than keeps pace with the supply.[47]

The violent crimes were also the crimes of mystery and drama; the crimes that provided raw material for novels, poems, and plays; the crimes par excellence, as the public thought of them. Pamphlets, trial transcripts, last words of condemned men were part of American popular culture. There were hundreds of these fugitive writings: John Erpenstein, who gave his wife a bread-and-butter sandwich, liberally sprinkled with arsenic, was credited with writing the "Life, Trial, Execution and Dying Confession of John Erpenstein, Convicted of Poisoning His Wife, and Executed in Newark, N. J., on March 30, 1852. Written by himself and translated from the German." Professor John W. Webster murdered Dr. George Parkman, in the Harvard Medical School, in 1849; publishers rushed many versions of the background and trial of his sensational crime into print. The Fall River tragedy—the murder of Lizzie Borden's parents in 1892—has enlivened American literature ever since.[48]

It was this type of crime, too, which evoked the raw hatred that could mold a mob and lead a man to be lynched. It was this type of crime in which trial by jury was frequent, and in which the jury was free to apply its "unwritten laws"; in which justice was, in theory, tailored to the individual case. Here, too, were the cases in which the defense of insanity was invoked. Juries, to be sure, probably went their own way; they excused men for insanity, or did not excuse, in accordance with their own moral code and common sense, rather than the science of their time. But those scientific notions had at least a marginal and indirect effect. And in the 19th century, almost for the first time, lawyers and doctors engaged in a grand and continuing debate about the meaning of criminal responsibility, and the scope of the insanity defense.

The dominant definition of legal insanity was the so-called M'Naghten rule, named after a mad Englishman, for whose case the rule was first announced, in 1843.[49] Simply put, a defendant could not be excused from responsibility unless he was "labouring under such a defect of reason . . . as not to know the nature and quality of the act he was doing; or . . . that he did not know what he was doing was wrong." This "right or wrong" test was a pleasing platitude: it seemed to soothe the moral sense of the legal community; in any event it won rapid acceptance. In a few American states, this "right or wrong" test was supplemented by another, the "irresistible impulse" or "wild beast" test. If a man, said Chief Justice John F. Dillon of Iowa in 1868, knew that his act was wrong, but "was driven to it by an uncontrollable and irresistible impulse, arising, not from natural passion, but from an insane condition of the mind" he was not to be held responsible.[50] The idea of irresistible impulse strikes the modern ear as somewhat romantic, not to say medically absurd; but the wild-beast test was broader than the M'Naghten test alone; and some of the best psychiatrists of the day believed in irresistible impulse.[51] A third rule stood all by itself in New Hampshire. This was Chief Justice Charles Doe's rule, enunciated in *State* v. *Pike* (1869). Here the test was no test at all: the question to be answered in each case was whether the criminal act was the "offspring or product of mental disease. . . ." Neither delusion, nor knowledge of right and wrong was, as a matter of law, a test of mental disease. Rather, all symptoms and "all tests of mental disease" were "purely questions of face," within the province and power of the jury alone to determine and decide.[52]

Arguments over these various "tests" were really arguments over the form of stereotyped instructions, to be read to the jury. What distinguished the tests was the degree of autonomy they (apparently) gave to the jury. Whether the jury listened, or cared, or understood is another question. In a few great cases, the tests acted as a dark and bloody battle-ground for war between contending schools of psychiatry. Most notable was the weird trial of Charles Guiteau, who murdered President Garfield in 1881. Guiteau's behavior, before and after (and during) the trial, was bizarre, to say the least; but probably no test, however worded, could have persuaded the jury not to send the President's killer to the gallows.[53]

It would not be totally wrong to interpret the debate as evidence of moral sensitivity among those concerned with the criminal law—at least a horror of putting incompetent people to death. But, as we have seen, the criminal law was a two-edged sword. The other edge was the regulatory edge, and here, if anything, moral coloring faded away. The criminal law was both more and less than the moral steward of society. Small economic crimes—shooting a deer out of season—did not require a guilty and dangerous mind like murder and rape. To get a felony conviction, for crimes against property, the prosecution at common law had to show a specific intent to act illegally. Injury to property was not a crime unless it was malicious; there "had to be a definite motive of hatred, revenge, or cruelty, as well as an intent to cause the injury." In the 19th century, this requirement loosened. It was the behavior that was dangerous, not just the mind of the actor; the behavior had to be stamped out. "The demand for protection of the wealth of the country . . . has led to liability for intentional but nonmalicious injury to property."[54] Motive or attitude was secondary. In the New York penal code of 1881, the fact that a defendant "intended to restore the property stolen or embezzled, is no ground of defense, or of mitigation of punishment."[55] The code made it a crime to destroy or injure property "unlawfully or wilfully" (sec. 654).[56] Similarly, "metaphysical difficulties" about whether a corporation could form an "intent" to commit a crime were brushed aside; originally, a corporation could not be indicted at all; and as late as the 1850's scattered cases held that corporations were criminally liable only for acts or omissions that did not require a criminal "intent."[57] It was still theoretically true in 1900 that a corporation could not be convicted of rape or treason; but most cases that tried and convicted corporations arose under statutes on economic crime—creating a nuisance, charging too much interest, breaking the Sabbath, or, as in one case, "permitting gaming upon its fairgrounds."[58]

For some crimes, the presumption of innocence or regularity—the principle that the state must specifically prove that a man was guilty or an action irregular, overcoming the presumption that no wrong had been done—was turned topsy-turvy by statute. The object was to toughen the regulatory blade of the criminal law. In the New York penal code, the "insolvency of a moneyed corporation" was "deemed fraudulent" unless "its affairs appear, upon investigation, to have been administered fairly, legally, and with . . . care and diligence" (sec. 604). In Indiana, under a law of 1891, a prima-facie case of "intent to defraud" the depositor was made out, when a bank failed or suspended within thirty days of accepting a deposit.[59] There was no-nonsense toughness in liquor statutes, too. Dry states outlawed the sale of hard liquor; but it was not easy to catch violators red-handed. So, in New Hampshire it was *"prima facie* evidence" of violation of liquor laws if the defendant "exposed" any bottles with liquor labels "in the windows of, or upon the shelves within his place of business," or if his store had a "sign, placard, or other advertisement" for liquor, or if he possessed coupon receipts showing he had paid his federal tax as a dealer or wholesaler in liquor, or if a person delivered liquor "in or from any store, shop, warehouse, steamboat . . . or any shanty or tent . . . or any dwelling-house . . . if any part . . . be used as a public eating-house, grocery, or other place of common resort." In Iowa, possession of liquor, "except in a private dwelling house," created a presumption of guilt. . . .[60]

RAYMOND A. MOHL

2

POVERTY, PAUPERISM, AND SOCIAL ORDER IN THE PREINDUSTRIAL AMERICAN CITY, 1780-1840

Raymond Mohl's article suggests that a conceptual framework borrowed from sociology, "the social order," helps to explain events in American cities in the early national period. Where other articles in this collection have focused on official agencies and institutions and their relationship to "Law and Order," Mohl emphasizes some of the sources for social disorder in preindustrial cities. In effect he documents the social conditions which led to the creation of the American system of criminal justice as we know it today. He also points out that the means to promote social order which nineteenth-century Americans adopted have failed to accomplish their ends—just as other means, like elaborately organized urban police departments, have also failed.

In recent years, increasing numbers of historians have made use of social science concepts and typologies as a means of broadening their understanding of the past. One such effort, Robert Wiebe's *The Search for Order*, has reinterpreted American history in post–Civil War years. Essentially, this study postulated the erosion of community and the growth of loose, disorderly, and impersonal human relationships in the urban, industrialized society of the late nineteenth century. The new conditions fostered a quest for order and direction. Some men sought to restore familiar patterns and defend the old order; others tried to build new institutions, to develop more cosmopolitan type relationships to

From *Social Science Quarterly* (March, 1972), pp. 934–948.

replace patterns prevalent in the old "island" community.[1] This conceptual framework, largely borrowed from sociology, has had a great influence in redirecting the thinking of historians about the post–Civil War period and the development of an industrialized society. It is suggested here, however, in an exploratory way, that these societal changes began much earlier, that a breakdown of community and a search for order occurred in preindustrial America—a pattern clearly evident in early nineteenth-century cities and typically manifested in concern over the question of poverty and pauperism.

Between the American Revolution and the industrial take-off of the mid-nineteenth century, American cities underwent a profound and, to contemporaries, disturbing transformation. Historians have noted the extent to which colonial society was deferential in character—that is, a hierarchical society in which men knew their place and accepted it. The egalitarian ideology of the American Revolution and the reality of social and economic change in the early nineteenth century destroyed deference and the certainty in social relationships it fostered. To be sure, most of the large colonial towns experienced economic depressions, poverty, disease, overcrowding, crime, violence, and social conflict. Yet few of these problems threatened for long to upset the elite-dominated, community-centered nature of pre-Revolutionary urbanism. Colonial institutions maintained more than a semblance of order and stability. But in the early decades of the nineteenth century, old and established institutions of family and faction, church and government, social class and community became ineffective, broke down under new urban conditions. Small, usually orderly, and relatively well-regulated in colonial years, the seaport cities became large, unstable, and socially fragmented.[2]

Extremely rapid population growth speeded these changes in preindustrial American cities. A small city of little more than 30,000 in 1790, New York grew by more than 80 percent during the following decade. In the same ten-year period, Baltimore almost doubled its population. Between 1790 and 1830 New York had an overall population growth rate of 549 percent. Similarly, over the same four decades Baltimore, Boston, and Philadelphia expanded at rates of 497 percent, 367 percent, and 266 percent, respectively. As economic historian George Rogers Taylor has suggested, these growth rates exceeded the total rate of population expansion, the growth rate of the same cities in the 40 years after 1860, and the contemporary growth rate of large British cities. The growth rates of the port cities remained high between 1830 and 1860 as well.[3]

Rapid population increase contributed to emergence of a disorderly society. While new transportation technology permitted upper and middle class movement to suburbs, even during these early years, the cities themselves became increasingly congested. Several wards of New York City, for example, had average densities above 170 persons per acre by 1840. Most big cities experienced housing shortages. By the 1830's European immigrants and native rural migrants crowded into boarding houses, cellars, attics, newly converted tenements, and make-shift quarters along waterfronts and on the outskirts of business districts. These new residential patterns destroyed the homogeneity of earlier years and altered everyday relationships among city dwellers. Heavy population concentrations fostered impersonality and stimulated social tensions. Population growth also forced physical expansion of urban centers—a haphazard process in the early nineteenth century. The gridiron pattern typically applied in Philadelphia and New York seemed efficient and businesslike, but the jumble of land uses and the absence of space for parks, squares, and neighborhood gathering places had a socially disintegrating effect.[4]

Increasingly heavy immigration during the period contributed not only to urban population growth, but to social fragmentation as well. Only a small stream in the 1790's, and interrupted several times in later years by war and depression, the immigrant influx hit flood tide after the 1820's. Almost 93,000 immigrants arrived in New York during the 1820's, and more than 400,000 came during the 1830's. New York City annually received between one-half and two-thirds of all newcomers, although not all remained in the metropolis. By 1850, the foreign-born made up almost half of New York's total population. By the same year, Irish immigrants alone composed more than 25 percent of Boston's population. The newcomers—mostly Irish and German workers and laborers and their families—added ethnic and religious diversity, challenged earlier majorities of English, Protestant stock, and altered the social complexion of city life in the United States. Nativists argued, moreover, that because the primarily Catholic foreigners constituted "the materials for mobs and rebellions," they threatened social stability and cohesiveness. The Irish especially became the butt of nativist hostilities. Poverty-stricken, for the most part without marketable skills, and morally offensive to old stock Americans, they crowded growing slums in seaport cities and contributed to urban disorder.[5]

Increasing class distinctions also fostered disorder. To be sure, upward economic mobility was always possible, but some historians have suggested that even eighteenth-century society was becoming more stratified and unequal. James Henretta, for instance, has shown that the class of propertyless laborers in colonial Boston grew twice as rapidly as the city's total population. Others have demonstrated increasing disparities in property distribution as the nineteenth century advanced, especially in urban commercial and business centers. Despite the rhetoric of egalitarianism in the "age of the common man," the fact is that a kind of permanent proletariat was emerging in early nineteenth century cities—composed largely of day laborers and unskilled, propertyless workers, immigrants, and blacks. Combined with the decline of deference, the reality of a larger, often discontented, lower class eroded the fixity of the old order and the values and norms which had sustained it.[6]

Moreover, the disorder attendant on a large lower class was multiplied by geographic mobility and population turnover. According to early nineteenth-century observers, the lower stratum of society in New York City was characterized by a "floating" population of transients and migrants. One writer described the poor as "constantly on the wing." Many were immigrants passing in or out of the city; others were native Americans who drifted temporarily to the city from neighboring countryside, or who sought new opportunities in the west after exhausting possibilities in the city. The same pattern prevailed in other cities as well. Stephan Thernstrom has estimated population turnover in preindustrial Boston at 25 percent per year. Even within the urban community, the poor moved constantly from place to place. On three different days in January, 1810, for example, the superintendent of New York's poorhouse listed one Ann Haviland, a widow on outdoor, or home, relief at three different addresses. And non–New Yorkers were always amazed at the spectacle of disorder presented every May 1, the city's traditional moving day, when, because of the uniform expiration of leases, rich and poor alike filled the streets moving furniture and belongings to new residence. Mobility undermined community as effectively as class distinction.[7]

Simultaneous economic changes had a similar impact. In pre-Revolutionary times work patterns reinforced the cohesive community. Men worked in small shops with a few other apprentices and journeymen, along with the shop owner—a master craftsman. Such work patterns transferred skills and, as Sam Warner has suggested for colonial Philadelphia, the incentive for shop ownership to the rising generation of craftsmen. The colonial city worker identified with his community and with the master craftsman—an employer who only temporarily stood above the worker in economic and social status. By the 1820's, however, cities like New York, Philadelphia, and Boston poised at the threshhold of the industrial era. As the cities became important processing and manufacturing centers, the factory increasingly replaced the small shop and machines the skilled craftsman. Immigrants and farm girls took up places in the new factories, further altering work patterns. At the same time, industrial beginnings produced new forms of economic complexity and interdependence. Workers, in turn, became increasingly subject to the business fluctuations, depressions, and unemployment which characterized the economic transformation of the period. Moreover, changes in the social organization of work brought specialization of tasks, lessened the importance of skill, and destroyed security, independence, and incentive for workers. The decline of handicraft industry, in other words, undermined the urban worker's identification with community. These changes had a very real impact on worker behavior, as evidenced by the emergence of a strong, but short-lived, trade union movement complete with picketing, strikes, and labor violence in the 1820's and 1830's.[8]

The development of factory-type work—observable as early as the 1790's—also had an impact on urban business leadership. A mercantile elite dominated political, economic, and social life of the cities through the Federalist period. Manufacturing in colonial years merely supplemented the commercial base of the economy. But with emerging industrialism, home industries and transportation interests began to challenge entrenched merchant capitalists; new and specialized business concerns and corporations began to rival old mercantile families. By the 1820's and 1830's "expectant capitalists" sought democratization of business life and supported President Jackson's attack on that symbol of financial power and privilege, the Second Bank of the United States. Corresponding developments occurred in American politics, as state constitutional conventions made universal white male suffrage the rule by the end of the 1820's. In every seaport city, as manufacturing increasingly rivaled commerce in economic importance, and as politics became more egalitarian and subject to professional political bosses and ward heelers, the old merchant elites suffered a relative decline in power, position, and social status.[9]

Other developments also reflected the growing ferment and disorder of the preindustrial American city. Municipal governments failed to cope with a multiplicity of urban problems; city services lagged far behind residential need. The essentially negative municipal controls and restrictive regulatory policies of the colonial era no longer sufficed in the larger, more diverse city of the early nineteenth century. Inadequate facilities for sewage and garbage disposal made cities like New York, as diarist George Templeton Strong wrote in the late 1830's, "one huge pigstye." Indeed, in the absence of real public responsibility, roving pigs rivaled city scavengers in efficiency—a sure indication, one British traveler suggested, of "something wrong" with municipal administration. Poor water supply and distorted medical conceptions rendered public health measures useless; epidemics of yellow fever and cholera periodically ravaged the cities.

Despite constant complaints from citizens about crime and violence, no city had a professional police force before 1840. Volunteer fire companies concentrated more on fighting one another than the frequent blazes which could destroy whole sections of a city at a time. The city required positive government to counter disorder, but mayors and councilmen failed to provide it. As the sense of community broke down, so also did municipal government.[10]

Social and economic change, then, undermined the orderly, well-regulated society of the colonial town. Institutions which had fostered community, tempered conflict, kept order, and maintained social control in the small city became ineffective in the distended, disorderly seaport cities of the early nineteenth century. The new conditions of an expansive but unsettled urban society imposed qualitative changes on the lives of city dwellers. Established middle-class norms and values held little meaning for the European and native newcomers who crowded the cellars and tenements of the growing cities. The struggle for adjustment and survival absorbed most of their energies. Technology and immigration threatened the position of workers. Heterogeneity, diversity, and division marked emerging residential patterns. Some observers thought they detected a widening gap between rich and poor—a disturbing sign of disunity and declining identification with community. For the rich, they said, the self-interested and all-consuming concern for private wealth had corrupting influences. Yet, the poor, somehow lacking this same acquisitive drive, remained equally corrupt. The role of the family seemed diminished; educators and preachers complained about the lessened influence of parents over children. Alarmed middle-class moralists noted rising rates of urban crime, violence, delinquency, and immorality. Nativists worried intensely about "internal subversion" purportedly plotted by Catholics, Freemasons, and abolitionists. Heightened ethnic, religious, class, and racial tensions resulted in a wave of urban riots and violence, clearly reflecting social unrest and fragmentation. The mob threatened the fragile foundations of American liberty. For a society which prized uniformity, stability, and order, which saw conformity as synonymous with cohesiveness and community, these social changes were especially disturbing. For those who defined the public good in terms of self-interest, disorder meant bad business and violence posed a very immediate personal danger. For those who identified with a virtuous and communal past, the signs of social anarchy seemed very real.[11]

For the merchant elite and for most native, middle-class Americans, urban pauperism and dependency typified all that was wrong with society in the early nineteenth century. Like the contemporary British political economists from whom they borrowed intellectually, nineteenth-century Americans accepted the idea of permanent economic inequality among men, but postulated an essential distinction between poverty and pauperism. Poverty seemed natural and ineradicable, the normal condition of the laboring classes. Few expected unskilled workingmen and immigrants to live much above a subsistence level. Furthermore, the self-reliant, laboring poor outwardly conformed to the Protestant work ethic and presented little threat to established order.[12]

Pauperism, however, meant dependency—an unacceptable kind of inequality. It contradicted the basic assumptions and requirements of a stable society. It undermined virtue and order. It violated the work ethic; it represented a constant economic drain on productive members of society. It denied the optimistic and often-repeated assertions of American progress. Paupers were idle, ignorant, immoral, impious, and vicious, civic and urban spokesmen said. They begged, stole, disturbed the peace, drank to excess, and, in the parlance of the times, committed "shameful enormities." They sought charity but avoided work. They refused to conform. Because a good portion of them were the same foreigners blamed for other disturbing changes, they were labeled unAmerican too. Pauperism, in short, seemed a destructive evil which threatened social values and norms and thus became intolerable.[13]

As the well-regulated society began to break down in American cities after 1800, as the pace of immigration, urbanization, and industrial change accelerated, pauperism became increasingly observable, a daily evident symbol of social disorder. New York City serves as a case in point. In February 1784 a local newspaper reported more than nine hundred families on the relief rolls, a result of the social and economic dislocations of the American Revolution. In January 1805 Mayor DeWitt Clinton sought legislative appropriations for ten thousand impoverished New Yorkers forced on the public bounty by severe winter weather. City records show that between April 1814 and April 1815 more than 16,000 individuals received public outdoor relief, while the new municipal poorhouse supported almost 3,000 others. In that single year, more than one fifth of the city's inhabitants sought public relief. Private charitable societies aided thousands more. Investigators in 1817 estimated that 15,000 people depended entirely on public and private charity.[14] Editors and correspondents constantly filled columns of the city's newspapers with complaints about throngs of beggars, vagrants, peddlers, prostitutes, public drunks, homeless, wandering children, and other "suspicious characters." Relief-seekers were variously described as "a parcel of drones," "a worthless scum," and "thieves in the garb of misery." The magnitude of the problem seemed ominous, the visibility of the poor seemed threatening. For the nineteenth-century establishment, for those, that is, who sought restoration of old norms and familiar patterns, an assault against pauperism and associated "vices" became a primary objective.[15]

Almost uniformly, the merchants and middle-class men who led the civic and reform organizations traced dependency to the poor themselves. They found causes of pauperism in drunkenness, impiety, idleness, extravagance, immorality, and the ease with which public and private charity could be obtained. Few failed to associate pauperism with the "vicious and immoral habits" observable in city slums. Character deficiency seemed the cause of economic insufficiency. Humanitarian leaders and city officials from Boston to Baltimore postulated these views with regularity. Despite the obvious relationship between lengthened welfare rolls and depressed economic conditions, by the 1820's pauperism came to be treated as a moral problem whose solution was central to the reestablishment of social order.[16]

Given their concern about social disintegration and their assumptions about the causes of pauperism, the reformers had few alternatives. The conviction that the poor brought poverty upon themselves implied that moral improvement, rather than charity and relief, would cure dependency. Indeed, the fear of suffering, some reformers argued, was "a wholesome moral discipline" which forced the poor to work and save, but the certainty of relief in time of need tended to destroy character and self-reliance. Charity simply deepened dependency; poorhouses made paupers. Stemming from individual moral defects, pauperism could be ended only by character building and moral reform. Thus, the urban humanitarians abandoned the older benevolent precept that charity was a religious obligation and a human duty. Accepting lower-class vices as the causes of pauperism, the moral reformers again and again asserted the need for encouraging opposing virtues. The character of the poor could be improved and dependency eliminated, said the New York Society for the Prevention of Pauperism in 1819, only "by inculcating religion, morality, sobriety, and industry, and by diffusing useful knowledge among the indigent and laboring people." The reformers sought to purge the poor of their sins and vices, bring moral uplift to the slums, and end poverty with virtue and religion. The assumptions of such a program to regulate lower-class behavior stimulated, even demanded, a far-reaching humanitarian activism.[17]

A fantastic array of new voluntary associations institutionalized the anti-pauperism energies of the merchant elite and the middle class. The New York Society for the Prevention of Pauperism, which functioned between 1817 and 1823, has already been mentioned. Baltimore had a similarly named society about the same time, while Philadelphia reformers sponsored a Society for the Promotion of Public Economy and a Society for Bettering the Condition of the Poor. Bostonians supported a Society for the Moral and Religious Instruction of the Poor, and, by the 1830's, a Society for the Prevention of Pauperism. Each of these important groups sought to end dependency through moral reform and by reducing what seemed excessive charity and relief.[18]

In addition each city sported dozens of specialized charities for every imaginable humanitarian purpose: to aid widows and orphans, immigrants and blacks, debtors and prisoners, aged females and young prostitutes; to supply the poor with food, fuel, medicine, employment, Bibles, and religion; to promote morality, temperance, piety, thrift, and industrious habits; to educate poor children in charity schools, free schools, almshouse schools, and Sunday schools; to reform drinkers, gamblers, criminals, juvenile delinquents, ungodly sailors, and Sabbath-breakers. New York City alone boasted more than 100 such organizations by 1825. Led and supported by the same people—mostly merchants, businessmen, and professionals—these groups consciously combined charity with moral and religious exhortation. Many abandoned charity altogether for moral reform. They used benevolence for what they considered important social purposes: to restore urban order and ensure security for established society. Evangelical preacher Lyman Beecher saw in these voluntary societies "a sort of disciplined moral militia" which would "uphold peace and good order in society" and "save the nation from civil war and commotion." They became, as one historian has suggested, "special kinds of defense organizations." In the early nineteenth century, the network of benevolent associations replaced the less formal, but now ineffective, institutions and social controls of colonial years.[19]

The new philanthropic associations became primary instruments for the achievement of social order. Education for the poor, for instance, was thought of primarily as a means of creating a moral, docile, hard-working, and law-abiding lower class. The New York African Free School typically aimed to make blacks "safe and useful members of society" and "quiet and orderly citizens." The New York Free School Society attempted to disseminate "fixed habits of industry, decency, and order." The Boston Children's Friend Society promoted moralistic schooling among the poor to "give stability to our valued institutions." The Boston Farm School urged education for potential delinquents from the slums as a means of "increasing the security of life and property."[20]

Similarly, it was argued that Sunday schools, which proliferated rapidly in every city after 1816, promoted "habits of order, submission, [and] industry," checked "destructive habits," increased "the public safety," and made the poor contented with their "station" in life. "Are you friends to social order?" asked a writer in a religious periodical, *The Evangelical Guardian,* in 1818. Then "engage in Sunday schools that you may be instrumental in teaching the rising generation how to preserve that order." As the Boston Sunday School Union noted in 1836, the poor were taught "self-control, and subjection, and the lesson of subordination."[21] As disseminators of societal traditions and values, schools in the preindustrial city provided formal indoctrination in middle-class morality. By demanding ethical conformity, by providing models of decency and decorum, by imposing values upon the lower classes from above, they also became protectors of social order. As one public school society argued, the moral training of the poor became "an act of self-preservation."[22]

A widespread campaign to evangelize city slums revealed similar purposes. Formed in 1816, the American Bible Society and a myriad of local auxiliaries optimistically attacked pauperism and urban disorder with scripture. When the New York Bible Society in 1820 asked why the city's courts overflowed with vicious criminals and its streets with beggars and paupers, the answer seemed logical and self-evident—"it is because," they said, "Bibles are not sufficiently distributed among them." Active in the growing southern manufacturing city of Richmond, the Bible Society of Virginia urged Biblical learning as the best method of restraining "bad passions" and producing "reverence of the laws." Bible reading made men virtuous and useful, sober and industrious; it stimulated "steady habits and correct moral deportment"; it served "the purposes of virtue and social order" and strengthened "the fabric of civil society."[23]

Other organizations supplied similar doses of evangelical religion for similar purposes. Bible society views were reinforced by a simultaneous proliferation of religious tract societies. Short pamphlets of four to twelve pages contained pointed moral messages and were widely disseminated in the larger cities. The New York Religious Tract Society alone distributed more than two million such pamphlets between 1812 and 1825. Their social purposes were obvious. A religious tract in every home, contended an evangelical advocate, was the surest guardian against "vice, anarchy, and violence," the best safeguard against revolution.[24] In addition, city mission organizations built free churches in the slums, sponsored Sunday schools and Bible lectures, held prayer meetings for seamen, and sent visitors to exhort and pray with the poor in their homes. One of the primary functions of such missions was to "save the bulwarks of freedom ... from threatened overthrow." Few disagreed with Presbyterian preacher William Engles, who noted in 1833 that these urban missionaries helped "secure the national stability."[25] At the same time, some city governments paid the salaries of poorhouse preachers. The New York

City Common Council supported such a practice because, they said, religion was "highly beneficial not only to the morals, but to the industry of the Lower Classes." Sabbatarians offered their program as "one of the most efficient expedients for the prevention of pauperism."[26] The removal by evangelical means of such vices as intemperance, idleness, crime, and Sabbath-breaking would bring salvation to the poor, eliminate pauperism, and improve civil and social order. Thus, the voluntary and interdenominational religious associations became instruments in the more general attack on pauperism and dependency, protective devices against urban disorder.

Numerous urban associations focused on concomitant problems; all symbolic of the social confusion which characterized the nineteenth-century preindustrial city. Temperance advocates argued that lower-class drinking habits destroyed incentive to work, undermined morality, and thus severed a main prop of the social order.[27] Some groups promoted work programs for the poor, either as a deterrent to relief, as a means of building character, or "to inure them to labour."[28] Others founded such self-help agencies as savings banks and fuel savings funds to stimulate thrift and self-reliance.[29] Still others organized societies for the prevention of vice and immorality, groups usually dedicated to publicizing social evils or lobbying for protective legislation.[30] Carrying the evangelical crusade to extremes, some radical moral reformers launched campaigns against theaters, candy stores, oyster shops, card playing, smoking, pornography, prostitution, masturbation, and obscene graffiti on school fences and church pews—all part of the "tide of vice" which seemed to characterize lower-class neighborhoods of growing cities.[31]

Threatened by the symptoms of social and economic change, merchants and middle-class urbanites turned benevolence into moral reform; stewardship became a means of social control. Concerned about the breakdown of urban order, they built a network of new institutions to restore the familiar, stable, well-regulated society they had known in the past. In attacking pauperism, they struck out at what seemed the most disturbing element in the changing city. Their perception of their society and their assumptions about pauperism narrowly limited their choice of alternatives to moral reform. But by moralizing about the poor, they conveniently overlooked the social and economic inequities of the urbanizing, industrializing, capitalistic environment. They gave high priority to social order, but generally neglected fulfillment of human needs.

These problems seem just as real in mid-twentieth century. Nurtured by the idea of the United States as the land of opportunity, Americans continue to moralize about the poor and ignore more fundamental causes of dependency. Indeed, the demand to get the lazy bums off welfare rivals in intensity the calls to lower taxes and support your local police. The bulk of modern welfare programs have been stretched upon a framework fashioned by nineteenth-century moralism. And it may equally be true, as Frances Fox Piven and Richard A. Cloward have recently suggested, that the welfare system continues to function as a means of social control, with relief programs expanding during and after periods of large-scale disorder and violence, and contracting as social turbulence subsides.[32] Entrenched poverty and seeming social disorder symbolize a deeply troubled society for contemporaries, as indeed it did for early nineteenth-century urbanites. Although admittedly exploratory and tentative, the conclusions offered here urge consideration of a useful conceptual framework which helps explain some aspects of the social development of early nineteenth-century American cities.

JOSEPH M. HAWES

3

PRISONS IN EARLY NINETEENTH-CENTURY
AMERICA: The Process of Convict Reformation

Joseph Hawes traces the development of the first penitentiary system in the United States and describes the expectations of the founders of the Auburn and Pennsylvania systems of prison discipline. He also shows that the differences between these early rival systems went beyond the surface manifestations of architecture and methods of inmate control. In particular the religious persuasion of the backers of the rival prisons was of paramount importance. The difference is most clearly revealed by examining the process by which the convicts would be reformed. The examination of the process of convict reformation also reveals that early prison reformers had not thought clearly about how reformation was to be achieved. Divine intervention proved to be the core of the process and elaborate prison buildings the lasting result.

On March 9, 1787, the Society for Promoting Political Inquiries met at Benjamin Franklin's house in Philadelphia to hear Benjamin Rush, a well-known physician, give a paper entitled "An Inquiry into the Effect of Public Punishments upon Criminals and upon Society." According to Rush, punishment had three purposes: "to *reform* the person who suffers it . . . to *prevent* the perpetration of crimes, by exciting terror in the minds of spectators; and, . . . to *remove* these persons from society who have manifested, by their tempers and crimes, that they are unfit to live in it." At that time, Pennsylvania had just eliminated the death penalty for most crimes and had not yet fully determined what to do with convicted criminals. One solution to this problem had been the use of public humiliation and requiring convicts to labor on public roads. Rush opposed these public punishments because they tended "to make bad men worse and to increase crimes by their influence upon society." It was also "of such short duration as to produce none of these changes in body or mind, which are absolutely necessary to reform obstinate habits of vice." Because men who suffered this punishment lost their sense of shame they were encouraged to commit more crimes.[1]

What Rush proposed to replace public punishment was a system of imprisonment. The convicts would be confined in a large house in a remote part of the state, and the prison should be constructed in order to emphasize its psychological impact on the inmate:

Let its doors be of iron; and let the grating, occasioned by opening and shutting them, be increased by an echo from a neighboring mountain, that shall extend and continue a sound that shall deeply pierce the soul. . . . To increase the horror of this abode of discipline and misery, let it be called by some name that shall import its design.

Rush believed that imprisonment itself would be especially effective. "An attachment to kindred society," he wrote, "is one of the strongest feelings in the human heart. A separation from them, therefore, has ever been considered as one of the severest punishments that can be inflicted upon man." Rush thought that the loss of personal liberty for an indefinite period of time was "a punishment so severe, that death has often been preferred to it."[2]

Rush's remarks had been delivered to a receptive audience. Pennsylvania was noted for humanitarianism, and the legislature had passed a law in 1786 reducing the number of capital crimes. Before the Revolution in 1776, a group of Quakers in Philadelphia formed the Philadelphia Society for Assisting Distressed Prisoners. This group, which disbanded when the British occupied Philadelphia during the Revolution, had provided prisoners with food and clothing. After the war and shortly after Rush read his paper, the members revived the society and gave it a new name, the Society for Alleviating the Miseries of Public Prisons.[3]

The members met at the German Schoolhouse on Cherry Street in Philadelphia on May 8, 1787. They resolved that the "follies or crimes of our fellow creatures" did not cancel "the obligations of benevolence," and they determined to recommend "degrees and modes of punishment" which would, "instead of continuing habits of vice, become the means of restoring our fellow creatures to virtue and happiness." They began visiting the prisons of Philadelphia, and in a memorial to the Pennsylvania legislature in January, 1789, they reported on conditions in the Walnut Street Jail. They found that "the men and women had general intercourse with each other, and . . . that they were locked up together in the rooms at night." There were, the memorialists noted, three great evils in the jail: "the mixture of the sexes—the use of spiritous liquors and the indiscriminate confinement of debtors and persons committed for criminal offenses." They also sent a memorial to the Pennsylvania legislature outlining a new system of imprisonment. They thought that "punishment by more *private* or even *solitary* labor, would more successfully tend to reclaim the unhappy objects; as it might be conducted more steadily and uniformly, and the kind and portion of labor better adapted to the different abilities of the criminals."[4]

Before the American Revolution, colonial criminal codes did not usually include imprisonment as a punishment. Prisons and jails were places for those awaiting trial, witnesses in criminal actions, and debtors. Penal theory stressed the deterrent effect of capital punishment. The idea was that the threat of death would make would-be criminals reconsider a contemplated criminal act. Capital punishment also satisfied society's demand for retribution for the wrong it had suffered. Noncapital punishment involved whipping, fines, or public humiliation. There is little evidence in colonial penal practice that reformation of the convict was a principal aim.[5]

In 1790, the Pennsylvania legislature, probably as a result of the memorials it had received from the Society for Alleviating the Miseries of Public Prisons, passed a law calling for the renovation of the Walnut Street Jail in Philadelphia. The jail would be designed to receive and separate two classes of prisoners. Those who had been found guilty of more serious offenses would be confined in solitary cells which were six feet wide, eight feet long, and nine feet high. There were also thirty-six rooms, which measured eighteen by twenty feet, in which those convicted of lesser offenses were to be confined. The convicts in the larger rooms were to work in shops during the day. The idea was that by making the prisoners work (presumably they had been driven to crime by economic want) they would learn a trade and thus be able to make an honest living. The first director of the renovated prison was Caleb Lownes, a member of the Society for Alleviating the Miseries of Public Prisons. However, since prisoners from all parts of Pennsylvania could be sent to the Walnut Street Jail, it soon became overcrowded, and its purposes were perverted. Often convicts were pardoned in order to make room for new inmates. In protest against these conditions, Lownes resigned.[6]

Before it had become overcrowded, the renovated Walnut Street Jail had seemed to work fairly well. It was a decided improvement over the old jail on High Street. Convicts were promised early release for cooperative behavior, and they were paid for their labor. Lownes recalled several years after he had resigned that the streets seemed safer to him. He thought that the rate of recidivism had declined, and that there had been fewer escapes. Despite its later failure the Walnut Street Jail served as a model for prisons in other states.[7]

In 1794, a New York Quaker, Thomas Eddy, came to Philadelphia to inspect the Walnut Street Jail. The jail was not yet overcrowded, and he returned home determined to erect a similar institution in his home state. The New York legislature modified the state's penal code in 1796, and, following Pennsylvania's lead, made imprisonment the principal form of punishment. Newgate Prison in Greenwich was the state's first prison. Other states soon followed New York (Massachusetts and Maryland in 1804, and Vermont in 1809), but all of them had copied the large rooms at Walnut Street and had ignored the cells. Like the Walnut Street Jail, those modeled after it soon became overcrowded and ineffective.[8]

The failure of the Walnut Street Jail and Newgate set back the movement to create a reformatory penal system begun by Benjamin Rush and the members of the Society for Alleviating the Miseries of Public Prisons and carried on by men like Thomas Eddy. But the failure did indicate that the reformers had not had any clear program for the prisons they had erected. Although these new prisons were supposed to reform their inmates, just how they were to accomplish this had not been clearly established. There was the generally accepted idea that idleness and crime were closely related and that labor in prison would provide the prisoner with a means of earning a living and the habits of industry so vital to success. Since prisoners spent only a short amount of time in the prison, even this rudimentary system of reformation had little effect. But with the new criminal codes which provided for imprisonment as the principal means of punishment, it would be difficult to abandon the prisons. The problem, now that imprisonment was in effect, was to find a way to make it fulfill the aims of punishment according to Benjamin Rush: to reform criminals, to deter would-be criminals, and to protect society from dangerous individuals.

In 1801, Eddy, who was disturbed by the failure of Newgate in New York, wrote *An Account of the State Prison,* in which he argued for reformation as the most important purpose of imprisonment. Eddy believed that solitary confinement in cells offered the best means to accomplish the desired reformation. He had served as inspector of prisons for the state of New York in the 1790's, but he resigned in 1802, because he did not agree with the methods then being used in the prisons. He believed that the failure of the early New York prisons to reform their inmates was due to the prisons' reliance on the congregate or large-room plan of confinement.[9]

Eddy's belief in the effectiveness of cells in reforming criminals probably came from the Quakers' ideas about human psychology. One of the central tenets of the Society of Friends was the doctrine of the "inner light"—the belief that every individual could receive divine inspiration. This divine intervention was essential if a person hoped to be saved—or reformed. But in order to receive this inspiration a person had to be properly receptive. He would have to renounce all "creaturely" concerns and open himself to divine forgiveness. Thus salvation, and by analogy, reformation, would require a period of soul-searching, of penitence and solitude before the workings of the divinity could begin. Reformation, then, would have to be accomplished on an individual basis. The convict would have to be totally isolated, alone with his reflections. In solitude he would repent, suppress his creaturely concerns, and, receiving divine intervention, be reformed. He could then return to society as a new man, unlikely to sin again.[10]

By 1816, the overcrowded conditions at Newgate in New York had become intolerable, and a new prison was begun at Auburn. It was built on the old congregate plan and contained 28 rooms, each of which would house from 8 to 12 inmates. But growing sentiment in favor of the cellular system of confinement had developed, and in 1819, the New York legislature provided for the construction of a new wing at Auburn on the cellular plan. The cells were three and one half feet wide, seven feet long, and seven feet high. When the wing was finished in 1821, a new system of classification was installed—apparently at the instigation of the New York legislature. There were to be three classes of convicts: hardened criminals, who were to be kept in solitary confinement; a middle group who would alternate between solitary confinement and labor; and a group of the most tractable prisoners who would work in association during the day and retire to solitary cells at night. The board of inspectors at Auburn outlined the new rules in 1821, and commented on the purpose of solitary confinement as they saw it:

The end and design of the law is the prevention of crimes, through fear of punishment, the reformation of offenders being of minor consideration. . . . Let the most obdurate and guilty felons be immured in solitary cells and dungeons; let them have pure air, wholesome food, comfortable clothing, and medical aid when necessary; cut them off from all intercourse with men; let not the voice or face of a friend ever cheer them; let them walk their gloomy abodes, and commune with their corrupt hearts and guilty consciences in silence and brood over the horrors of their solitude, and the enormity of their crimes, without the hope of executive pardon.[11]

Clearly the intent of the inspectors was to make solitary confinement at

Auburn as brutal and dehumanizing as possible. Within two years this aspect of the classification system had to be abandoned because of its effect on the convicts. Many of them showed severe mental aberrations as a result of their confinement.

In 1823, the governor of New York pardoned most of the inmates who had been thus confined. Of the original 80 convicts put in solitary, twelve were eventually returned to Auburn, having been convicted of new crimes after their release. The failure of solitary confinement at Auburn was a serious blow to penal reformers, and some voices now questioned the basic idea of imprisonment. There was talk of returning to public corporal punishment for minor offenses and to capital punishment for major crimes. But the scheme proposed for the more tractable convicts offered a viable compromise. The inmates at Auburn would work in groups during the day and retire to solitary cells at night. When the convicts were together every effort would be made to see that there was no communication between them. This was the "Auburn" or "silent" system.[12]

It would seem that the failure of solitary confinement at Auburn would have ended the matter, but some of the advocates of cellular confinement were not convinced that the Auburn experiment had been a fair trial. They could point to the obvious aim of the New York prison inspectors to make solitary confinement a thoroughly terrifying experience. They could argue that the New York approach did not agree with Quaker ideas of human nature. The cell was not, in the Quaker view, supposed to be a dungeon; it was supposed to be a place for reflection and penitence. It should be a place of light (even of hope) not a place of darkness and of fear. The trouble with the Auburn experiment was that it had been based on improper theory and conducted in cells that were too small, too dark, and too terrifying. The idea should not be abandoned simply because it had been tried out in an improper way. Perhaps, they suggested, the Auburn experiment had not been meant to succeed.

In 1818, while the state of New York was building Auburn, Pennsylvania began work on a new prison at Pittsburgh. It was to be constructed on the cellular plan, and Pennsylvania prison reformers hoped that it would become the standard for the country. It took eight years to finish the Western Penitentiary; in the meantime the Pennsylvania legislature authorized the construction of a new penitentiary near Philadelphia. Like the western institution it was to be built entirely on the cellular plan. Before the penitentiary at Cherry Hill just outside Philadelphia could be finished, there was growing evidence that something might be wrong with the plan of solitary confinement. By the late 1820's, most of the Pennsylvania reformers knew about the disastrous results of the Auburn experiment with solitary confinement. Now there seemed to be difficulties at the Western Penitentiary as well. This building had been designed as a large semicircle with 190 individual cells. The cells were too small to permit any work in them, and the walls of the prison were not soundproof. According to foreign observers, the "sole occupation [of the convicts] consisted in mutual corruption." Thus prisoners were not effectively separated from each other. Critics of the system of exclusive cellular confinement pointed to the ineffectiveness of the Western Penitentiary and concluded that the entire idea was unworkable. . . . But the Society for Alleviating the Miseries of Public Prisons was nothing if not persistent. In December, 1827, they sent another of their memorials to the Pennsylvania legislature. They urged the legislature to hold fast to the "principle of solitary confinement, that great scheme of Christian benevolence." They were aware of the difficulties with solitary confinement; it had been represented as being "extremely barbarous." "The idea has been inculcated," they noted,

that every offender, on his entrance into prison, is to be immured in some narrow, gloomy cell, out of sight or hearing of any of his species—insanity, idiocy, and great physical evil have been predicted as the certain consequences of so dreadful a system.

But this grim picture, "the whole of this horrible creation is," they said, "the offspring either of ignorance or misconception." The trouble might have come from the terminology:

Perhaps the term *separate* rather than *solitary* confinement would more appropriately describe the kind of durance which we propose to inflict. Completely to separate one prisoner from another: to take away every possible chance of communication in prison, and mutual recognition after discharge, is what we greatly desire.—Suitable books and private religious instruction we would afford to all: but if labour should be introduced, we hope that no other will ever be permitted than such as can be performed in their private separate apartments, and that this will be employed as an alleviation, not an aggravation of their punishment.[13]

Meanwhile, the voices in opposition to the Pennsylvania Society's ideas were growing in number.

In 1824, a young agent for the American Tract Society, Louis Dwight, decided to devote his energies to prison reform. Dwight had intended to become a clergyman, but an injury from inhaling "exhilirating gas" at a chemistry lecture at Yale had made him unable to carry out the normal duties of a minister. In his travels he had often visited jails and prisons and the conditions he found there so impressed him that he decided to make the improvement of prisons his major life work. "I had rather be in prisons, contending against sin," he wrote in 1825, "than to receive the honors of LaFayette." In June, 1825, Dwight and a group of ministers and reformers established the Boston Prison Discipline Society.[14]

The new society announced that "with this acknowledgment of the Divine Redeemer, as our support and our guide, we proceed to develop these principles and facts, concerning Prison Discipline which we believe to be important." Although there was much to disapprove of in American prisons, the Boston Prison Discipline Society (and in practice this meant Dwight) did find one prison that it could praise without reservation. Auburn was the ideal that should inspire every state:

The whole establishment from the gate to the sewer is a specimen of neatness. The unremitted industry, the entire subordination and subdued feelings of the convicts, has probably no parallel among an equal number of convicts. In their solitary cells, they spend the night, with no other book but the Bible; and at sunrise, they proceed in military order, under the eye of the turnkeys, in solid columns, with the lock march, to their workshops; thence, in the same order, at the hour of breakfast, to the common hall, where they partake of their wholesome and frugal meal in silence.

Now the Prison Discipline Society became an ardent champion of the Auburn system, and a long and bitter controversy over the proper system of prison discipline—that is, the internal arrangements of the prisons—began to take shape.[15]

In Pennsylvania the failure of the Western Penitentiary, the failure of solitary confinement at Auburn, and the apparent success of the new system at Auburn were enough to cause the legislature to reexamine its commitment to the solitary system. In 1826, the legislature charged a three-man commission with finding the best possible system of prison discipline. They agreed that solitary confinement without labor should not be adopted. It would be "a total expense to the State," and it "produces bodily infirmities, disease and insanity." A compromise position other than the one adopted at Auburn could be adopted: solitary confinement with labor in the cells. This would answer the major objections to solitary confinement without labor, but it still had disadvantages. Only certain occupations could be practiced in the cells. Constant cellular confinement, with or without labor, was detrimental to health, and because the prisoners would work alone and without much external discipline, the profits, if any, from convict labor would be low. So the commission recommended that the ideas of the Philadelphia reformers be dropped and that the design of the new prison be changed to the Auburn plan. But the new prison at Cherry Hill was finished on the original plan, and the recommendations of the legislative commission were ignored.[16]

The new prisons in the United States now became the object of European study, and a stream of foreign visitors came to pass through the prisons, take notes on prison architecture, watch the prisoners at work or in their cells, and talk at length with the warden. Among the best known—and most important because of their careful observation—were two French noblemen, Alexis de Tocqueville and Gustave de Beaumont, and the secretary of the London Prison Discipline Society, William Crawford.[17]

In their report, Tocqueville and Beaumont discussed the history of prison reform in the United States and then turned to the theory of imprisonment. "We believe," they wrote,

that society has the right to do everything necessary for its conservation, and for the order established within it. And we understand perfectly well, that an assemblage of criminals, all of whom have infringed the laws of the land, and all of whose inclinations are corrupted, and appetites vicious, cannot be governed in prison according to the same principles, and with the same means, as free persons, whose desires are correct, and whose actions are conformable to the laws.[18]

Tocqueville and Beaumont were equally concerned with the actual practices in American prisons. They noted that American prisons seemed to be most effective at preventing "moral contagion," but confessed that the actual workings of reformation remained something of a mystery. Consequently, prison officials regarded this vital but mysterious function as the province of religion. Tocqueville and Beaumont also noted the different theories that supporters of the Auburn and Pennsylvania systems advocated. "Can there be," they said of the Pennsylvania system,

a combination more powerful for reformation than that of a prison which hands over the prisoner to all the trials of solitude, leads him through reflection to remorse, through religion to hope; makes him industrious by the burden of idleness, and which, while it inflicts the torment of solitude, makes him find a charm in the converse of pious men, whom otherwise he would have seen with indifference, and heard without pleasure?

When they turned from theory to practice, Tocqueville and Beaumont found some aspects of the prison at Cherry Hill that seemed both inefficient and wasteful. The prison had cost $432,000; much of this sum had been spent for "enormous unnecessary expenses." They thought that most of the expenses "had no other object than the armament of the edifice. Gigantic walls, gothic towers, a wide iron gate, give to this prison the appearance of a fortified castle of the middle ages. . . ."[19]

By contrast, the initial expense of erecting the prison at Auburn had been much lower, and a large portion of current operating costs were covered by the returns from the inmates' labors. But the workings of the Auburn system were quite different. In theory both systems operated to prevent "evil communication," and both systems claimed as one of their chief goals the reformation of the convict. They differed principally in the means they used to accomplish these ends.

To understand the workings of the Auburn system Tocqueville and Beaumont talked with the warden of the prison at Sing Sing, New York, Captain Elam Lynds. Captain Lynds had been one of the officers at Auburn when it opened. Lynds explained that the purpose of the strict discipline that was a central feature of the Auburn system was "to maintain uninterrupted silence and uninterrupted labor; to obtain this it is equally necessary to watch incessantly the keepers as well as the prisoners. . . ." The French noblemen asked Captain Lynds how the systems promoted reformation. "I do not believe in *complete* reform," he answered,

except with young delinquents. Nothing in my opinion is rarer than to see a convict of mature age become a religious and virtuous man. I do not put great faith in sanctity of those who leave the prison. I do not believe that the counsels of the chaplain or the meditations of the prisoner, make a good Christian of him. But my opinion is that a great number of old convicts do not commit new crimes, and that they even become useful citizens, having learned in prison a useful art, and contracted habits of constant labor.

Tocqueville and Beaumont concluded that the Pennsylvania system produced "more honest men," while the Auburn system produced "more obedient citizens."[20]

William Crawford, the secretary of the London Prison Discipline Society, came to the United States to study the rival systems in 1833. When he visited the prison at Cherry Hill, he was most interested in learning if the rumored effects of solitary confinement—that it was extremely unhealthy and that it caused insanity—were true. "I was indeed struck," he writes, "by the mild and subdued spirit which seemed to pervade the temper of the convicts, and which is essentially promoted by reflection, solitude, and the absence of corporal punishment." Crawford concluded that the system there was "a safe and efficacious mode of prison management," and that it had "no unfavourable effect upon the mind or health."[21]

Crawford also visited Auburn. He found the physical facilities appropriate and acceptable, but he did not fully approve of the system of discipline:

The convict is prohibited from speaking to any fellow prisoner. He is required to pursue his labour with downcast eyes. If in any case he is detected in looking off his work, in gazing at or attempting to exchange communication with another prisoner, he is flogged by the overseer with a whip (a "cat" or "cow-hide"), in the presence of his associates. The correction is certain and immediate. The quantity of punishment is entirely dependent on the will of the overseer, against whose acts there is no appeal.

But the system was not working. Convicts found ways to communicate, and the punishments produced no lasting effects. "It is true," Crawford wrote, "that the dominion of the lash produces instantaneous and unqualified submission, but this obedience is but of a temporary nature. It imparts no valuable feeling and presents no motive that is calculated to deter eventually from the commission of crime and amend the moral character."[22]

Crawford and Beaumont and Tocqueville concluded that the Pennsylvania system, although more expensive to operate, was superior, but Louis Dwight and the Boston Prison Discipline Society remained convinced that the Auburn system was better. There the differences between the two systems rested until 1845. Annually, the Boston Prison Discipline Society issued a report which praised the Auburn system and condemned the Pennsylvania system. The supporters of separate confinement remained silent and in effect depended on foreign observers to champion their cause. Over the years some of the members of the Boston society began to wonder about the statements in their annual reports. One of the members who questioned Dwight's views was the noted reformer Samuel Gridley Howe. "I thought that the course which our society had been led by the secretary to adopt," Howe wrote, "was uncourteous and unjust, and so expressed myself to him repeatedly." But Dwight paid no attention to Howe.[23]

The annual meeting of the Boston Discipline Society in 1845 took up the controversy over the secretary's fairness to the Pennsylvania system and chose a committee to investigate the matter. Besides Dwight and Howe the committee included Horace Mann and Charles Sumner. Howe wrote a report specifying the bias against Pennsylvania in previous reports, but the committee refused to approve his draft. The 1846 meeting also refused to include Howe's minority report in the *Annual Report* for that year, and so Howe published his report on his own. Howe noted that "we have carefully searched the reports since 1838 and have not found a line of unqualified praise of any feature of the Pennsylvania system." But, Howe said, there were aspects of the system at Cherry Hill worthy of praise and features at Auburn that were less than desirable.[24]

It would appear that the controversy over the two rival systems turned mostly on the questions of expense and effectiveness. Since most of the new state prisons built in the United States in the early nineteenth century conformed to the Auburn plan, it seemed to have captured the minds of Americans concerned with prisons. Howe thought the Auburn system prevailed because it was cheaper, because it had been advocated so ably and so long by Dwight and the Prison Discipline Society in Boston, and because it was a considerable improvement over the older prisons. The surface issue was a debate over what kind of prison to construct, one that required perpetual solitude and produced little revenue or one that provided solitary confinement at night and the more profitable congregate labor by day. Certainly the difference in initial and operating costs between the two systems was an important factor in the relative popularity of them, but there was another significant difference that explains the concern of men like Howe.[25]

Both systems claimed to reform most of their inmates. Both sought through extraordinary means to prevent the convicts from communicating with each other, and both stressed the importance of religion in the process of reformation. Where they differed most was in the means by which they sought to accomplish these ends. The Auburn plan relied on corporal punishment to enforce the rule of silence; at Pennsylvania, solitude was to be guaranteed through the construction of the building. At Auburn, a combination of influences was supposed to produce the desired reformation. Solitude at night provided time for reflection. Labor by day gave the convicts orderly work habits; a strict system of discipline enabled the convicts to control their vicious impulses; and a system of religious instruction completed the process. The Eastern Penitentiary had no system of strict discipline and therefore did not rely on corporal punishment. Otherwise, the process of reformation there was similar. The way the prisons differed most was in the relationship between religion and reformation.

Tocqueville and Beaumont had noted that reformation was, at the root, a mysterious process, a process basically religious, and so the prison chaplain assumed a central role. Under the Auburn system he was charged with both "reforming" the convicts and determining if a convict's reformation was genuine. The theory of reformation was that the poor misguided convict should be led away from his evil ways and to the contemplation of proper and wholesome ideas. The best way to do this was to exhort him to forsake his past and be reformed. Bible reading and personal conversations with the chaplain would supplement the sermons. Related to the efforts to encourage religious faith and discipline among the sinners in prison was the system of discipline employed at Auburn. It sought to encourage habits of industry and obedience that would make the ex-convict a good citizen as well as a good Christian. Thus the prison chaplain at Auburn did not serve to mitigate the harshness of the discipline; he reinforced it.[26]

The chaplains saw their work as the recovery of lost souls, and they believed that they were doing especially righteous work. In 1830, B. C. Smith, the chaplain at Auburn, reported that the two years he had served at the prison were the "most useful, certainly the happiest, portion of my life." Tocqueville and Beaumont noted that "because their aim is great," religious reformers "pursue it with ardor, and the nobleness of their undertaking elevates at once their office, and the functions of those who, in concert with them, work for the reformation of the criminals; it gives altogether to the penitentiary establishment a greater interest and a much higher morality." In its seventh *Annual Report,* the Prison Discipline Society of Boston claimed that the process of reformation in prisons operating on the Auburn system was enjoying considerable success:

The testimony on this subject from the chaplains, the Sabbath school teachers, the letters from discharged convicts, and their friends and neighbors, in some instances, is encouraging in a high degree. Why should it be otherwise? When did God ever refuse to crown with his blessing institutions where order, temperance, industry, good government, moral and religious instruction, are the order of the day? Where the Sabbath, the Bible, the place of prayer, and the minister of the gospel are honored?

Clearly religious instruction and the system of discipline under the Auburn system were closely related—both in keeping "order" within the prison and in the process of reformation.[27]

Chaplain Smith at Auburn reported that in his talks with convicts he "dealt plainly with them." "I have dwelt, emphatically," he said,

upon their depravity and guilt in trampling upon the laws of God and of their country; endeavored to awaken remorse in their consciences; to convince them of the justice of their punishment; to induce them to yield strict and humble obedience to all the regulations of the prison; to press home upon them the duty of immediate repentance and amendment..."[28]

Echoing Chaplain Smith, Jonathan Dickerson, the chaplain at Sing Sing, argued that "a humane, though firm and rigid prison discipline, so far from operating against the happy tendencies of the gospel, will serve as a handmaid and assistant to it." These two aspects, Dickerson continued, worked a mutual benefit:

Where *moral influence* and *divinely appointed means* are made to bear a conspicuous part as essentially necessary in humbling and reforming these men, the system is served; the discipline is aided, strengthened, and sanctified, as it were, thereby, and the whole machinery will co-operate, and move on most *harmoniously, impressively,* and, under God, with *amazing effects* upon the consciences of these men.[29]

Thus, before the process of reformation could properly begin, it was necessary to make the convicts humble, "to awaken remorse in their consciences," and "to convince them of the justice of their punishment." Once these things had been done, then the convicts would, presumably, be ready to turn away from their old ways.

Sometimes, in the mind of the chaplain at least, the convicts were grateful for the opportunity to reform. In 1833, Chaplain Smith of Auburn reported that "the general state of feeling among the convicts is gratifying in the highest degree. It is not merely that of humble acquiescence in their punishment," he continued, "but of fervent gratitude that they have been arrested, and brought under a course of discipline and instruction, which has opened their eyes upon the infatuation of their former course of life." This gratitude, Smith hastened to assure his readers, did not come from "any lenity in the management of the convicts." It came from the design of the system:

Every object, and every movement, is repulsive to their feelings. Their mental suffering is, in most cases, intense. I do not believe there are ten convicts in prison, who would not gladly purchase a remission of one half their term of sentence at the expense of every farthing of property they ever possessed.[30]

Thus Smith would have his readers believe that the convicts were both grateful and miserable. They were glad they had been arrested, but they hated prison. Prison was thus a place for two functions: punishment and reformation, and the convicts, Smith assures us, found the punishment irksome and the process of reformation something wonderful.

Such a dual, almost schizophrenic response, seems unlikely. What actually was at work, according to Tocqueville and Beaumont, was a pattern of deception encouraged by the system itself. Indeed, this deception worked so well that Smith contradicted himself. "The criminal," Tocqueville and Beaumont noted, has an interest in showing to the chaplain, with whom alone he has moral communications, profound repentance for his crime, and a lively desire to return to virtue. If these sentiments are not sincere, he nevertheless will profess them. On the other hand, the man who sacrifices his whole existence to the pursuit of an honorable end, is himself under the influence of an ardent desire which must sometimes lead to errors. As he desires with ardor the reformation of the criminals, he easily gives credence to it.[31]

Smith had contradicted himself because the system worked against itself. In the first place, the two aims of punishment and reformation were themselves antithetical. In spite of the theory it had become clear that punishment did not in and of itself reform. The process of reformation, when reduced to its essentials, was that of divine intervention, and was therefore not punitive. The chief agents of reformation, the chaplains, were expected to serve as the evaluators of their own work. And, the voice of public opinion seemed to say that punishment should be severe, but that convicts should be reformed. It is no wonder that the prisons tried to do both.

Society's attitude toward the convict was always somewhat contradictory. Even among those special friends of the convict, the inmates of prisons were a class to be treated without respect. As the *Christian Examiner* put it in 1836, in response to criticism of the harsh discipline in the Auburn system:

We think it is carrying the sentiment of sympathy for the dignity of human nature somewhat far, to talk with so much indignation of applying the whip to the back of these hardened, perverse, and otherwise incorrigible rogues, who alone can ever be exposed to it. [How can this be] degrading, forsooth, to one who has already reached the lowest degradation of which human nature seems capable, and who prefers resistance, however hopeless, to submission to rules which are likely to benefit him as much as he is capable of being benefited?[32]

Already in 1836, the advocates of penal reform who espoused the Auburn system were beginning to recognize that reformation and punishment—at least the particular blend in that system—did not mix very well. And, forced to choose between the two, even the religiously motivated reformers chose punishment.

The process of reformation at the Eastern Penitentiary in Pennsylvania was similar but with an important difference. Under the Auburn system, the chaplain was basically an active agent for reform. He preached to the inmates and sought them out, talking "plainly" with them all the while.

Steeped in the traditions and approaches of evangelical protestantism, the advocates of the Auburn system believed that the prisoners should be coerced into reform. They would be both exhorted and disciplined. Before anything else they would have to be humbled and made to acquiesce in the process they were experiencing. If they did not cooperate, then these "hardened, perverse, and otherwise incorrigible rogues" could be whipped or otherwise physically punished. The system at Cherry Hill was more subtle; the chaplain, although far from passive, was less active, less given to exhortation and more given (at least in theory) to gentle persuasion. According to the famous reformer Dorothea Dix:

> The separate system reveals, in all parts of its administration, a more direct application and exercise of Christian rule and precepts, than any other mode of prison government. It brings the officer into communication with the prisoner, not as the commander, and not as the guard, watchful and wary, noting of necessity each movement and act; but as the kind governor and attendant, seldom called on to exercise other than beneficial influences. . . .[33]

The Pennsylvania system reflected the basic assumptions of the Quakers— that men may not be directly coerced into proper righteousness; they must be inspired.

Thus the two systems, which had a common background and which shared much of the same philosophy, nonetheless were fundamentally different. The difference lay primarily in the emphases of Quakers and evangelical protestants. The Quakers preferred a noncoercive, practically passive, approach to reform and religion. These matters, with the Quakers, were private, personal, and the product of the divine kindling of the individual's inner light. For the Baptists and Congregationalists who supported the Prison Discipline Society of Boston and advocated the Auburn system, religion and reform were active human pursuits. This view is exemplified in the life of Louis Dwight and in the career of the famous evangelist Charles Grandison Finney. As Perry Miller wrote of him: "He simply stood up and said over and over, 'all men may be saved if they will.' . . . Or as he put it in one brief sentence: 'Don't wait for feeling, DO IT.'" The evangelical protestants would urge men to repent and reform; they would force them to be obedient and even to claim that they were reformed. The Quakers, perhaps more humane, would provide a place for penitence, contemplation, and—it was hoped—reformation. The solitary confinement of the Pennsylvania system, though supported as more gentle and less brutal than the Auburn system, was probably no less terrible to the convicts. It stressed self-discipline rather than obedience, but it was more expensive than the Auburn system, and it may have been no more effective.[34]

ANTHONY PLATT

4

THE TRIUMPH OF BENEVOLENCE:
The Origins of the Juvenile Justice System in the United States

By looking at the child-saving movement at the end of the nineteenth century, Anthony Platt reveals the origins of the American juvenile justice system and also provides some insight into the ideological assumptions underlying that system. He argues that a widely shared "liberalism" has caused historians and criminologists to view the reforms of the Progressive Era as basically humanitarian and leading to the fulfillment of the promise of American life. The emphasis on reform, he continues, has tended to perpetuate the fundamental ills of society even as the reformers sought to ameliorate harmful conditions. After outlining the "myth" of the origins of the juvenile justice system, Platt argues that "the child-saving movement tried to do for the criminal justice system what industrialists and corporate leaders were trying to do for the economy—that is, achieve order, stability, and control while preserving the existing class system and distribution of wealth." Child saving was a middle-class movement and attracted the support of leading industrialists. The development of a system of juvenile justice came in the context of the humanitarian, reformist child-saving movement. Both delinquent and dependent children fell into the orbit of the new system, whose main purpose was social control rather than individual betterment. Since its inception, the system has come to be "an esoteric craft reserved for specialists and outside the competence of ordinary citizens."

In conclusion, Platt finds the system and its components to be "dismal failures" and rejects the view that "generational problems" are the cause of the failure. He sees many parallels between present efforts to reform the juvenile justice system and the child-saving movement. Today's reforms, like those of the Progressive Era, are designed primarily for control and not to serve the people as a whole.

The modern system of crime control in the United States has many roots in penal and judicial reforms at the end of the nineteenth century. Contemporary programs which we commonly associate with the "war on poverty" and the "great society" can be traced in numerous instances to the programs and ideas of nineteenth century reformers who helped to create and develop probation and parole, the juvenile court, strategies of crime prevention, the need for education and rehabilitative programs in institutions, the indeterminate sentence, the concept of "halfway" houses, and "cottage" systems of penal organization.

The creation of the juvenile court and its accompanying services is generally regarded by scholars as one of the most innovative and idealistic products of the age of reform. It typified the "spirit of social justice," and, according to the National Crime Commission, represented a progressive effort by concerned reformers to alleviate the miseries of urban life and to solve social problems by rational, enlightened, and scientific methods.[1] The juvenile justice system was widely heralded as "one of the greatest advances in child welfare that has ever occurred" and "an integral part of total welfare planning."[2] Charles Chute, an enthusiastic supporter of the child-saving movement, claimed that "no single event has contributed more to the welfare of children and their families. It revolutionized the treatment of delinquent and neglected children and led to the passage of similar laws throughout the world."[3] Scholars from a variety of disciplines, such as the American sociologist George Herbert Mead and the German psychiatrist August Aichhorn, agreed that the juvenile court system represented a triumph of progressive liberalism over the forces of reaction and ignorance.[4] More recently, the juvenile court and related reforms have been characterized as a "reflection of the humanitarianism that flowered in the last decades of the 19th century"[5] and an indication of "America's great sense of philanthropy and private concern about the common weal."[6]

Histories and accounts of the child-saving movement tend either to represent an "official" perspective or to imply a gradualist view of social progress.[7] This latter view is typified in Robert Pickett's study of the House of Refuge movement in New York in the middle of the last century:

In the earlier era, it had taken a band of largely religiously motivated humanitarians to see a need and move to meet that need. Although much of their vision eventually would be supplanted by more enlightened policies and techniques and far more elaborate support mechanisms, the main outlines of their program, which included mild discipline, academic and moral education, vocational training, the utilization of surrogate parents, and probationary surveillance, have stood the test of time. The survival of many of the notions of the founders of the House of Refuge testifies, at least in part, to their creative genius in meeting human needs. Their motivations may have been mixed and their oversights many, but their efforts contributed to a considerable advance in the care and treatment of wayward youth.[8]

This view of the nineteenth century reform movement as fundamentally benevolent, humanitarian, and gradualist is shared by most historians and criminologists who have written about the Progressive Era. They argue that this reform impulse has its roots in the earliest ideals of modern liberalism and that it is part of a continuing struggle to overcome injustice and fulfill the promise of American life.[9] At the same time, these writers recognize that reform movements often degenerate into crusades and suffer from excessive idealism and moral absolutism.[10] The faults and limitations of the child-saving movement, for example, are generally explained in terms of the psychological tendency of its leaders to adopt attitudes of rigidity and moral righteousness. But this form of criticism is misleading because it overlooks larger political issues and depends too much on a subjective critique.

In the following pages we will argue that the above views and interpretations of juvenile justice are factually inaccurate and suffer from a serious misconception about the functions of modern liberalism. The prevailing myths about the juvenile justice system can be summarized as follows: (1) The child-saving movement in the late nineteenth century was successful in humanizing the criminal justice system, rescuing children from jails and prisons, developing humanitarian judicial and penal institutions for juveniles, and defending the poor against economic and political exploitation. (2) The child-savers were "disinterested" reformers, representing an enlightened and socially responsible urban middle class, and opposed to big business. (3) The failures of the juvenile justice system are attributable partly to the overoptimism and moral absolutism of earlier reformers and partly to bureaucratic inefficiency and a lack of fiscal resources and trained personnel.

These myths are grounded in a liberal conception of American history which characterizes the child savers as part of a much larger reform movement directed at restraining the power of political and business elites. In contrast, we will offer evidence that the child-saving movement was a coercive and conservatizing influence, that liberalism in the Progressive Era was the conscious product of policies initiated or supported by leaders of major corporations and financial institutions, and that many social reformers wanted to secure existing political and economic arrangements, albeit in an ameliorated and regulated form.

Although the modern juvenile justice system can be traced in part to the development of various charitable and institutional programs in the early nineteenth century,[11] it was not until the close of the century that the modern system was systematically organized to include juvenile courts, probation, child guidance clinics, truant officers, and reformatories. The child-saving movement—an amalgam of philanthropists, middle-class reformers, and professionals—was responsible for the consolidation of these reforms.[12]

The 1890s represented for many middle-class intellectuals and professionals a period of discovery of "dim attics and damp cellars in poverty-stricken sections of populous towns" and "innumerable haunts of misery throughout the land."[13] The city was suddenly discovered to be a place of scarcity, disease, neglect, ignorance, and "dangerous influences." Its slums were the "last resorts of the penniless and the criminal"; here humanity reached the lowest level of degradation and despair.[14] These conditions were not new to American urban life, and the working class had been suffering such hardships for many years. Since the Haymarket Riot of 1886, the centers of industrial activity had been continually plagued by strikes, violent disruptions, and widespread business failures.

What distinguished the late 1890s from earlier periods was the recognition by some sectors of the privileged classes that far-reaching economic, political, and social reforms were desperately needed to restore order and stability. In the economy, these reforms were achieved through the corporation, which extended its influence into all aspects of domestic and foreign policies so that by the 1940s some 139 corporations owned 45 percent of all the manufacturing assets in the country. It was the aim of corporate capitalists to limit traditional laissez-faire business competition and to transform the economy into a rational and interrelated system, characterized by extensive long-range planning and bureaucratic routine.[15] In politics, these reforms were achieved nationally by extending the regulatory powers of the federal government and locally by the development of commission and city manager forms of government as an antidote to corrupt machine politics. In social life, economic and political reforms were paralleled by the construction of new social service bureaucracies which regulated crime, education, health, labor, and welfare.

The child-saving movement tried to do for the criminal justice system what industrialists and corporate leaders were trying to do for the economy—that is, achieve order, stability, and control while preserving the existing class system and distribution of wealth. While the child-saving movement, like most progressive reforms, drew its most active and visible supporters from the middle class and professions, it would not have been capable of achieving significant reforms without the financial and political support of the wealthy and powerful. Such support was not without precedent in various philanthropic movements preceding the child savers. New York's Society for the Reformation of Juvenile Delinquents benefited in the 1820s from the contributions of Stephen Allen, whose many influential positions included mayor of New York and president of the New York Life Insurance and Trust Company.[16] The first large gift to the New York Children's Aid Society, founded in 1853, was donated by Mrs. William Astor.[17] According to Charles Loring Brace, who helped to found the Children's Aid Society, "a very superior class of young men consented to serve on our Board of Trustees; men who, in their high principles of duty, and in the obligations which they feel are imposed by wealth and position, bid fair hereafter to make the name of New York merchants respected as it was never before throughout the country."[18] Elsewhere, welfare charities similarly benefited from the donations and wills of the upper class.[19] Girard College, one of the first large orphanages in the United States, was built and furnished with funds from the banking fortune of Stephen Girard;[20] and the Catholic bankers and financiers of New York helped to mobilize support and money for various Catholic charities.[21]

The child-saving movement similarly enjoyed the support of propertied and powerful individuals. In Chicago, for example, where the movement had some of its most notable successes, the child savers included Louise Bowen and Ellen Henrotin, who were both married to bankers;[22] Mrs. Potter Palmer, whose husband owned vast amounts of land and property, was an ardent child saver when not involved in the exclusive Fortnightly Club (the elite Chicago Woman's Club) or the Board of Lady Managers of the World's Fair;[23] another child saver in Chicago, Mrs. Perry Smith, was married to the vice-president of the Chicago and Northwestern Railroad. Even the more radically minded child savers came from upper-class backgrounds. The fathers of Jane Addams and Julia Lathrop, for example, were both lawyers and Republican senators in the Illinois legislature. Jane Addams's father was one of the richest men in northern Illinois, and her stepbrother, Harry Haldeman, was a socialite from Baltimore who later amassed a large fortune in Kansas City.[24]

The child-saving movement was not simply a humanistic enterprise on behalf of the lower classes against the established order. On the contrary, its impetus came primarily from the middle and upper classes, who were instrumental in devising new forms of social control to protect their privileged positions in American society. The child-saving movement was not an isolated phenomenon but rather reflected massive changes in productive relationships, from laissez-faire to monopoly capitalism, and in strategies of social control, from inefficient repression to welfare state benevolence.[25] This reconstruction of economic and social institutions, which was not achieved without conflict within the ruling class, represented a victory for the more "enlightened" wing of corporate leaders, who advocated strategic alliances with urban reformers and support of liberal reforms.[26]

Many large corporations and business leaders, for example, supported federal regulation of the economy in order to protect their own investments and stabilize the marketplace. Business leaders and political spokesmen were often in basic agreement about fundamental economic issues. "There was no conspiracy during the Progressive Era," notes Gabriel Kolko. "There was basic agreement among political and business leaders as to what was the public good, and no one had to be cajoled in a sinister manner."[27] In his analysis of liberal ideology in the Progressive Era, James Weinstein similarly argues that "few reforms were enacted without the tacit approval, if not the guidance, of the large corporate interests." For the corporation executives, liberalism meant "the responsibility of all classes to maintain and increase the efficiency of the existing social order."[28]

Progressivism was in part a businessmen's movement, and big business played a central role in the progressive coalition's support of welfare reforms. Child labor legislation in New York, for example, was supported by several groups, including upper-class industrialists who did not depend on cheap child labor. According to Jeremy Felt's history of that movement, "the abolition of child labor could be viewed as a means of driving out marginal manufacturers and tenement operators, hence increasing the consolidation and efficiency of business."[29] The rise of compulsory education, another welfare state reform, was also closely tied to the changing forms of industrial production and social control. Charles Loring Brace, writing in the mid-nineteenth century, anticipated the use of education as preparation for industrial discipline when, "in the interests of public order, of liberty, of property, for the sake of our own safety and the endurance of free institutions here," he advocated "a strict and careful law, which shall compel every minor to learn to read and write, under severe penalties in case of disobedience."[30] By the end of the century, the working class had imposed upon them a sterile and authoritarian educational system which mirrored the ethos of the corporate workplace and was designed to provide "an increasingly refined training and selection mechanism for the labor force."[31]

While the child-saving movement was supported and financed by corporate liberals, the day-to-day work of lobbying, public education, and organizing was undertaken by middle-class urban reformers, professionals, and special interest groups. The more moderate and conservative sectors of the feminist movement were especially active in antidelinquency reforms.[32] Their successful participation derived in part from public stereotypes of women as the "natural caretakers" of "wayward children." Women's claim to the public care of children had precedent during the nineteenth century, and their role in child rearing was paramount. Women, generally regarded as better teachers than men, were more influential in child training and discipline at home. The fact that public education also came more under the direction of women teachers in the schools served to legitimize the predominance of women in other areas of "child saving."[33]

The child-saving movement attracted women from a variety of political and class backgrounds, though it was dominated by the daughters of the old landed gentry and wives of the upper-class nouveaux riches. Career women and society philanthropists, elite women's clubs and settlement houses, and political and civic organizations worked together on the problems of child care, education, and juvenile delinquency. Professional and political women's groups regarded child saving as a problem of women's rights, whereas their opponents seized upon it as an opportunity to keep women in their "proper place." Child saving became a reputable task for any woman who wanted to extend her "housekeeping" functions into the community without denying antifeminist stereotypes of woman's nature and place.[34]

For traditionally educated women and daughters of the landed and industrial gentry, the child-saving movement presented an opportunity for pursuing socially acceptable public roles and for restoring some of the authority and spiritual influence which many women felt they had lost through the urbanization of family life. Their traditional functions were dramatically threatened by the weakening of domestic roles and the specialized rearrangement of the family.[35] The child savers were aware that their championship of social outsiders such as immigrants, the poor, and children, was not wholly motivated by disinterested ideals of justice and equality. Philanthropic work filled a void in their own lives, a void which was created in part by the decline of traditional religion, increased leisure and boredom, the rise of public education, and the breakdown of communal life in large, crowded cities. "By simplifying dress and amusements, by cutting off a little here and there from our luxuries," wrote one child saver, "we may change the whole current of many human lives."[36]

The child-saving reformers were part of a much larger movement to readjust institutions to conform to the requirements of corporate capitalism and the modern welfare state. As the country emerged from the depressions and industrial violence of the late nineteenth century, efforts were made to rescue and regulate capitalism through developing a new political economy, designed to stabilize production and profits. The stability and smooth functioning of this new order depended heavily on the capacity of welfare state institutions, especially the schools, to achieve cultural hegemony and guarantee loyalty to the state. As William Appleman Williams has commented, "It is almost impossible to overemphasize the importance of the very general—yet dynamic and powerful—concept that the country faced a fateful choice between order and chaos."[37] In order to develop support for and legitimize the corporate liberal state, a new ideology was promoted in which chaos was equated with crime and violence, and salvation was to be found in the development of new and more extensive forms of social control.

The child savers viewed the "criminal classes" with a mixture of contempt and benevolence. Crime was portrayed as rising from the "lowest orders" and threatening to engulf "respectable" society like a virulent disease. Charles Loring Brace, a leading child saver, typified popular and professional views about crime and delinquency:

> As Christian men, we cannot look upon this great multitude of unhappy, deserted, and degraded boys and girls without feeling our responsibility to God for them. The class increases: immigration is pouring in its multitudes of poor foreigners who leave these young outcasts everywhere in our midst. These boys and girls . . . will soon form the great lower class of our city. They will influence elections; they may shape the policy of the city; they will assuredly, if unreclaimed, poison society all around them. They will help to form the great multitude of robbers, thieves, and vagrants, who are now such a burden upon the law-respecting community. . . .[38]

This attitude of contempt derived from a view of criminals as less than human, a perspective which was strongly influenced and aggravated by nativist and racist ideologies.[39] The "criminal class" was variously described as "creatures" living in "burrows," "dens," and "slime"; as "little Arabs" and "foreign childhood that floats along the streets and docks of the city—vagabondish, thievish, familiar with the vicious ways and places of the town";[40] and as "ignorant," "shiftless," "indolent," and "dissipated."[41]

The child savers were alarmed and frightened by the "dangerous classes" whose "very number makes one stand aghast," noted the urban reformer Jacob Riis.[42] Law and order were widely demanded:

The "dangerous classes" of New York are mainly American-born, but the children of Irish and German immigrants. They are as ignorant as London flashmen or costermongers. They are far more brutal than the peasantry from whom they descend, and they are much banded together, in associations, such as "Dead Rabbit," "Plug-ugly," and various target companies. They are our *enfants perdus,* grown up to young manhood.... They are ready for any offense or crime, however degraded or bloody.... Let but Law lift its hand from them for a season, or let the civilizing influences of American life fail to reach them, and, if the opportunity offered, we should see an explosion from this class which might leave this city in ashes and blood.[43]

These views derived considerable legitimacy from prevailing theories of social and reform Darwinism which, *inter alia,* proposed that criminals were a dangerous and atavistic class, standing outside the boundaries of morally regulated relationships. Herbert Spencer's writings had a major impact on American intellectuals; Cesare Lombroso, perhaps the most significant figure in nineteenth-century criminology, looked for recognition in the United States when he felt that his experiments on the "criminal type" had been neglected in Europe.[44]

Although Lombroso's theoretical and experimental studies were not translated into English until 1911, his findings were known by American academics in the early 1890s, and their popularity, like that of Spencer's works, was based on the fact that they confirmed widely held stereotypes about the biological basis and inferior character of a "criminal class." A typical view was expressed by Nathan Allen in 1878 at the National Conference of Charities and Correction: "If our object is to prevent crime in a large scale, we must direct attention to its main sources—to the materials that make criminals; the springs must be dried up; the supplies must be cut off."[45] This was to be achieved, if necessary, by birth control and eugenics. Similar views were expressed by Hamilton Wey, an influential physician at Elmira Reformatory, who argued before the National Prison Association in 1881 that criminals had to be treated as a "distinct type of human species."[46]

Literature on "social degradation" was extremely popular during the 1870s and 1880s, though most such "studies" were little more than crude and racist polemics, padded with moralistic epithets and preconceived value judgments. Richard Dugdale's series of papers on the Jukes family, which became a model for the case-study approach to social problems, was distorted almost beyond recognition by anti-intellectual supporters of hereditary theories of crime.[47] Confronted by the evidence of Darwin, Galton, Dugdale, Caldwell, and many other disciples of the biological image of behavior, many child savers were compelled to admit that "a large proportion of the unfortunate children that go to make up the great army of criminals are not born right."[48] Reformers adopted and modified the rhetoric of social Darwinism in order to emphasize the urgent need for confronting the "crime problem" before it got completely out of hand. A popular proposal, for example, was the "methodized registration and training" of potential criminals, "or these failing, their early and entire withdrawal from the community."[49]

Although some child savers advocated drastic methods of crime control—including birth control through sterilization, cruel punishments, and lifelong incarceration—more moderate views prevailed. This victory for moderation was related to the recognition by many progressive reformers that short-range repression was counterproductive as well as cruel and that long-range planning and amelioration were required to achieve economic and political stability. The rise of more benevolent strategies of social control occurred at about the same time that influential capitalists were realizing that existing economic arrangements could be successfully maintained only through the use of private police and government troops.[50] While the child savers justified their reforms as humanitarian, it is clear that this humanitarianism reflected their class background and elitist conception of human potentiality. The child savers shared the view of more conservative professionals that "criminals" were a distinct and dangerous class, indigenous to working-class culture, and a threat to "civilized" society. They differed mainly in the procedures by which the "criminal class" should be controlled or neutralized.

Gradually, a more "enlightened" view about strategies of control prevailed among the leading representatives of professional associations. Correctional workers, for example, did not want to think of themselves merely as the custodians of a pariah class. The self-image of penal reformers as "doctors" rather than "guards" and the medical domination of criminological research in the United States at that time facilitated the acceptance of "therapeutic" strategies in prisons and reformatories.[51] Physicians gradually provided the official rhetoric of penal reform, replacing cruder concepts of social Darwinism with a new optimism. Admittedly, the criminal was "pathological" and "diseased," but medical science offered the possibility of miraculous cures. Although there was a popular belief in the existence of a "criminal class" separated from the rest of humanity by a "vague boundary line," there was no good reason why this class could not be identified, diagnosed, segregated, changed, and incorporated back into society.[52]

By the late 1890s, most child savers agreed that hereditary theories of crime were overfatalistic. The superintendent of the Kentucky Industrial

School of Reform, for example, told delegates to a national conference of corrections that heredity is "unjustifiably made a bugaboo to discourage efforts at rescue. We know that physical heredity tendencies can be neutralized and often nullified by proper counteracting precautions."[53] E. R. L. Gould, a sociologist at the University of Chicago, similarly criticized biological theories of crime as unconvincing and sentimental. "Is it not better," he said, "to postulate freedom of choice than to preach the doctrine of the unfettered will, and so elevate criminality into a propitiary sacrifice?"[54]

Charles Cooley, writing in 1896, was one of the first American sociologists to observe that criminal behavior depended as much upon social and economic circumstances as it did upon the inheritance of biological traits. "The criminal class," he observed, "is largely the result of society's bad workmanship upon fairly good material." In support of this argument, he noted that there was a "large and fairly trustworthy body of evidence" to suggest that many "degenerates" could be converted into "useful citizens by rational treatment."[55]

Although there was a wide difference of opinion among experts as to the precipitating causes of crime, it was generally agreed that criminals were abnormally conditioned by a multitude of biological and environmental forces, some of which were permanent and irreversible. Strictly biological theories of crime were modified to incorporate a developmental view of human behavior. If, as it was believed, criminals are conditioned by biological heritage and brutish living conditions, then prophylactic measures must be taken early in life. "We must get hold of the little waifs that grow up to form the criminal element just as early in life as possible," exhorted an influential child saver. "Hunt up the children of poverty, of crime, and of brutality, just as soon as they can be reached."[56] Efforts were needed to reach the criminals of future generations. "They are born to crime," wrote the penologist Enoch Wines, "brought up for it. They must be saved."[57] New institutions and new programs were required to meet this challenge.

The essential preoccupation of the child-saving movement was the recognition and control of youthful deviance. It brought attention to, and thus "invented" new categories of youthful misbehavior which had been hitherto unappreciated. The efforts of the child savers were institutionally expressed in the juvenile court which, despite recent legislative and constitutional reforms, is generally acknowledged as their most significant contribution to progressive penology. There is some dispute about which state first created a special tribunal for children. Massachusetts and New York passed laws, in 1874 and 1892 respectively, providing for the trials of minors apart from adults charged with crimes. Ben Lindsey, a renowned judge and reformer, also claimed this distinction for Colorado, where a juvenile court was, in effect, established through an educational law of 1899. However, most authorities agree that the Juvenile Court Act, passed by the Illinois legislature in the same year, was the first official enactment to be recognized as a model statute by other states and countries.[58] By 1917, juvenile court legislation had been passed in all but three states and by 1932 there were over six hundred independent juvenile courts throughout the United States.[59]

The juvenile court system was part of a general movement directed towards developing a specialized labor market and industrial discipline under corporate capitalism by creating new programs of adjudication and control for "delinquent," "dependent," and "neglected" youth. This in turn was related to augmenting the family and enforcing compulsory education in order to guarantee the proper reproduction of the labor force. For example, underlying the juvenile court system was the concept of *parens patriae* by which the courts were authorized to handle with wide discretion the problems of "its least fortunate junior citizens."[60] The administration of juvenile justice, which differed in many important respects from the criminal court system, was delegated extensive powers of control over youth. A child was not accused of a crime but offered assistance and guidance; intervention in the lives of "delinquents" was not supposed to carry the stigma of criminal guilt. Judicial records were not generally available to the press or public, and juvenile hearings were typically conducted in private. Court procedures were informal and inquisitorial, not requiring the presence of a defense attorney. Specific criminal safeguards of due process were not applicable because juvenile proceedings were defined by statute as civil in character.[61]

The judges of the new court were empowered to investigate the character and social background of "redelinquent" as well as delinquent children; they concerned themselves with motivation rather than intent, seeking to identify the moral reputation of problematic children. The requirements of preventive penology and child saving further justified the court's intervention in cases where no offense had actually been committed, but where, for example, a child was posing problems for some person in authority, such as a parent or teacher or social worker.

The role model for juvenile court judges was doctor-counselor rather than lawyer. "Judicial therapists" were expected to establish a one-to-one relationship with "delinquents" in the same way that a country doctor might give his time and attention to a favorite patient. Juvenile court-rooms were often arranged like a clinic, and the vocabulary of its partici-pants was largely composed of medical metaphors. "We do not know the child without a thorough examination," wrote Judge Julian Mack. "We must reach into the soul-life of the child."[62] Another judge from Los Angeles suggested that the juvenile court should be a "laboratory of human behavior" and its judges trained as "specialists in the art of human relations." It was the judge's task to "get the whole truth about a child" in the same way that a "physician searches for every detail that bears on the condition of the patient."[63] Similarly, the judges of the Boston juvenile court liked to think of themselves as "physicians in a dispensary."[64]

The unique character of the child-saving movement was its concern for predelinquent offenders—"children who occupy the debatable ground between criminality and innocence"—and its claim that it could transform potential criminals into respectable citizens by training them in "habits of industry, self-control and obedience to law."[65] This policy justified the diminishing of traditional procedures and allowed police, judges, probation officers, and truant officers to work together without legal hindrance. If children were to be rescued, it was important that the rescuers be free to pursue their mission without the interference of defense lawyers and due process. Delinquents had to be saved, transformed, and reconstituted. "There is no essential difference," noted a prominent child saver, "between a criminal and any other sinner. The means and methods of restoration are the same for both."[66]

The juvenile court legislation enabled the state to investigate and control a wide variety of behaviors. As Joel Handler has observed, "the critical philosophical position of the reform movement was that no formal, legal distinctions should be made between the delinquent and the dependent or neglected."[67] Statutory definitions of "delinquency" encompassed (1) acts that would be criminal if committed by adults; (2) acts that violated county, town, or municipal ordinances; and (3) violations of vaguely worded catch-alls—such as "vicious or immoral behavior," "incorrigibility," and "truancy"—which "seem to express the notion that the adolescent, if allowed to continue, will engage in more serious conduct."[68]

The juvenile court movement went far beyond a concern for special treatment of adolescent offenders. It brought within the ambit of governmental control a set of youthful activities that had been previously ignored or dealt with on an informal basis. It was not by accident that the behavior subject to penalties—drinking, sexual "license," roaming the streets, begging, frequenting dance halls and movies, fighting, and being seen in public late at night—was especially characteristic of the children of working class and immigrant families. Once arrested and adjudicated, these "delinquents" became wards of the court and eligible for salvation.

It was through the reformatory system that the child savers hoped to demonstrate that delinquents were capable of being converted into law-abiding citizens. Though the reformatory was initially developed in the United States during the middle of the nineteenth century as a special form of prison discipline for adolescents and young adults, its underlying principles were formulated in Britain by Matthew Davenport Hill, Alexander Maconochie, Walter Crofton, and Mary Carpenter. If the United States did not have any great penal theorists, it at least had energetic administrators—like Enoch Wines, Zebulon Brockway, and Frank Sanborn—who were prepared to experiment with new programs.

The reformatory was distinguished from the traditional penitentiary in several ways: it adopted a policy of indeterminate sentencing; it emphasized the importance of a countryside location; and it typically was organized on the "cottage" plan as opposed to the traditional congregate housing found in penitentiaries. The ultimate aim of the reformatory was reformation of the criminal, which could only be achieved "by placing the prisoner's fate, as far as possible, in his own hand, by enabling him, through industry and good conduct to raise himself, step by step, to a position of less restraint . . ."[69]

Based on a crude theory of rewards and punishments, the "new penology" set itself the task of resocializing the "dangerous classes." The typical resident of a reformatory, according to one child saver, had been "cradled in infamy, imbibing with its earliest natural nourishment the germs of a depraved appetite, and reared in the midst of people whose lives are an atrocious crime against natural and divine law and the rights of society." In order to correct and reform such a person, the reformatory plan was designed to teach the value of adjustment, private enterprise, thrift, and self-reliance. "To make a good boy out of this bundle of perversities, his entire being must be revolutionized. He must be taught self-control, industry, respect for himself and the rights of others."[70] The real test of reformation in a delinquent, as William Letchworth told the National Conference of Charities and Correction in 1886, was his uncomplaining adjustment to his former environment. "If he is truly reformed in the midst of adverse influences," said Letchworth, "he gains that moral strength which makes his reform permanent."[71] Moreover, reformed delinquents were given every opportunity to rise "far above the class from which they sprang," especially if they were "patient" and "self-denying."[72]

Reformation of delinquents was to be achieved in a number of different ways. The trend from congregate housing to group living represented a significant change in the organization of penal institutions. The "cottage" plan was designed to provide more intensive supervision and to reproduce, symbolically at least, an atmosphere of family life conducive to the resocialization of youth. The "new penology" also urged the benefits of a rural location, partly in order to teach agricultural skills, but mainly in order to guarantee a totally controlled environment. This was justified by appealing to the romantic theory that corrupt delinquents would be spiritually regenerated by their contact with unspoiled nature.[73]

Education was stressed as the main form of industrial and moral training in reformatories. According to Michael Katz, in his study of nineteenth-century education, the reformatory provided "the first form of compulsory schooling in the United States."[74] The prominence of education as a technique of reform reflected the widespread emphasis on socialization and assimilation instead of cruder methods of social control. But as George Rusche and Otto Kirchheimer observed in their study of the relationship between economic and penal policies, the rise of "rehabilitative" and educational programs was "largely the result of opposition on the part of free workers," for "wherever working-class organizations were powerful enough to influence state politics, they succeeded in obtaining complete abolition of all forms of prison labor (Pennsylvania in 1897, for example), causing much suffering to the prisoners, or at least in obtaining very considerable limitations, such as work without modern machinery, conventional rather than modern types of prison industry, or work for the government instead of for the free market."[75]

Although the reformatory system, as envisioned by urban reformers, suffered in practice from overcrowding, mismanagement, inadequate financing, and staff hiring problems, its basic ideology was still tough-minded and uncompromising. As the American Friends Service Committee noted, "if the reformers were naive, the managers of the correctional establishment were not. Under the leadership of Zebulon R. Brockway of the Elmira Reformatory, by the latter part of the nineteenth century they had co-opted the reformers and consolidated their leadership and control of indeterminate sentence reform."[76] The child savers were not averse to using corporal punishment and other severe disciplinary measures when inmates were recalcitrant. Brockway, for example, regarded his task as "socialization of the anti-social by scientific training while under completest governmental control."[77] To achieve this goal, Brockway's reformatory became "like a garrison of a thousand prisoner soldiers," and "every incipient disintegration was promptly checked and disinclination of individual prisoners to conform was overcome."[78] Child saving was a job for resolute professionals who realized that "sickly sentimentalism" had no place in their work.[79]

"Criminals shall either be cured," Brockway told the National Prison Congress in 1870, "or kept under such continued restraint as gives guarantee of safety from further depredations."[80] Restraint and discipline were an integral part of the "treatment" program and not merely expediencies of administration. Military drill, "training of the will," and long hours of tedious labor were the essence of the reformatory system, and the indeterminate sentencing policy guaranteed its smooth operation. "Nothing can tend more certainly to secure the most hardened and desperate criminals than the present system of short sentences," wrote the reformer Bradford Kinney Peirce in 1869.[81] Several years later, Enoch Wines was able to report that "the sentences of young offenders are wisely regulated for their amendment; they are not absurdly shortened as if they signified only so much endurance of vindictive suffering."[82]

Since the child savers professed to be seeking the "best interests" of their "wards" on the basis of corporate liberal values, there was no need to formulate legal regulation of the right and duty to "treat" in the same way that the right and duty to punish had been previously regulated. The adversary system, therefore, ceased to exist for youth, even as a legal fiction.[83] The myth of the child-saving movement as a humanitarian enterprise is based partly on a superficial interpretation of the child savers' rhetoric of rehabilitation and partly on a misconception of how the child savers viewed punishment. While it is true that the child savers advocated minimal use of corporal punishment, considerable evidence suggests that this recommendation was based on managerial rather than moral considerations. William Letchworth reported that "corporal punishment is rarely inflicted" at the State Industrial School in Rochester because "most of the boys consider the lowering of their standing the severest punishment that is inflicted."[84] Mrs. Glendower Evans, commenting on the decline of whippings at a reform school in Massachusetts, concluded that "when boys do not feel themselves imprisoned and are treated as responsible moral agents, they can be trusted with their freedom to a surprising degree."[85] Officials at another state industrial school for girls also reported that "hysterics and fits of screaming and of noisy disobedience, have of late years become unknown. . . ."[86]

The decline in the use of corporal punishment was due to the fact that indeterminate sentencing, the "mark" or "stage" system of rewards and punishments, and other techniques of "organized persuasion" were far more effective in maintaining order and compliance than cruder methods of control. The chief virtue of the "stage" system, a graduated system of punishments and privileges, was its capacity to keep prisoners disciplined and submissive.[87] The child savers had learned from industrialists that persuasive benevolence backed up by force was a far more effective device of social control than arbitrary displays of terrorism. Like an earlier generation of penal reformers in France and Italy, the child savers stressed the efficacy of new and indirect forms of social control as a "practical measure of defense against social revolution as well as against individual acts."[88]

Although the child-saving movement had far-reaching consequences for the organization and administration of the juvenile justice system, its overall impact was conservative in both spirit and achievement. The child savers' reforms were generally aimed at imposing sanctions on conduct unbecoming "youth" and disqualifying youth from the benefit of adult privileges. The child savers were prohibitionists, in a general sense, who believed that social progress depended on efficient law enforcement, strict supervision of children's leisure and recreation, and enforced education. They were primarily concerned with regulating social behavior, eliminating "foreign" and radical ideologies, and preparing youth as a disciplined and devoted work force. The austerity of the criminal law and penal institutions was only of incidental concern; their central interest was in the normative outlook of youth, and they were most successful in their efforts to extend governmental control over a whole range of youthful activities which had previously been handled locally and informally. In this sense, their reforms were aimed at defining, rationalizing, and regulating the dependent status of youth.[89] Although the child savers' attitudes to youth were often paternalistic and romantic, their commands were backed up by force and an abiding faith in the benevolence of government.

The child-saving movement had its most direct impact on the children of the urban poor. The fact that "troublesome" adolescents were depicted as "sick" or "pathological," imprisoned "for their own good," addressed in paternalistic vocabulary, and exempted from criminal law processes, did not alter the subjective experiences of control, restraint, and punishment. It is ironic, as Philippe Aries observed in his historical study of European family life, that the obsessive solicitude of family, church, moralists, and administrators for child welfare served to deprive children of the freedoms which they had previously shared with adults and to deny their capacity for initiative, responsibility, and autonomy.[90]

The child savers' rhetoric of benevolence should not be mistaken for popular democratic programs. Paternalism was a typical ingredient of most reforms in the Progressive Era, legitimizing imperialism in foreign policy and extensive state control at home. Even the corporate rich, according to William Appleman Williams, "revealed a strikingly firm conception of a benevolent feudal approach to the firm and its workers" and "were willing to extend—to provide in the manner of traditional beneficence—such things as new housing, old age pensions, death payments, wage and job schedules, and bureaus charged with responsibility for welfare, safety, and sanitation."[91] But when benevolence failed—in domestic institutions such as schools and courts or in economic policies abroad—government officials and industrial leaders were quick to resort to massive and overwhelming force.[92]

This is not to suggest that the child savers and other progressive movements did not achieve significant reforms. They did in fact create major changes. In the arena of criminal justice they were responsible for developing important new institutions which transformed the character of the administration of juvenile justice. But these reforms, to use Andre Gorz's distinctions, were "reformist" rather than "structural":

> Structural reform . . . does not mean a reform which rationalizes the existing system while leaving intact the existing distribution of powers; this does not mean to delegate to the [capitalist] State the task of improving the system.

> Structural reform is by definition a reform implemented or controlled by those who demand it. Be it in agriculture, the university, property relations, the region, the administration, the economy, etc., a structural reform *always* requires the creation of new centers of democratic power. Whether it be at the level of companies, schools, municipalities, regions or of the national Plan, etc., structural reform always requires a *decentralization* of the decision making power, a restriction on the powers of State or Capital, an extension of popular power, that is to say, a victory of democracy over the dictatorship of profit.[93]

By this definition, then, the child-saving movement was a "reformist reform." It was not controlled by those whom it was supposed to benefit; it did not create new centers of democratic power; it extended and consolidated the powers of the state; and it helped to preserve existing economic and political relationships.

During the last seventy years, the juvenile justice system has grown into a massive and complex bureaucratic organization, staffed by judges, prosecutors, public defenders, probation and parole officers, counselors, child guidance experts, correctional officers, guards, and bailiffs. It is significant that the exclusion of "amateurs" and volunteers from decision-making positions was one of the first tasks undertaken by "professional" child savers at the beginning of this century.[94] With the exception of a few attempts to develop community controlled antidelinquency programs —for example, the Cincinnati experiment in 1917 and the Chicago Area Project in the 1930s[95]—the job of controlling delinquency has become an esoteric craft reserved for specialists, a craft outside the competence of ordinary citizens.[96] In addition to the earlier problems of the child-saving movement—its class exploitation, repressive benevolence, and elitism—the modern juvenile justice system also helps to maintain racism, sexism, and working-class powerlessness.

Even by its own standards, the juvenile justice system has seriously failed. One out of every nine persons under the age of eighteen years is referred by the police to the juvenile court on delinquency charges; one out of every six boys (boys are arrested five times more often than girls) is referred to juvenile court.[97] Arrests of young persons for crimes increased 47 percent between 1960 and 1965, while each year, according to a conservative estimate, 100,000 youths are held in custody institutions. Youth arrests exceed adult arrests, and in the large urban centers literally millions of young people are arrested annually. A high proportion—as much as 75 percent in some cities—of the victims of the juvenile justice system are Third World.

On purely utilitarian grounds, reformatories and detention centers are also a dismal failure in deterring or reducing crime.[98] The task of these institutions is to educate or coerce youth into conformity and submission, to make them accept society's prevailing values, and to prepare them for future roles as punctual and disciplined workers, contented housewives and secretaries, and competitors for "service" jobs as maids, janitors, garbage collectors, and other forms of "dirty work." Under the present system, successful "rehabilitation" is impossible because people cannot have their basic needs met in a society practicing class exploitation, racism, and sexism. It is not surprising, then, that the "graduates" of reformatories invariably return to crime as a means of survival or that many eventually end up in Folsom, Attica, Soledad, and other heavy security prisons.

The increase in delinquency and ineffectiveness of the juvenile justice system are not simply attributable to "youth" or "generational problems." This description obscures the class and racial composition of youths processed through the system. While it is true that middle-class youths are being arrested in increasing numbers, especially for drug-related offenses, the overwhelming majority of arrestees are poor and Third World. Middle-class youths are kept out of state institutions with the help of expensive attorneys, private psychiatrists, and (in extreme cases) referrals to private military schools. Most white middle-class residents have community control of their suburban police and are able to prevent officials from channeling their children to juvenile court.

The most serious and militant challenge to established authority in recent years has come from urban black youth.[99] The Kerner Report observed that there was enough evidence by 1966 to indicate that a large proportion of "riot" participants were youths. It also suggested that "increasing race pride, skepticism about their job prospects, and dissatisfaction with the inadequacy of their education, caused unrest among students in Negro colleges and high schools."[100] The events of recent years support and go beyond this finding—especially in urban schools, which are more and more becoming the locus of youthful protest.

Young blacks between the ages of fifteen and twenty-four were the most active participants in the urban riots of the 1960s.[101] These youths were not known to be psychologically impaired or suffering from any special personality problems. Juveniles arrested in the 1967 Detroit riot were found by a psychological team to be less emotionally disturbed than typical arrestees.[102] Furthermore, the recent riots not only were viewed by nonrioting blacks as a legitimate form of protest, but they also served to mobilize the younger segments of the black community and educate them to the realities of their caste position in American society. As William Grier and Price Cobbs observed:

Today it is the young men who are fighting the battles, and for now, their elders, though they have given their approval, have not joined in. The time seems near, however, for the full range of the black masses to put down the broom and buckle on the sword. And it grows nearer day by day. Now we see skirmishes, sputtering erratically, evidence if you will that the young men are in a warlike mood. But evidence as well that the elders are watching closely and may soon join the battle.[103]

One of the most significant features of the new black militancy is the increased political consciousness of youths, who are developing Afro-American organizations in high schools, forming youth chapters in political organizations, demanding cultural autonomy and community control in education, and challenging arbitrary authority. Massive student boycotts occurred in Chicago and New York in 1968 in support of extensive demands, including locally controlled schools and holidays to commemorate the birthdays of Martin Luther King, Malcolm X, Marcus Garvey, and W. E. B. DuBois. White high school youths, notably in New York and Berkeley, developed union organizations to oppose the war and to express their solidarity with the struggles of Third World youth. High school activists have generally impressed school officials with the sophistication and legitimacy of their demands; some ameliorative concessions were made to students while more fundamental disputes over school control and decentralization are still being contested.

The militant activities of black and other Third World youth, the development of political organizations in high schools, opposition to the war and draft, the increasing rebelliousness and use of drugs, opposition to stereotypes about the immaturity of youth, and the recruitment of young persons into militant political organizations—all these events in the

1960s indicated that a radical political movement was developing and that agencies of social control were both ineffective and counterproductive. In the same way that the child savers created the juvenile justice system at the end of the last century in order to rescue capitalism and avert radical change, the state has begun to develop new strategies of control and amelioration in response to recent militancy.

Following the 1967 National Crime Commission and various riot and violence commissions, efforts are currently under way to streamline and professionalize the administration of criminal justice by introducing rational management procedures, removing private citizens from the affairs of specialists, and developing techniques for managing an increasingly recalcitrant and hostile youth population. A cautious pragmatism guides the contemporary reformer, for crime control has become a task for hardheaded professionals attempting to rescue antiquated criminal justice bureaucracies with methods engineering and an updated Taylorism.

As in the child-saving movement, the new strategies of control are two-pronged—some are benevolent, ameliorative, and reformist, while some are explicitly coercive and authoritarian. The Crime Commission, which represents the more "enlightened" wing of the contemporary reform movement, primarily focuses on ways of extending controls over "hard-to-reach" youth and devising new methods of control within existing institutions.[104] The "two-pronged" approach proceeds upon the premise that the solution to delinquency lies in creating more systematic and pervasive institutions of control, together with making conventional and legal activities more attractive to youth.

The more benevolent strategies of reform presently under development include youth service bureaus, community relations programs, and the provision of lawyers in juvenile court. Public officials have in some instances recognized the potential power of youth by agreeing to negotiate student demands, creating special programs of job training, and consulting with youth and gang leaders in the development of community projects. Often this recognition is motivated by an awareness that youth organizations, like the Blackstone Rangers in Chicago, are becoming more and more capable of mobilizing vast numbers of young people with a view to political or even guerrilla action.

The most significant ameliorative reform in recent years is the "constitutional domestication" of the juvenile court. For several years, critics have pointed out that the juvenile court violates constitutional guarantees of due process and stigmatizes youths as "delinquents," thereby performing functions similar to those of the criminal courts. The United States Supreme Court recognized the constitutional argument for the first time in 1967 when it delivered an opinion on the juvenile court in the *Gault* case. The Court added clear procedural guidelines to its earlier statement in the *Kent* case (1966) that the "admonition to function in a 'parental' relationship is not an invitation to procedural arbitrariness." Speaking for the majority in the *Gault* case, Justice Fortas held that juveniles are entitled to (1) timely notice of the specific charges against them; (2) notification of the right to be represented by counsel in proceedings which "may result in commitment to an institution in which the juvenile's freedom is curtailed"; (3) the right to confront and cross-examine complainants and other witnesses; and (4) adequate warning of the privilege against self-incrimination and the right to remain silent. The right to counsel is the fundamental issue in the *Gault* case (1967:36) because exercise of the right is designed to assure procedural regularity and implementation of related principles:

A proceeding where the issue is whether the child will be found to be "delinquent" and subjected to the loss of his liberty for years is comparable in seriousness to a felony prosecution. The juvenile needs the assistance of counsel to cope with problems of law, to make skilled inquiry into facts, to insist upon the regularity of the proceedings, and to ascertain whether he has a defense and to prepare and submit it.[105]

The *Gault* decision followed shortly after the President's Crime Commission had made even stronger recommendations concerning the right to counsel:

Counsel must be appointed where it can be shown that failure to do so would prejudice the rights of the person involved . . . Nor does reason appear for the argument that counsel should be provided in some situations but not in others; in delinquency proceedings, for example, but not in neglect. Wherever coercive action is a possibility, the presence of counsel is imperative. . . . What is urgent and imperative is that counsel be provided in the juvenile courts at once and as a regular matter for all who cannot afford to retain their own. . . . Counsel should be appointed . . . without requiring any affirmative choice by child or parent.[106]

Although the *New York Times* greeted *Gault* as a landmark decision demanding "radical changes,"[107] it seems unlikely that the decision will generate anything more than a few modest alterations in existing arrangements for handling delinquents. Whereas the *Gault* decision may introduce some measure of due process in juvenile court, it also runs the risk of making juvenile court more orderly and efficient at the expense of substantive fairness. The "constitutional domestication" of the juvenile court will mean, *inter alia,* that the intake of delinquency cases will be sharply reduced; but it is unlikely to have much impact on the mechanical expediency of lower-court justice or on the penal character of juvenile institutions. Furthermore, studies of defense lawyers in juvenile courts suggest that the implementation of due process will fall far short of the ideal adversary system suggested by the Supreme Court. Lawyers in juvenile courts bring to their job commonsense notions about adolescence and "troublesome" behavior. Their views on youth and delinquency are really no different from those of other adult officials (teachers, social workers, youth officers, etc.) who are charged with regulating youthful behavior. Juveniles get the same kind of treatment in court that they get in school or at home, and lawyers accept this as one of the inevitable and appropriate consequences of adolescence.[108]

Although providing lawyers for youth is one of the ameliorative concessions of the contemporary reform movement, the main focus has been on improving efficiency in the juvenile court through narrowing its formal jurisdiction, developing more refined classification systems, and creating new institutional arrangements (Youth Service Bureaus, for example) to handle less serious crimes on a local and informal basis. The same period, however, has seen the creation of police gang intelligence units, infiltration of youth groups by police spies, the presence of heavily armed riot and "tactical" units, and the routine coercive measures to support benevolent policies. Rather than increasing opportunities for self-determination by youth, public officials have opted for closer supervision in order to decrease opportunities for the exercise of illegal or collective power.[109] Intelligence units are expanding and developing counterinsurgency techniques to manage gangs.[110] The size of the gang intelligence unit in Chicago, for example, increased from 38 to 200 within a few years.[111] In many cities, schools have taken hard-line action against organizers, since some authorities feel that "riots are unleashed against the community" from high schools and the granting of concessions to students might encourage further rebellions.[112] As in Vietnam, authorities quickly resort to the use of force when "pacification" fails; and as the contradictions become more apparent and the control system more unsuccessful, the methods of coercion become similarly more explicit and more desperate.

Contemporary efforts to restructure the juvenile justice system have many parallels with the child-saving movement, though the state today has far more technological resources and a capacity to create more sophisticated and dangerous strategies of control. Academics have in general helped to legitimize and provide technical assistance to these new developments, albeit in the name of liberal ideology. They continue to accept state definitions of crime, to promote reforms within the framework of corporate capitalism, to underestimate the importance of historical and macroscopic analysis, and to encourage defeatist attitudes about the possibility of radical change. The answer to economic and political oppression is not to be found in such liberal reforms as youth service bureaus or the provision of public defenders. The old models need to be completely dismantled and replaced by institutions which serve and are democratically controlled by the people. While undertaking this task, we must also discard false ideologies and break free from the myths which distort our views of the past and limit our vision of the future.

RICHARD M. BREDE

5

COMPLAINANTS AND KIDS: The Role of Citizen Complainants in the Social Production of Juvenile Cases

Richard Brede's article focuses on the role of citizen complainants in cases involving juveniles. His basic point is that citizens call in the police to solve or ameliorate a social problem involving young people. Calling the police leads to an encounter in which the police must decide if the juveniles should be arrested. The police will make their decision by applying "social definitions of deviant or criminal acts provided . . . by community residents." The citizen complainant usually regards an arrest of young people as a solution to his problem. In discussing the implications of this process Brede relies on material collected in a participant observer project in Chicago which involved three ethnically and socioeconomically different police districts. Brede reminds us that "police work is overwhelmingly a reactive process" and then raises two important questions: "Whose rules do the police enforce?" and "What practical and moral interests are served when juvenile offenders are taken into custody?"

Over the past dozen years or so, sociologists have expressed a topical concern with the police and their various relationships with the public at large or with identifiable segments of the public. Such titles as Reiss's *The Police and the Public* and Bayley and Mendlesohn's *Minorities and the Police* stand as exemplars of this focused concern. Now despite differences in types of policing organizations studied, the scope and size of the research enterprises, and methods used to investigate police

---

From *Journal of the Kansas Trial Lawyers* (Summer, 1977), pp. 4–15.

behavior which otherwise distinguish such studies from one another, a common underlying orientation toward the police unites the vast bulk of them. Here reference is made to the fact that most police-public studies are more or less explicitly founded on a working definition that "sees" the police as the "cutting edge" of the legal order. The police, that is, are defined primarily in terms of the ways in which they are structurally linked up with and functionally contribute to the overall criminal justice system. Speaking to this point, Reiss has argued that a sociological concern with police encounters with citizens is warranted because such important social transactions constitute "the microcosm that generates all cases for processing in the criminal justice system."[1]

What I have called the cutting-edge perspective has thus served as an orienting image for studies of the police and public and has in fact exerted a powerful influence on the kinds of police behavior believed worth examining topically. Once it is conceded that the police provide a screening or filtering function for the criminal justice system, it makes good sense to conduct research into the ways in which police officers routinely go about locating, identifying and selecting persons to be legally processed as "cases" by other agents within the system for administering criminal justice. Accordingly, research has been accomplished in such areas as judgmental criteria in use by police officers in initiating street-level contacts with suspect persons,[2] the use of paid informers and undercover agents in securing and maintaining police access to illegal activities transacted in private settings,[3] social constraints and practical understandings surrounding police decisions to invoke the law by making an arrest,[4] and statistical correlates of police decision making in screening offenders, principally juvenile offenders, for court appearances.[5]

Such research is obviously relevant to a sociological understanding of how police officers initiate encounters with suspects and the social circumstances under which they take them into custody. However, the nearly total preoccupation with "cutting-edge" research on the police side of police-public relationships has left virtually unexamined the various social roles played by citizen complainants in mobilizing the police on their own behalf. And although a considerable amount of evidence indicates that police work with both adult and juvenile offenders consists largely in responding to citizen reports of criminal actions and citizen identifications of persons responsible for committing them,[6] more is presently known about citizens who are criminally victimized and do not notify the police than is known about citizens who do report crimes to the police and moreover furnish police officers with information (or other situational evidence of crime) intended to lead to the identification and location of offenders. In short, there is currently more research interest in what Conklin has called the "dark figure" of crime (e.g., crime that occurs but goes unreported) than there is in researching the organization of social contacts between citizen complainants and the police.[7]

The present paper adopts a rather different frame of reference toward social contacts between police officers, citizen complainants and juvenile offenders. Briefly stated, *the perspective offered here is that citizen-initiated contacts with the police are situated social acts whose principal object is the solution or amelioration of a perceived interpersonal problem existing between the complainant and a specific juvenile or group of juveniles.* What I wish to call attention to with this general conception of public-police encounters is that such encounters become focused around social definitions of deviant or criminal acts (or definitions of social conditions felt to warrant official police attention) provided for the police by community residents who witness or otherwise learn about such acts or conditions and make reports to the police. Problems reported to the police may center around substantive legal concerns, as when a complainant (or member of the complainant's family) is victimized by a juvenile through a robbery, burglary, or assault. On the other hand, problems may be of exceedingly minor legal significance but involve important moral interests, as the following problem examples show:

Two 16 year-old boys had rented Honda motor bikes for the afternoon. They stopped their bikes in front of a high school closed for summer vacation and tried to enter the building to use the latrine. Finding the entrance locked, they urinated on shrubs growing by the door. Across the street, a father and his daughter were busy washing the family car. Seeing the boys so engaged, the father took his daughter inside and called the police. The boys were arrested and charged with disorderly conduct. (Field Notes.)

Gang boy: This one time we were at this restaurant where we used to hang around, you know, and we were always bothering the guy [owner] in there. One time we started throwing snow balls at him, and he called the cops, you know, and they picked us up. We didn't tell the cops we were throwing at him. We said we were throwing at each other and that some snow balls just went inside the place, you know. He talked to those cops a long time, man. Then they took us down to [District B] and put us up for disorderly. (Tape-recorded interview.)

No matter what the specific nature of the perceived interpersonal problem—a dispute stemming from the loss or damage of personal property, a criminal victimization, a violation of situated rules of interpersonal propriety, or a conflict over personal or official authority—a citizen complainant holds a juvenile accountable (or a juvenile is found to be accountable) and his arrest by the police is defined as a problem solution.

Later in this paper it will be shown that much more of relevance to the sociology of law and order in America attaches to the decision to take a juvenile into custody than the fact that he is ritually inducted into the system for administering juvenile justice, as clearly fateful and consequential as that decision may be for the juvenile concerned. Such police actions are weighty and consequential for citizen complainants as well, since from their standpoint both practical and moral interests are intimately bound up in the decision to arrest.[8] And, as Maureen E. Cain has recently observed, sociologists interested in the study of law and law enforcement might profitably conceptualize the police as an "institutionalized group expected by those who support it to be predominantly oriented to the maintenance of their rules in a specific way, i.e., by preventing specific offenses or types of offense or by dealing with specific rule-breakers."[9]

This definition begs the issue of whose rules the police in fact enforce. After first setting the scope and method of the present article, I will take up this issue by considering the following interrelated topics: Who are the complainants in juvenile cases; what conditions, acts or incidents do they report to the police; and what legally substantive or moral interests of complainants are served by the police when they take a juvenile into custody.

Data on which this article is based were collected as part of the Policing of Juveniles Project, an eighteen-month participant observer study focusing on everyday aspects of police handling of juvenile offenders in the city of Chicago. As initially conceived, the project called for descriptive observations of police behavior in three of Chicago's twenty-one police districts. Since we were at the time interested in describing variations in police handling practices (including variations in police decision-making), police districts were selected because they served distinct or identifiable racial or ethnic populations. Thus, District A serves an all-Black community located on Chicago's South Side; District B serves a mosaic of ecologically specific and spatially adjacent ethnic and racial groupings, including Black, Polish, Italian, Chicano, and Puerto Rican neighborhood enclaves; and District C serves an inner-city area comprised of some middle- and upper-middle-class whites, together with concentrations of American Indians, Cubans, and southern white newcomers to the city.

In addition to participant observer reports of police behavior, we collected all arrest reports completed on juvenile offenders taken into custody and officially processed by the police in each target district during one police period (28 days). These data were examined for content and sorted into "police cases" on the basis of who initiated the complaint that eventually led to taking a juvenile into custody. The citizen-complainant types thus elicited included juvenile complainants, child protectors, adult victims, property caretakers, and juvenile removers. Percentage comparisons for complainant types in each police district are given in Table 5.1 A brief discussion of each complainant type follows.

TABLE 5.1. PERCENTAGE OF JUVENILE CASES INITIATED BY CITIZENS

Complainant type	District A	District B	District C
Juvenile complainants	5	2	2
Child protectors	20	15	19
Adult victims	31	30	28
Property caretakers	30	22	21
Juvenile removers	13	22	21
Citizen-iniated, unable to classify	1	10	10
Total percentage	100	101	101
Total number	(112)	(72)	(64)

Despite the fact that juveniles are often criminally victimized by other juveniles, our data suggest that they are seldom complainants in their own right. Furthermore, a reading of the content of juvenile complainant cases indicates that on those occasions when they do plead their cause to the police, something like the following is likely to happen. A juvenile claiming to be a battery victim stopped a passing squad car, reported the incident and pointed out the offender. The arresting officer's report reads:

AR 168R
   Patrol [number] stopped by victim and stated he was involved in a fight with [female offender] and received a laceration on fingers of left hand, inflicted by [female offender]. Both were arrested and turned over to Youth Officers [District A].

With the arrest of both juveniles involved in the fight, the distinction between juvenile offender and victim-complainant is in effect obliterated. The case is handled as a fight between two juveniles, both of whom are processed as "offenders." This pattern is reproduced in substantially the same form in other cases where juveniles register complaints against each other over matters like fights.

AR 76R
Subject arrested fighting with [name of co-offender]. This occurred at [address]. Brought into [District B] Youth Office by arresting officers.

AR 15R
Arrestee choked complainant causing partial loss of voice, while fighting.

Arrestee fighting on school grounds with complainant [in preceding case].

The police practice followed in responding to juvenile complainants seems to be largely confined to cases where the arresting officers for one reason or another cannot readily determine who is the offender and who is the victim. If two juveniles, both of whom have been fighting, each give conflicting accounts to the police as to who started it and over what, and if each claims to be the victim-complainant, the police take both into custody on the basis of "cross complaints." However, even in the absence of competing assertions about who has been victimized and by whom, the police appear to be generally reluctant to recognize complaints lodged by juveniles (particularly complaints made about parents) as legitimate ones when all they have to go on is the juvenile's word for it—as the following case suggests:

A uniformed patrolman entered the Youth Office with a teen-age Puerto-Rican girl. The patrolman said to her, "Here, tell him." The girl said she had been badly treated at home and had moved in with her aunt at the aunt's request. She seemed very embarrassed to say that her stepfather "gets fresh" with her and that this is the reason for leaving home. She further said that both her mother and stepfather wanted her to move back home but that she was afraid to be alone in the house with the stepfather. Youth Officer ————— took her name and address and told the girl, "You know what to do when your stepfather comes after you? You fight." He gestured that she can protect herself by kicking or hitting the stepfather in the groin. The girl seemed to understand and left the Youth Office. Officer ————— later said, "You can never tell about these deals—that's only one side of the story." (Field Notes.)

Observations of like instances confirm the view that while the police listen to complaints brought to their attention by juveniles, the likelihood of their getting involved in such matters in an official capacity is remote. And in part their reluctance is to be explained by the fact that there usually is another side to the story.

A twelve-year-old boy walked into the [District C] station and told the desk sergeant that he wished to have his father placed under arrest and lodged in jail. The boy was referred to the Youth Officer who determined the nature of the boy's grievance: The father's excessive and unpredictable use of physical force against family members over inconsequential matters, the latest being an unfilled milk pitcher on the dinner table. The Youth Officer drove the boy to his home to interview the father and acquaint him with his son's allegations. The father's account of the milk pitcher incident differed considerably from his son's, being just a further instance of the boy's unwillingness to assume responsibility around the house. His wife was silent during most of this, a fact the father interpreted as her "being against him." The father further stated that his son's actions were hasty and that he wished to punish his father. The father accompanied the Youth Officer to the car. At this time the father flatly stated that problems between he and his son were his business and of no concern to the police. (Field Notes.)

The comparatively few cases we observed where the police officially respond to interpersonal difficulties reported by juvenile complainants does not mean that the police are unwilling to confirm the legal rights of juvenile victims nor necessarily to deny them legal protection. Rather, the data suggest that rights of juveniles are more typically confirmed and upheld when cases are brought to police attention by child protectors.

As might be expected, within the category of child protectors, parents are by far the major source of complaints reported to the police. This fact does not in itself invite comment. It is understood parents might well seek police protection for their children when they have been threatened by another youth, robbed, when they have been the victim of rape or rape attempts, or when their property (e.g., a bicycle or a wagon) has been stolen. However, most child protector cases initiated by parents do not show this pattern at all. Instead we find the following:

AR 152R
Above subject taken into custody on complaint of victim's father [name]. [Offender] arrested at school [name]. Subject pushed victim to ground on way to school.

AR 13R

[Offender] is being accused by [victim] as the youth who cut her with a piece of glass on 19 March 1968 near [address]. Victim appeared at [District A] with her mother.

AR 1R

The offender was accused by [mother of victim] of striking the victim [name]. Turned over to Youth Officers [District C].

AR 76R

Beat [number] arrested above person with his brother [name] for committing a battery upon [complainant's] son.

AR 47R

Patrol [number] sent to [address] interviewed complainant who stated that the person who attacked his daughter was in [school]. Received permission from principal [name] and was accompanied by asst. principal [name] to room [number] where offender was picked out of a room of students. Subject taken to [District A].

Incidents recounted in these arrest reports are not too dissimilar in nature from those considered earlier involving juvenile complainants who laid claim to being battery victims, except for the fact that child protectors resolve for the police much of the definitional ambiguity that surrounds the task of deciding who is victim and who is offender. And, as indicated in the last arrest report presented above, child protectors go to some length to supply information which enables the police to identify and locate juvenile offenders. Other observations support this.

An off-duty policeman brought two 13 year old girls and his 12 year old son into the Youth Office and said the girls had squirted the boy in the face with an unidentifiable liquid contained in a squirt gun; the liquid had irritated his eyes and the complainant was concerned that it might have caused damage to his son's eyes. He further said that when he learned of the incident he contacted the girls and asked them what they had put in the squirt gun and why they had used it on his son. The girls would not tell him, so he brought them to the Youth Officer. When the girls' parents arrived, the Officer learned that both girls had earlier that day tried to discourage the complainant's son from "coming around and bothering them." They also said that on several previous occasions the boy had forced them off the sidewalk by riding his bicycle at them and swerving away at the last minute. They had they said filled a squirt gun with water and dish-washing detergent and squirted him as he passed by on his bicycle. The boy confirmed this and was told by the Youth Officer to stay away from the girls in the future. (Field Notes.)

Arrest reports and field observations indicate that child protecting is not the sole province of parents or persons with a kinship relation to juvenile victims. Child protecting functions are also performed by other adults who can be thought of as having a temporary custodial relationship with juvenile victims.

AR 4R

On Mar. 20, 1968 at about 2:30 a.m. [arresting officer] was on routine patrol in the vicinity of [street intersection] when he observed a bus driver of an east bound bus and a citizen chasing a male/negro youth. [Arresting officer] gave chase and apprehended [offender] after being told by both the driver and citizen that the citizen was assaulted on the bus and that his glasses were broken. When [arresting officer] attempted to take the youth into custody, [offender] struck him and had to be subdued. [Offender] was taken to [District B] where he began to fight and strike at anyone within reach. The youth swore and spit at anyone who tried to speak with him and would not give any information to anyone. [Offender] was handcuffed, searched and identified and his mother [name] was immediately notified and when she arrived the youth attempted to strike her several times. The odor of alcohol was strong about his person.

AR 26R

Beat [number] stopped by civilian [news manager] who stated that one of his paperboys had been robbed 8 March 68. Complainant stated he knew where offender lived. Officers went to location and victim pointed out two offenders. Beat [number] transported all individuals concerned to [District A].

AR 58R

Beat [number] sent to [name of school] to talk to principal. Above named youth was identified by [victims] as the person responsible for stopping them on the street in the vicinity of [school] and threatening them with a stick if they did not give him a nickel apiece.

The fact that adults other than parents also serve as child protectors should not obscure one important similarity that can be found in such police cases. Child protectors ordinarily do not witness directly those actions they subsequently report to the police as offenses. Rather, they learn about them from juvenile victims; and in some instances, child protectors may be unaware for weeks or longer that an offense against a juvenile has in fact been committed.

AR 115R

[Offender] arrested by [arresting officers] on complaints of parents of [1st victim] and parents of [2nd victim]. Both parents stated that [offender] committed the act twice on both girls of sexual intercourse in his apartment located at [address], basement on or about [date].

Both children taken to [hospital] for examination by [doctor] who stated to both parents that no previous tears apparent. [Mother of 2nd victim] stated that she had asked the doctor if the time factor was a factor and he stated to [mother] that it would be difficult to tell, at this time. Reporting officers also interviewed [victims] and both told the same story stated above.

While we cannot be precise at this time with regard to information-exchange processes through which child protectors learn about crimes committed against juveniles, child protector reports to the police are largely reconstructive in nature. Based on personal knowledge the victim has about the circumstances of the offense or specific knowledge he has about the offender, child protectors reconstruct for the police, often with the victim's assistance, a plausible account of what happened to the victim, detailing the nature of the offense, where it occurred, and where the juvenile responsible can be found. But, whether detailed or not, accounts provided by child protectors impose a definitional structure or set of rulings on interpersonal problems between juveniles, establishing for arresting officers the legal identities of those victimized and those held to be accountable.

One of the leading characteristics of child protector cases is the rather indirect and reconstructive relationship that child protectors have to the actions that they report to the police. A similar point can be made for some of the cases brought to police attention by adult victims; namely, those cases where an adult victim reports a criminal offense to the police without being able to supply definitive information about the person(s) responsible for it. A person whose automobile is stolen or whose home is burglarized during his absence often has little more than suspicions about who might have been responsible for the crime.

The handling of such cases is a complicated business; and I can do little more at this time than suggest the barest outline of how this work gets done. On receiving a complaint that a person's home has been burglarized, patrolmen responding to the call make a report of the incident, exhausting the complainant's knowledge about the crime, including whatever speculations the complainant may offer about person(s) likely to have committed it. The patrolman's report typically contains information on the circumstances surrounding the discovery of the crime and a description of the articles found to be missing. The case is then assigned to the detective division charged with investigating and solving crimes of that nature (e.g., Burglary Division, Robbery Division, Homicide-Sex Division, and so on).

Once assigned, these cases are cleared by arrest in a variety of ways, two of which are indicated below. In the first arrest report presented, the arrest of two juveniles resulted from a detective investigation of a burglary during which detectives learned that the two had given generous amounts of money to their friends.

AR 248R

On 11 March 68, at approximately 0100 hrs. [offender] and [co-offender] entered into the apartment of [complainant] and took a grey metal box containing $3000.00 USC and three $500.00 war bonds. The war bonds were destroyed in the furnace in the basement of [offender's] building. After being informed of his right to counsel and his right to silence, [offender] stated that he opened the apartment door with a caseknife and that he and [co-offender] went into the apartment and went to the bedroom. [Offender] stated that the occupants of the apartment were not in the bedroom and that he opened the bottom dresser drawer and found the metal box. [Offender] stated that he and [co-offender] then went out the backdoor and jumped the fence and went into his basement. [Offender] then stated that he pried open the box and after a casual look threw the bonds into the furnace. [Offender] stated that he and [co-offender] split the money and he got about $1,250.00 USC. [Offender] stated that he went out the front of the basement and went into his house. [Offender] stated that he gave his mother $140.00 USC and told her he won it playing cards. [Offender] stated that he went to several stores in [part of town] and spent about $700.00 to $800.00 USC on clothing. [Offender] stated that he gave some money to several friends. [Offender] stated that he spent all his split of the money.

The second arrest report deals with an arrest for Grand Theft Auto. Though the case had been assigned for investigation to detectives in the Auto Theft Division, uniformed patrolmen made the actual arrest.

AR 252R

On 5 March 68 [offender] was observed by [arresting officers] in the driver seat of [complainant's car], which was previously reported stolen under [case number]. Upon questioning at scene, [offender] told officers it was his brother's auto, then later changed to his uncle's. Check showed auto to be stolen and [offender] and [co-offender] were arrested and taken to [District A] for investigation. At that time [offender] gave birthdate [that indicated that he was over 16 years of age] and was being processed as adult when mother came into district, identified him and produced birth certificate showing him to be 16 years old. [Detectives from Auto Theft Division] were at [District A] for investigation and scheduled and completed complaints against [co-offender] for Grand Theft Auto. [Parole Officer] notified of this arrest and stated [offender] would be remanded back to I.Y.C. custody for violation of parole. Auto was returned to owner at [District

A] after complaints were signed and investigation completed by detectives. After being informed of his right to counsel and his right to remain silent, [offender] stated he would make a statement. He said he observed the car at [street intersection] between 11:00 and 12:00 p.m., and saw that it was running, with ignition removed. He entered auto and drove to [address] where he met [co-offender]. He was joined by [co-offender] and they both stayed in auto listening to radio, until approached by arresting officers.

In the two cases considered above, adult victims play a passive part in the actual arrest of a juvenile: they report that crimes have been perpetrated against them but do not take a hand in apprehending the offender. However, the bulk of police arrest reports examined and our field observations of such cases indicate that actions taken by adult victims are directly relevant to the production of juvenile cases in two major ways. First, adult victims provide eyewitness identifications of juveniles who commit crimes against them; and second, adult victims also perform a detaining function by holding for the police juveniles they have apprehended themselves. Both of these complainant actions are reflected in police arrest reports presented below, grouped for convenience into those cases where an adult complainant witnesses a crime committed against him, and those cases where an adult victim catches a juvenile and holds him for the police.

AR 7R

Beat [number] while on patrol was stopped by the victim [name] and he stated that he had just been robbed by two youths, one armed with a knife. Upon touring the area, the two offenders were apprehended at [address]. Both offenders turned over to youth officers [District B].

AR 54R

Above arrested with [names of co-offenders]. The three arrestees were seen by complainant attempting to remove liquor bottle from dispenser. Dispenser and bottle damaged.

AR 81R

The above arrested for riding a bicycle on the sidewalk being older than 13 years old. Also involved in small accident with complainant, however there is no proof that it was intentional and was merely an accident.

AR 83R

[Offender] was arrested after he was observed coming out of an apartment located at [address] with a tool chest and two lawn chairs by complainant. [Offender] was in the company of [co-offender]. When arrested both boys admitted breaking into the apartment and taking a tool chest, the lawn chairs and 3 wrist watches.

AR 120R

Arrested for theft of purse from doctor's office at [address]. Complainant observed offender take purse.

AR 148R

Victim seen offender put a white substance into the carburetor of her auto. Damage to auto amounted to $6.00.

AR 70R

Patrol [number] stopped on the street by [victim] who stated the arrestee had just snatched her purse containing $11.00 USC. Also arrested [co-offenders].

AR 86R

Beat [number] sent to [address] by the CCR. Complainant was reporting that a boy had snatched her black leather purse containing $2.00 USC, misc. cards and papers. While report was being made out the above walked past squad car. Complainant stated there goes the boy who snatched my purse. He was placed under arrest, taken to [District A], turned over to youth officer.

AR 43R

Arrestee along with [co-offender] was discovered by the complainant trying to gain access to his grocery store and auto without his consent.

AR 59R

Complainant was sitting in living room and heard noise in the rear of the house. She went to investigate and observed a [person] standing on an object and cutting the screen on the window. While writing the report with complainant in squad car she observed offender walking down the street. Offender a juvenile turned over to [District A] youth officers.

AR 240R

CC Radio call see complainant, a robbery victim [name] age 44. Upon arrival at the scene, officer [name and beat number] was informed by the complainant that he had just been held up at gunpoint by two juveniles and his valuables taken from him. At this time Beat [number and officer] appeared on the scene and they put the complainant in one of the squad cars and toured the vicinity and the complainant told them the culprits had gone north and as they were patroling they spotted two youths whom they apprehended. The two youths [names] were identified by the complainant as the ones who held him up. The complainant stated that the [offender] had the gun and that as he was coming out of the building at [address] where he is employed, he was approached by [offender] and [co-offender] and that [offender] put the gun up to his face while the [co-offender] grabbed him from behind and told him to give them all of his money. They proceeded to search him and took from him a watch (Timex) valued at $10.00 and about $15.00 in US Currency. The gun used in the armed robbery was a Rohm .22 Cal short pistol [inventory number and serial number] and when asked where he got the gun [offender] told reporting officer that he had found it in the old house by the railroad tracks at [address]. [Offender] states that he and [co-offender] were the persons involved in the armed robbery. He was asked if he knew [victim] and he answered, "Yes, he is the one we held up, and I am the one who had the gun and stuck it in his face and asked him for his money and I put my hands in his pocket and took about $13.00 and then I took the watch also." [Offender] stated that he talked [co-offender] into coming with him and that [co-offender] had nothing to do with him and that [co-offender] had nothing to do with the holdup except that he had been on the scene at the time of the crime.

A second grouping of arrest reports deal with actions adult complainants take after discovering an offense.

AR 3R

Beat [number] sent by CC to laundromat at [address] disturbance, upon arrival interviewed victim [name]. She stated while she was doing her wash, a boy now known as [offender] grabbed her purse and ran. A few minutes later offender was seen by victim peeking around building. She apprehended same and held for police. Taken to [District C] turned over to youth division.

AR 38R

Beat [number] assigned by CCR to [address] on youths being held for police for damage to property. Upon arrival, the above officers were met by [victim and two witnesses]. Complainant stated that [offenders] were jumping on her 1968 Chevrolet and damaged the right front fender. [Complainant] also stated that when she came out, the above youths ran, but they were apprehended by her and two witnesses and held for the police. They were brought into [District B] to be processed.

AR 133R

Beat [number] assigned by CC to above location holding boy for police. Above arrestee was caught by complainant stealing a battery and electric drill from [address].

The foregoing police reports clearly reveal the integral part played by adult victims in bringing about the arrest of a juvenile. As complainants on their own behalf, adult victims typically take more direct and purposive action than simply picking up a telephone receiver and calling the police to report a crime. While their chief contribution to the production of juvenile cases lies in providing eyewitness identifications of juvenile offenders, they do engage in actions that might be called "detaining before arrest" by holding or otherwise detaining juveniles they have defined as offenders. What this in effect means is that by the time the police arrive on the scene, adult victims have things pretty well in hand. Black and Reiss have noted that arresting officers frequently abdicate their discretionary powers by deferring to those complainants who express a preference for the arrest of a juvenile.[10] To this observation we might add that a good part of the legwork connected with the actual apprehension of juveniles is accomplished by the time the police arrive. As will be seen, the actions called "detaining before arrest" reach a high point in cases initiated by property caretakers.

A number of business enterprises and public institutions employ special caretakers who are charged with certain custodial responsibilities with regard to merchandise, equipment, or other objects that are on display in these places. Store security guards are probably the most familiar of these caretaker types and account for a large number of complaints against juveniles for the crime of shoplifting.

AR 68R
    Beat [number] arrested the above, on signed complaint of [security guard] working as guard for [name of supermarket]. The above arrested for shoplifting. Item was a 24¢ package of crackers.

AR 86R
    Beat [number] sent by CCR to investigate holding teens for the police at [name of department store]. Upon arrival spoke to officer [name] the house det. who stated above person apprehended along with [co-offender] for shoplifting.

AR 105R
    Above arrested by [department store] security guard for shoplifting. Above stole 2 packages nuts and bolts 29¢ each, 2 packages of fishing leaders 90¢ each, 1 dog leash 99¢. Total value $3.37.

AR 115R
    Above offender arrested by security officer [name] security officer for [department store] after he observed above offender put 4 decks of cards and 1 bottle of cologne under coat.

AR 52R

> Above arrested by security officer at [discount store]. Offender had in his possession 9 45 rpm records. Turned over to youth officer.

AR 156R

> The above arrested in [supermarket] in company of [co-offenders] on complaint of security officer [name] who observed them. [Offender] had taken 3 boxes of Demet Turtles and 4 packs of Kool cigarettes. Each had articles in their possession.

AR 117R

> Above subject arrested at [department store] by the security officer for shoplifting a gold color costume jewelry ring value one dollar. Security officer stated he found the unpaid for ring in the offender's purse.

By visually monitoring the behavior of shoppers, security guards discharge their custodial duties by identifying juveniles in the act of shoplifting or attempting to leave the store without paying for merchandise. Juveniles so identified are then detained by security guards and held for the police.

Security guards are, however, not alone in identifying and detaining juveniles. Store managers are also complainants in shoplifting cases and perform the same detaining actions.

AR 112R

> Above arrested on complaint of manager of store [name]. He stated [offender] did steal 1 box of cookies value 49¢.

AR 36R

> [Offender] arrested this date at the [supermarket] by complainant [manager's name] who observed [offender] attempt a theft of $2.23 worth of foods and attempt to leave store without paying for same.

AR 88R

> Above subject in company with his brother caught in act of shoplifting by comp. who is asst. mgr. of [supermarket]. Comp. signed.

AR 65R

> Beat [number] sent by CCR to [address] to investigate holding a prisoner. [Complainant], the manager of [drug store] at that location, stated that the above arrestee was observed by a citizen who was parked out front tossing T.V. tubes out of the door. The citizen intervened and informed the manager who recovered the T.V. tubes val. at $83.63. Transported offender into [District A] and turned over to youth officer for disposition.

Complainant actions we have called "detaining before arrest" are found in their most conspicuous form in the preceding arrest reports, where store or supermarket caretakers do the work of identifying offenders and offenses. All actions preparatory to an actual arrest are carried out by security guards or store managers before the police arrive. The arresting officers are forced to respond to situations where offender-offense identifications are complete and a juvenile is already in custody. This pattern is duplicated in other cases where adults register complaints on behalf of a business or institution.

AR 108R
Beat [number] sent by CC to meet CTA police at [address]. On arrival talked to CTA police who had the above and 4 other youths in custody for breaking the light bulbs on "L" platform. The above admitted breaking the bulbs.

AR 33R
Patrol [number] received call to investigate a disturbance with a youth. Upon arrival of reporting officers [principal of grade school] stated that arrestee and two others had broken a window and a pencil sharpener. Both valued at $13.00. Arresting officer has no knowledge of case.

AR 72R
Sent by CCR. Juvenile apprehended by complainant [janitor] with stones in his hand in the rear yard of building. There are 8 windows broken at [address of building].

While such cases occur with less frequency than cases where the formal charge is shoplifting, they add to our knowledge of the types of property caretakers who lodge complaints against juveniles. In addition to store security guards and store managers, we can include private police-force officers, building maintenance men, firemen, school principals, and park supervisors among those property caretakers who identify juvenile deviance.

At the same time, by expanding the roster of complainant types, we also draw attention to differing social circumstances surrounding the social production of a juvenile arrest. In cases considered up to now (especially those initiated by child protectors and adult victims) citizen complainants helped to simplify arrest procedures by sorting out, on the one hand, juvenile victims from juvenile offenders, and, on the other hand, by providing eyewitness identifications of juvenile offenders. Property caretakers are considerably more involved as interactants in the production of juvenile cases. Property caretakers both identify and apprehend juveniles before the police arrive, reducing in effect the actual arrest of a juvenile to a rubber stamping procedure.

Juvenile remover cases are defined in the present study as cases where adult complainants request police assistance in the removal of a "problem juvenile" whose behavior has challenged, threatened, or upset the ritual order of a social setting. In such cases, that is, a juvenile's behavior has exceeded what is allowable by others in the setting; and he has been identified by a complainant as a violator of what Denzin has termed relational propriety.[11] He is, in short, designated by other interactants in the setting as a candidate for removal.

Arrest reports covering these cases deal mainly with public behavioral settings, and the range of settings they deal with is not a very broad one. In what follows, we will explore arrests stemming from relational impropriety in city parks, restaurants, public transportation facilities, and public schools.

What is perceived by a complainant as relational impropriety is often a matter of how much of a given kind of behavior he is willing to put up with. Consider the following cases:

A patrolman entered the Youth Office with a 14 year old boy and a middle aged man. The man worked at a park and told Youth Officer ———— that "This kid has been a problem." The boy was told to sit on the bench and the man took a chair next to the Youth Officer's desk. "He uses that favorite phrase from the South Side. I don't have that crap simply because I won't put up with it. He's a wise kid. I tell him and his friends to get out and they won't leave. Then he spits on me." The boy interrupted and said, "My little brother spit on you. It wasn't me." Officer ———— indicated that he would call the boy's parents and asked the boy for his name and phone number. The boy tried to explain his presence in the park after he had been asked to leave, "Mr. ————, I went back in to tell my little brother to come out in the street . . . I got a witness." The boy's father arrived and wanted to know what the trouble was. Youth Officer ———— told the father that the complainant would explain. "Your son is very articulate. He knows all the four letter words not in the dictionary, like fuck you, motherfucker . . . he won't get out of the park when I tell him." The boy's father spoke angrily to his son: "I know one thing, you boys better learn to keep your filthy tongues . . . you're not supposed to sass an older person." The complainant spoke to Officer —————, "I've got a twenty year old girl working with me and I'm not going to have swearing at her." Officer ————— spoke to the boy: "Mr. ————— represents authority. All he would have to do is say 'I want to go to court' and I'd have no choice. What Mr. ————— suggests is that you stay out of the park at least until things cool down. When you want to go back to the park, talk to Mr. ————— and stick to your word." He then spoke to the boy's father; "If he was my son I'd lay him over my knee and he wouldn't walk for three weeks." The boy tried to explain, "All I was doing was swearing at the guys." Officer ———— said, "Did it do any good?" And to the father, "Take him on home." (Field Notes.)

AR 128R
    Beat [number] assigned by CCR to above location about a disturbance with teens. Upon arrival spoke to special policeman [name] who stated that above offender tossed rocks into the establishment although no one was injured. The special policeman said he asked offender to stay away from the hot dog stand earlier.

Though incidents reported in the above cases are quite different, the patience of both complainants was worn thin after a warning to leave the vicinity, and an arrest for disorderly conduct resulted when the problem juveniles refused to do so. It also happens, however, that police officers receive requests to remove juveniles from restaurants and other settings not because of anything specific that they have done, but because the complainant is concerned that they might do something.

AR 131R
    Above subject along with five other youths [name of gang] caused a disturbance in restaurant in that a rival gang member [name of gang] was identified by above subject's brother as the person who had beat him up the previous Saturday in a fight at [address] between the two gangs.

There are enough gang fights in the area where this incident took place to warrant the owner's concern. Still, it seems likely that problem juveniles are removed because of their nuisance value. A similar point can be made with regard to juveniles who violate the ritual order on public transportation facilities.

AR 123R
    Above arrested on west bound CTA bus causing a disturbance, smoking and disturbing other passengers.

AR 19R
    Beat [number] responded to CCR holding teens. Upon arrival met CTA police who had 3 youths in custody. The above offender was causing a disturbance by stopping an El train and holding it in station for two minutes.

AR 10R
    Above person arrested for disorderly conduct by the CTA police for causing a disturbance on the "L" train.

In the above cases, relational impropriety consists of causing a disturbance on a public conveyance by smoking where no smoking is the rule, arguing loudly or shouting where indifference to others is the accepted form, blocking the aisle while passengers are boarding or exiting the conveyance, or pulling the emergency cord and creating delays in scheduling. Causing a disturbance in any one of these taken-for-granted terms is cause for removal from the setting.

Removal of problem juveniles from school settings is quite another matter, owing principally to the fact that the social relationship within which impropriety is defined by a teacher is usually a more personal and intimate one than exists between a restaurant owner and patron or bus driver and passenger. Given the more personal nature of relationships between teachers and students in school settings, we might expect a greater level of tolerance or acceptance of loud, coarse, rude or recalcitrant behavior on a juvenile's part; and efforts to remove a problem juvenile from a school setting should reflect the complainant's perception of the inability of the relationship to contain the behavior identified as deviant.

Two arrest reports dealing with the removal of a problem juvenile do not conform to these speculations and moreover suggest a concern on the part of school administrators similar to that encountered in the complaint lodged by the restaurant owner—the removal of juveniles who may cause problems.

AR 110R

Beat [number] sent to investigate disturbance at [high school]. Principal [name] stated that [offender] is not student at [high school]. [Offender] arrested for trespassing.

AR 93R

The arresting officer arrested the above on complaint of principal [name and name of school] for disorderly conduct at [name of school] by coming into [high school] and not a student there, but a student at [name of high school].

The remaining arrest reports, however, relate to problems generated within the social order of the school, and more specifically within the social order of the classroom.

AR 4R

Above subject was causing a disturbance in [school] gym. Complainant, gym instructor, stated that subject kicked a door, and was smoking inside gym. Youth would not leave gym when told. Gym instructor felt it was necessary to call police and have the youth turned over to a youth officer.

AR 141R

Beat [number] sent to [name of school]. Informed by school official that [offender] is a uncontrollable student, fighting and talking all the time. He has no respect for his teachers. Turned over to youth officer.

AR 169R

Offender placed in custody for attacking and striking a teacher after he had requested that she leave the room. The offender continued to threaten the victim after she was in custody.

Here, school discipline problems that exceed routine measures established by the school for coping with them are transformed through complainant action into police problems. That is, a classroom discipline problem is brought to public attention and solved (at least temporarily) by the removal of the problem juvenile. Other classroom problems are potentially more serious in their consequences, as the following arrest reports indicate.

AR 164R

Above arrestee arrested for carrying a gun not loaded to the [name of school]. After the complainant, a teacher at [name of school] observed the arrestee with gun, she confiscated same and the boy then left the school, leaving the gun. Arrestee was contacted at his home and he and his parents were notified to appear at [District B] youth office and complied with notification.

AR 44R

[Offender] was arrested for having a zip gun in his possession in [school]. The youth was apprehended by [teacher], when he was observed in the classroom inserting a shell in the opening of what appears to be a zip gun. The youth was placed under arrest and turned over to youth officers. [Offender] states he found the gun outside the school exit.

AR 118R

[Arresting officer] assigned to [high school] was called into [room number]. [School counselor] stated that [offender] asked her to do him a favor. He stated that it was urgent and if she would keep this knife for him. He said he brought it to school to kill [assistant principal]. Knife was concealed on person under his shirt, tucked in front of pants, covered by an army coat. Knife is 8" carving knife. In conversation with [offender] in the presence of his mother at [District C] he states he came to school with the knife went to the main office of [high school] to see [assistant principal], he was busy so he went to attendance room and asked for an attendance slip because he was late. Then he saw [counselor] and asked her if she would do him a favor. She said yes. He took out the knife and handed it to her asking her to hold it for him and not tell anyone about it. She took the knife and said that she wouldn't tell anyone. A short while later [arresting officer] came into office and then [school principal] came in. [Officers from District C] arrived, [offender] was handcuffed, placed in a squad car and taken into [District C].

This article is in one sense a studied reaction to what I take to be the prevailing sociological perspective on the police today, particularly as that perspective has been applied in research on metropolitan policing organizations. In studies which collectively comprise what I have called the cutting-edge perspective, little in the way of serious or critical attention has been paid to roles played by citizen complainants in mobilizing the police and actively cooperating with them in the social production of juvenile cases. Thus, for example, LaFave in his landmark study of police arrests makes no mention of citizen complainants and in fact makes reference to complaints to the police only insofar as criminal courts occasionally issue writs or bench warrants authorizing a person's arrest.[12] While Wheeler has argued for a reformulation of criminal statistics that would express police arrests as a function of interactions between police officers, offenders, and citizen complainants, this important line of inquiry has been largely ignored.[13] More sociological interest has been focused on how the police (as the embodiment of the "long arm of the law" or the "thin blue line") intrusively reach into the everyday lives of people than has been directed to examining the social circumstances and occasions under which police assistance and intervention is specifically requested. More interest has been directed to factors which socially isolate the police from the public at large than has correspondingly been shown to working relationships that exist between police officers and civilians.[14]

I do not mean to say that such factors as police professionalism, social isolation of the police, the emergence of a police subculture or subculture of policemen, and styles of command and control within police departments have no direct bearing on the behavior of police officers. Of course they do, and numerous studies have shown the importance of such factors in accounting for police behavior.[15] Rather, the question now before us is, given the fact that police work is overwhelmingly a reactive process (i.e., an organized social response to complainant reports of interpersonal problems existing between themselves and specific juveniles), whose rules do the police enforce and what practical and moral interests are served when juvenile offenders are taken into custody.

Our data suggest that broad-ranging interpersonal problems are brought to police attention by citizen complainants; and judging from the concerted and purposive actions taken by complainants both before the police arrive and while the police are in their presence (e.g., providing eyewitness accounts and descriptions of juvenile offenders, locating offenders, and detaining them before arrest) we have strong indications indeed that complainants express a preference or even demand that the juvenile be taken into custody, because it is felt that the juvenile deserves arrest as a fitting punishment, property will subsequently be returned as a result of the arrest, or the complainant does not know what else to do with the juvenile under the circumstances.

When viewed from a legalistic standpoint, data which form the basis for this article suggest that most of such interpersonal problems are of minor legal significance—a conclusion which has found support in the work of Black and Reiss (see Table 5.2).

TABLE 5.2. PERCENTAGE OF JUVENILE CASES BY SERIOUSNESS OF OFFENSE AND POLICE DISTRICT

Type of Offense	District A	District B	District C
Serious Offenses	17%	16%	16%
Nonserious Offenses	83%	84%	84%
Total offenses	112	72	64

However, such knowledge about the legal significance of the problems they seek police help in resolving may be of only doubtful value to citizen complainants. Parents who enlist police aid in taming a neighborhood bully or seek "expert" advice for dealing with their own children, widows who have lost objects of sentimental value through theft, school teachers and administrators who cannot cope with unruly students or the occasional student who becomes dangerous, and store managers with standing orders to sign complaints against shoplifters regardless of dollar amounts involved, do not in all likelihood consult criminal statute books before calling the police. For such citizen complainants it is enough that the problem is serious to them and that they feel the police are likely to side with them, recognize their problem, and attempt to deal with it. It is in this fundamental sense that both the moral and legal interests of the citizenry are intimately tied to decisions to notify the police and decisions to take juveniles into custody; and it also is in this sense that the taking of juveniles into custody by the police can be viewed as solutions to interpersonal problems existing between juvenile offenders and members of the citizenry.

It is, I think, important to be mindful of this moral-legal nexus, particularly at a time when traditional methods of handling juvenile offenders are being roundly condemned and newer methods proposed. On close inspection of the kinds of problems brought to official police attention, it is instructive to recall the words of Austin Porterfield, who noted thirty years ago:

A real factor in the conflict of children with a community is the community itself, particularly that section of a community's population which is most likely to complain . . . And we may conclude . . . that no small part of the conflict with youth grows out of the peevishness, impatience, irresponsibility, and, in many cases, the criminalistic attitudes of the complainant.[16]

SAMUEL WALKER

6

THE RISE AND FALL OF THE POLICEWOMEN'S MOVEMENT, 1905-1975

Samuel Walker traces the history of the movement to add women to police departments in the United States from 1905 to 1975. He reminds us that the employment of women police officers "is nothing new and can be traced to the first decade of this century." Walker discusses the present controversy over the hiring of women police officers for routine patrol duties and notes that in the past most women in police departments either did clerical work or were assigned to juvenile divisions. Although this specialization provided opportunities for women in law enforcement, it also led to a stereotyped view of the proper role for a policewoman. Given the current intensity of the feminist movement in the United States and the continuing pressure of the federal government for equal employment opportunities, the history of policewomen provides little incentive for change. As Walker notes, the use of policewomen in the past "represented only a minor challenge at best to both the functions of the police and the image of the woman." Thus the history of the policewoman's movement can be viewed in two ways. Those who oppose the use of women on routine police patrols can argue that women have not had such duties in the past, while those who advocate the routine use of women in all police activities can point to the long history of policewomen and argue that the women performed their duties as adequately as men did without disrupting the structure and function of police departments.

From *A Critical History of Police Reform* (Lexington, Mass.: D. C. Heath and Co., 1977), pp. 85-94.

The deployment of women police officers on routine patrol has become one of the most controversial issues in American policing in the past few years. The male-dominated police establishment has been challenged by the combined forces of an aggressive women's movement and the principle of equal employment opportunity. The use of women police officers has also been recommended by such prestigious groups as President Johnson's Commission on Law Enforcement and the Administration of Justice. The effectiveness of women officers, meanwhile, has been demonstrated by experiments sponsored by the Police Foundation.[1] In spite of such strong pressure for change, however, the police establishment has remained largely hostile to the concept.

The present controversy centers on the use of women police officers on routine *patrol*—the activity that is generally regarded as the "backbone" of police work. The employment of women police officers itself, however, is nothing new and can be traced to the first decade of this century. For the most part, women police officers have been used for specialized tasks such as juvenile work or clerical jobs. The following paper examines the origins and development of the policewomen's movement in the United States. A study of the movement not only illuminates a significant phase of American police reform but also sheds some light on the role of the women's movement and its impact on an important social institution.

The policewomen's movement originated in the years 1905–1910. The first woman known to have held full police powers was Mrs. Lola Baldwin, appointed to the Portland, Oregon, police department in 1905. The city of Portland that year was the site of the Lewis and Clark Exposition. A number of civic-minded women became concerned that the fair would present dangerous temptations for children. Mrs. Baldwin was appointed to the police department and given the responsibility of protecting children from potential vices. To assist her, Mrs. Baldwin organized and directed a team of civic-minded women. The experiment proved satisfactory to those involved with it and, when the fair ended, Mrs. Baldwin was given a permanent position with the police department.[2]

In the next few years, a few other departments hired policewomen to perform similar tasks. The policewomen's movement as an aggressive and self-conscious movement began in 1910 with the appointment of Mrs. Alice Stebbins Wells to the Los Angeles police department. Like Mrs. Baldwin, Mrs. Wells was a social worker; she had attended theological seminary in Connecticut and had held several church-related social work positions prior to her appointment in Los Angeles. Her assignment, like Mrs. Baldwin's, was to prevent juvenile delinquency and to care for young women in trouble with the law.[3]

Soon after her appointment, Mrs. Wells became the leading spokesperson for the policewoman's movement. She spoke extensively across the country, addressing local women's groups and such national organizations as the International Association of Chiefs of Police and the National Conference of Charities and Corrections. In 1911, for example, she spoke in thirty-one different cities on one thirty-day tour. In 1915 she helped to organize the International Association of Policewomen. Her work bore fruit. By 1916 at least sixteen and perhaps as many as forty cities had appointed at least one policewoman.[4]

The careers of Mrs. Baldwin and Mrs. Wells suggest the dominant characteristics of the policewoman's movement. Three aspects in particular stand out. First, policewoman's duties were strictly limited to the handling of juveniles and adult females. It should be noted that the leaders of the movement actively sought this limited role. Second, the impetus for the movement came primarily from private women's groups and social work agencies, not from police departments themselves. Third, many of the first policewomen were selected by and, in some cases, paid either wholly or in part by private groups.

The policewoman's movement had its origins in the earlier campaign for matrons in local jails. In the earliest recorded instance, the American Female Reform Society of New York City demanded and obtained, in 1845, the employment of matrons in the city jails. The second recorded use of matrons occurred in Portland, Maine, in 1877. There, the Women's Christian Temperance Union succeeded in obtaining the employment of a matron. Initially, the matron was paid entirely by the local chapter of the W.C.T.U.; later, the city paid the first half and then all of her salary. The matron's movement gained momentum in the 1880's, with the W.C.T.U. leading the campaign. By the turn of the century most major cities had adopted the use of matrons. While in some cases women with social work backgrounds were hired, in others the job was reserved for the widows of deceased police officers.[5]

The policewoman's movement, like the matron's movement, emphasized the idea that children and female offenders required special treatment and that the "maternal" qualities of women suited them for such tasks. This limited conception of the proper role for policewomen, which was aggressively embraced by the leaders of the movement, proved to be the undoing of the movement in the long run. The movement reached its peak in the mid-1920's and declined steadily thereafter.

During its years of vigorous growth, from 1910 to 1924, the policewoman's movement encountered strong resistance from both the police establishment and from elected city officials. The International Association of Chiefs of Police, for example, regarded the movement with mixed feelings. The organization never went on record opposing the idea of policewomen, but it never gave it a very strong endorsement either. Social work agencies such as the National Conference of Charities and Corrections and the American Social Hygiene Association, along with local women's groups, were always the most enthusiastic supporters of the movement.

In some cities the appointment of the first policewoman was achieved with relative ease. This was true in Los Angeles, where the mayor appointed Mrs. Wells shortly after receiving a petition bearing one hundred signatures. In Chicago the campaign took about two years. In 1910 the chief justice of the municipal court appointed a committee of women social workers to study the problem of juvenile delinquency. The committee's report was quickly acted on by the mayor and the city council. The necessary legislation was passed in late 1912 and the first thirteen policewomen appointed in 1913.[6]

The appointment of the first policewoman in Cleveland, however, came only after an eight-year struggle. The campaign had its origins in two anti-vice efforts that began in 1910. Mayor Tom Johnson embarked on a campaign to eradicate prostitution and in 1915 finally closed down the city's quasi-official vice district. The anti-prostitution effort resulted in a dramatic increase in the number of women arrested by the police. In a parallel development, a group of civic reformers began in 1911 to inspect the dance halls in the city. The volunteers, many of them ministers, were eventually deputized by the police department and paid by municipal funds. Both the anti-prostitution and dance hall inspection campaigns stimulated interest in developing new techniques for handling female offenders and preventing juvenile delinquency.[7]

A brutal murder in 1916 aroused public opinion and launched the policewomen's movement in Cleveland. A sixteen-year-old girl was strangled in her rooming house by an employee of a well-known men's club. This convinced some civic reformers that there should be some means of protecting young women from the dangers that allegedly lurked in such men's clubs. A Women's Protective Association was quickly formed and funds raised to employ a "Special Investigator" who would perform such protective work. The association deliberately chose the title of "Special Investigator" out of fear that the title of "policewoman" would arouse too much opposition.[8]

The Cleveland Women's Protective Association petitioned city government for the appointment of policewomen but encountered strong opposition. In 1917 the city council rejected a bill to hire twenty-nine policewomen and create a Women's Bureau in the police department. Agitation lapsed during World War I, but resumed in 1921. The mayor expressed some interest in hiring policewomen in 1921 but left office without taking any action. Two years later the Women's Protective Association intensified its campaign, bringing in representatives from the American Social Hygiene Association to help lobby. Finally, in 1923, the city council passed the necessary legislation. But the public safety director opposed the idea and refused to make any appointments. Later that year the mayor appointed the first four policewomen on his own authority. Thus, even in reform-minded Cleveland, the struggle took the better part of eight years.[9]

The movement in Boston took almost as long. In 1912 the White Slave Traffic Commission recommended the appointment of policewomen in a report to the state legislature. Two years later, after a concerted lobbying effort by a coalition of women's groups, the legislature authorized cities in the state to hire policewomen. World War I intervened, however, and apparently no appointments were made. The campaign revived after the war and, in 1920, the legislature passed the Boston Policewoman's Act. The first six women were appointed in early 1921.[10]

The campaign in Baltimore was brief and relatively easy. Lobbying began in 1912 and the leader of the movement presented both Republican and Democratic legislators with a bill she had drafted. Many legislators, however, were "shocked and astonished" at the idea of women wearing police uniforms, patrolling the streets and "arresting Negroes and drunken men." When it was explained to them that "the women would not be uniformed, not have 'beats'; but that women and children in the community would be their care," they rather quickly changed their minds and passed the necessary legislation.[11]

The Baltimore effort clearly indicates the extent to which the policewomen's movement succeeded in overcoming opposition by emphasizing the traditional image of the woman as the guardian of children and other women. The national spokeswomen for the movement were even more explicit. Mary Hamilton, the first policewoman in New York City, wrote that "In many ways the position of a woman in a police department is not unlike that of a mother in a home. Just as the mother smoothes out the rough places, looks after the children and gives a timely word of warning, advice or encouragement, so the policewoman fulfills her duty."[12] Similar testimonials to the essential domesticity of policewomen pervaded the literature of the movement.

The policewomen's movement was a struggle on two fronts. On the one hand it had to overcome entrenched opposition to creating new roles for women. In addition to opposition from police officials and elected city leaders, Mary Hamilton reported that in at least one large Connecticut city the movement was denounced by other, more conservative women's groups. The struggle to carve out a new role was a heady experience.

Mary Hamilton spoke passionately of the "chance for a woman with ideas and initiative to do constructive, pioneer work—to make history in fact."[13]

At the same time, the policewomen's movement was part of a struggle within the police establishment to create a new role for the police. In this respect, the movement enjoyed a certain amount of support from a small group of reform-minded police administrators. The decade and a half before World War I was a period of ferment and change in American policing. In these years the concept of police "professionalism" emerged. The movement for professionalization paralleled and drew much of its inspiration and ideology from the broader Progressive movement. Reform-oriented administrators such as Richard Sylvester, Superintendent of the Washington, D.C., police, and August Vollmer, Chief of Police in Berkeley, California, along with civilian reformers such as Raymond B. Fosdick, emerged as the leaders of the professionalization movement.[14]

Police reform in the pre-World War I years was a diverse and hetero-geneous movement. All of the reformers agreed that the police should be removed from partisan political influence, that top administrators should be trained experts in their field, and that all policemen should receive some formal, job-related training.[15] One school of thought main-tained that professionalism should be defined in terms of managerial efficiency. By the 1930's this definition had clearly triumphed. But in the pre-World War I years another school of thought argued that the police could be an important instrument for broader social reform. The conven-tions of the IACP, for example, were highlighted by long debates over such questions as the control of gambling and prostitution, the merits of probation and parole, and the proper methods for handling juvenile offenders.

Perhaps the most important innovation in police thinking in this period was the idea of "crime prevention." The true mission of the police, some reformers argued, was not merely the arrest of law breakers but the prevention of crime. And the best way to prevent crime, they agreed, was to stop juveniles from entering lives of crime. This idea, in turn, provided the entering wedge for the policewomen's movement. After all, who were better qualified to offer counsel and guidance to children than women? As Mary Hamilton pointed out, it was not until the crime prevention role came to the fore in police thinking "that the need for policewomen arose."[16]

The policewomen's movement, then, capitalized on and helped to advance one of the important new ideas of police reform. One can per-haps explain the success of the movement from city to city in terms of the extent to which individual police departments were committed to crime prevention through juvenile work. Clearly the Los Angeles police embraced the idea enthusiastically, while the Cleveland police remained skeptical. Police thinking in this era was far from monolithic and, as the debates at the annual IACP conventions suggest, was quite diverse.

The policewoman was to fulfill her crime prevention role by patrolling, in plain clothes, those places where it was believed that children might come into contact with vice. Alice Stebbins Wells explained to the IACP delegates that "policewomen began by concerning themselves with the places of amusement where the young gather—the dance halls, the skating rinks, the picture shows, the parks and streets—through the curfew and other minor laws, and will continue to do so."[17] Eleanor Hutzel, the chief policewoman in Detroit, defined the responsibilities of the police-woman in these terms: "a patrol problem may be defined as any situation, arising in a public place, that is potentially harmful to a woman or child."[18]

This definition of the policewoman's duties opened the door for highly arbitrary practices. The policewomen's movement was animated by an extremely moralistic outlook. Mary Hamilton expressed this spirit when she warned that "danger lurks in parks, playgrounds, beaches, piers, and baths unless there is someone to watch over these pleasure haunts experienced enough to recognize a devastating evil, however well disguised."[19] The leaders of the policewomen's movement often tended to equate pleasure itself with vice. To protect children from such temptations, policewomen were to take them into protective custody. A World War II era manual advised that "one of the most important crime prevention functions of the policewoman is to discover young girls who are in hazardous situations and to take appropriate action before they become a problem to the community."[20]

"Protective custody" was a highly ambiguous concept and its implementation raised problems of civil liberties. In 1925 Mina Van Winkle of the Washington, D.C., police department was taken to court over the detention of a minor. The court ruled in her favor and thereafter police-women felt confident that their actions were justified. A 1945 government manual of instruction declared unambiguously that the policewoman "should not hesitate to take such action through fear of any violation of civil liberties. Her legal right to follow this procedure has been upheld by the courts." Taking a child into protective custody was not merely a right, but a duty.[21]

The protective work to be done by policewomen was seen as a clear alternative to traditional law enforcement work. Mary Hamilton cited as an example a situation where young boys were playing baseball in the streets. The policewoman would issue a warning and give counsel to the boys rather than make an arrest as a male police officer might do. Thus, the woman would give the police department a "gentler" image and, in the process, hopefully improve its public image.[22] Alice Stebbins Wells argued that the policewoman could also protect regular officers from delicate and often troublesome situations. The male officer jeopardized his reputation whenever he had to handle a female offender. Police-women were "a protection to the department." Mrs. Wells concluded her remarks to the IACP convention by reassuring the chiefs that "the policewoman is not going to take the place of the policeman."[23]

The new crime prevention role of the policewoman raised the question of training. Mrs. Wells pointed out that "when we realize that police work is unlike any other work previously done by women, we at once realize that there is no ready-made body from which to draw."[24] She might have added that there was also no body of knowledge or set of practices among male police officers upon which to draw. In 1910, when Mrs. Wells was first appointed, only a handful of American police departments offered any formal training for their officers. The policewomen's movement, by insisting on high standards of education and training, helped to advance the idea for all police officers. A double standard developed immediately. The Committee on Qualifications of the International Association of Policewomen proposed that policewomen should have at least a high school diploma, with additional college-level training, preferably in "recognized schools of social work. . . ." Moreover, "women police should have at least two years of social case work experience in a recognized agency with preference given to those who have had, in addition, administrative or executive responsibility in social service, in public affairs or in business."[25] These standards far exceeded those expected of male police officers.

The careers of the leading policewomen suggest that they did have a relatively high level of educational achievement. Mrs. Wells had attended theological seminary, while Mary Hamilton attended the New York University School of Philanthropy prior to her appointment. In the mid-1930's five of the top six officers of the Policewomen's Association of California had some college level education. One held a law degree, two were trained nurses and two others had some college education.[26]

The policewomen's movement enjoyed vigorous growth and maintained a strong identity for about fifteen years. Between 1910 and 1916 at least sixteen and perhaps as many as forty police departments hired police-women. By 1919 the number had risen to nearly sixty and a survey in 1925 revealed that at least 145 cities had at least one policewoman. In 1915, meanwhile, the leaders of the movement organized the International Association of Policewomen. The Association carried forward the organizing effort and, through the 1920's, published a monthly *Bulletin*. By the mid-1920's, however, the movement reached its peak and lost its momentum. The decline can, in large part, be attributed to the limits which it had set for itself.

Developments in New York City provide some insight into the decline of the movement. As early as 1924, Mary Hamilton described the emerging "crisis in the history of policewomen's endeavors." In 1921 the New York City police department established a special Women's Precinct, the first of its kind in the country. An old station house at 434 West 37th Street was renovated for the purpose and eventually looked "more like a charming club house for girls than an old-time police station." Mrs. Hamilton pointed out that this non–law enforcement image represented "the very essence of the principles for which the modern policewoman should stand."[27]

Nonetheless, Mrs. Hamilton sensed that the promise of the policewomen's movement had gone unfulfilled. The Women's Precinct soon "became more or less of a routine complaint bureau, to which men and women alike were assigned."[28] Henrietta Additon of the Philadelphia Big Sister Association also complained in 1924 that the precise role of the policewoman "has always been undefined and vague and as a result, the office of the policewoman has often been the dumping grounds for an assortment of miscellaneous duties."[29]

What had been an exciting and bold innovation in 1910 had, by 1925, become a routine and bureaucratized activity, increasingly on the periphery of police activities. The movement experienced little or no growth after the mid-1920's. An extensive survey in 1946 revealed that only 141 out of 417 major cities employed policewomen.[30] This represented virtually no progress in two decades. The movement had not even been able to capitalize on the opportunities raised by World War II when an acute manpower shortage and rising concern over juvenile delinquency briefly rejuvenated interest in the work of policewomen.[31]

The crisis that overtook the policewomen's movement was in large part one of ideology. Policewomen articulated no new ideas following the initial period of growth between 1910 and 1915. The various manuals and guides published from the 1930's onward were simply more elaborate statements of the same ideas set forth by Alice Stebbins Wells and Mary Hamilton. The special role of the policewoman as the guardian of youth increasingly became less of an opportunity for innovative work and more of a trap, a second-class position within the police establishment.

As the policewomen's movement stagnated intellectually, the movement for police professionalization continued to develop. By the late 1930's, under the influence of August Vollmer and his leading disciple

O. W. Wilson, professionalism acquired a very specific meaning. The professional department concentrated on the law enforcement and crime fighting aspects of police work, while incorporating the latest ideas of managerial efficiency. The social work aspects of policing, which had received considerable emphasis in the pre–World War I years, was in almost total eclipse. Social work activities were no longer valued as "real" police work.

The emerging concept of professionalism left policewomen in an extremely marginal position, since their role had always been defined in terms of social work functions. The quarterly reports of the Philadelphia Police Department's Juvenile Division from the 1950's provide a vivid picture of the policewomen's identity crisis. Reporting on a national policewomen's conference, the *Philadelphia Policewoman* commented that "At Syracuse it was emphasized—and in this we agree—that policewomen need not, perhaps should not be, social workers as was stated. Police duties are clearly defined by law, and the primary responsibility of policewomen involves law enforcement." Yet, the pages of the *Philadelphia Policewoman* clearly indicated a social work orientation. Policewomen were described as having "case loads" of between ten and sixty juveniles, while the unit's director relied heavily on moralistic rhetoric with frequent citations from Biblical scripture.[32]

By the late 1950's and early 1960's the policewomen's movement was in a state of almost total eclipse. The two most important textbooks on police administration from this period barely even mentioned policewomen. The seventh edition of *Municipal Police Administration,* published in 1971 by the International City Management Association, noted that "Policewomen should have co-equal status with patrolmen in regard to authority and responsibility, training, and, of course, compensation." But the text did not suggest what role the policewoman should play, nor did it confront the basic question of whether or not policewomen could serve on routine patrol.[33] O. W. Wilson's textbook, *Police Administration,* widely regarded as the "bible" on the subject, meanwhile advanced a blatantly anti-female viewpoint. While noting that women could be of considerable value in juvenile work and certain other police activities, Wilson argued that a woman was not qualified to head the juvenile unit. A male police officer would have wider police experience, would understand the activities of other units, and thereby would be better able to secure their cooperation. Moreover, men are "less likely to become irritable and overcritical under emotional stress" and are likely to be more effective as supervisors of women.[34] This idea represented a major setback for policewomen, since the policewomen's movement had always maintained that juvenile work should be located in a special unit headed by an experienced policewoman.[35]

The leading authority on police administration in the 1960's used an argument of female inferiority to deny policewomen a major role even in juvenile work. That the policewomen's movement had come to such a pass after fifty years should hardly be surprising. After all, O. W. Wilson's ideas about the "special" qualities of women were not unrelated to those of the leaders of the policewomen's movement five decades before. In retrospect, it appears that the policewomen's movement laid the foundation for its own decline. The introduction of policewomen and the idea of juvenile delinquency crime prevention were far less radical innovations than they appeared at the time. Rather, the policewomen's movement was a modest, liberal reform. Even its leading proponents emphasized the fact that it represented only a minor challenge at best to both the functions of the police and the image of the woman.

The history of the policewomen's movement provides some perspective on the present controversy surrounding the use of women police officers on patrol. Despite the intensity of the controversy, it is a far less radical innovation than it might appear. It does represent expanded job opportunities for women. It is also possible that, as its proponents hope, it will make available a large pool of recruits with somewhat higher educational levels than before. This purpose largely accounts for the interest of the Police Foundation in promoting women police.[36] But the use of women officers on patrol does not, in itself, represent any significant challenge to present police practices.[37] It is unlikely to affect such long-standing problems as police corruption, abuse of civilians, and poor relations with minority group communities. The history of the policewomen's movement suggests the relative ease with which a seemingly dramatic reform movement can be co-opted.

DENNIS SMITH

7

REFORMING THE POLICE: Organizational Strategies for the Urban Crisis

Smith raises the question of the role of the police in American society and also asks if the police themselves contributed to the climate of violence that characterized urban life in the late sixties and early seventies. His focus is on the organizational context in which the police function. He is not specifically critical of the personnel in police departments, for as he says "worse men might aggravate the present situation; better men might make it better." But Smith regards the study of the governance of the police as a neglected area. He reminds his readers of the distinction between government and administration and shows that many critics of the police have relied on a model of administration which would stress greater centralization in the name of efficiency. Smith argues, however, that a case can be made for decentralization of police administration.

The bulk of Smith's article focuses on how local control of police might improve police-community relations–particularly relations with minority areas. Thus the key to his argument is that local control of the police will lead to better police services in the ghetto and "as these take place, the prospect of an upward spiraling of citizen confidence and cooperation with the police, leading to greater effectiveness and more confidence, becomes imaginable." Decentralization without adequate provision for local control, however, will not accomplish any real change. Smith analyzes

This is a slightly revised version of a paper presented in a seminar examining the contemporary relevance of "the political theory of the compound republic," organized in 1969 by Vincent Ostrom of Indiana University. The inspiration and critical review he provided are gratefully acknowledged.

James Q. Wilson's proposal for decentralization and finds that "it fails to countenance the problem of the legitimacy of police organization." In summary then, Smith's paper calls for a greater awareness of the relationships between the police and America's pluralistic society.

The proposition to be explored in this paper is that urban police forces, as they are presently constituted, contribute significantly to the potential for a violent process of polarization of American society. A corollary to this proposition is that to increase the armed might of police organizations as a strategy for dealing with civil disorder is to compound their contribution to an escalation of hostility.

Is America approaching a second civil war? To ask the question is, in the view of some, an inflammatory act. While the risk of a self-fulfilling prophecy cannot be overlooked, the hope of a self-denying prophecy is of greater weight. Even if scholars remained silent, it is doubtful that American policemen would suppress their belief that they are now confronting a terrorist attack. An article by Terry Ann Knopf attempted to discount the theory of impending warfare. In "Sniping—A New Pattern of Violence?" she wrote:

> For some time now, many observers (including members of the academic community) have been predicting a change from spontaneous to premeditated outbreaks resembling guerrilla warfare. Their predictions have largely been based upon limited evidence such as unconfirmed reports of arms caches and the defiant, sometimes revolutionary rhetoric of militants.[1]

Although Knopf's assertion of "limited evidence" could have been questioned at the time she wrote (and additional evidence has appeared since then), the greatest weakness of her argument is that it is one-sided. The reports that police at least are increasing their armaments *are* confirmed. The creation of S.W.A.T. units in major urban police departments is perhaps the most widely publicized aspect of police preparation. In a discussion of social conflict in Latin America, sociologist Irving Louis Horowitz warns against dismissing the possibility that "counterinsurgency units precede in time the formation of insurgency units."[2] The implicit theory of conflict escalation underlying Horowitz's caveat needs to be applied to an analysis of a possible trend toward urban guerrilla warfare in the United States.

Even before the recent upsurge of violent attacks on American policemen, danger had come to be recognized as a salient element of the policeman's environment.[3] Whereas before the threat to life arose *in* the line of duty, today it appears simply *because* the policeman chose that line of work. The policeman in the past expected his life to be endangered while making an arrest or confronting an armed robber, but he did not expect to be killed while sitting in a parked car or walking unarmed through a neighborhood and by persons whose only crime was that they were bent on murdering a policeman. This pattern of violence raises serious questions about the social circumstances of its origin and about the political system which dismisses the currency of the phrase "kill the pig" as a personal rather than political structural pathology. However, the most important question may be "How will the policemen who survive the attacks respond?" Will they interpret the "unprovoked attacks" in the way banner headlines in major newspapers and magazines across the country have suggested,[4] as the beginning of an urban guerrilla revolt? If so, how will they deal with the "enemy"? To answer these questions, we must move to an analysis of the broad topic of the relationship between the police and the urban community.

Before beginning an analysis of the role of police in the urban crisis, a disclaimer is in order. The intention is not to discredit the personnel of police organizations. Though their behavior is crucial, the focus here will be on the organizational context—the logic of their situation—on which the behavior of policemen is predicated. Worse men might aggravate the present situation; better men might make it better. But unless the institutional arrangement currently used to provide police services in urban areas is altered, a rapid escalation of violence leading to war in the cities remains possible. With that assertion we must turn to an analysis of the police crisis in America.

The "discovery" of the police by American social science is a relatively recent occurrence. In the mid-1960's Arthur Niederhoffer maintained that "Climactic social upheavals in America have thrust police to the center of the public arena where their vital significance cannot be ignored."[5]

The "glass house" now occupied by police is not the result, as some have argued, of a "Communist attack on the U.S. Police."[6] Rather, a distinguishing characteristic of political association is the availability of coercive capabilities for use in constraining conflict. Understanding the behavior of police as specialized instruments of coercion is essential for a society in conflict. James Q. Wilson has phrased it, "the ability of the police to do their job well may determine our ability to manage social conflict, especially that which involves Negroes and other minority groups, and our prospects for maintaining a proper balance between liberty and order."[7] Perhaps an even more compelling reason to study the police is their pivotal position in deciding the question of whether the United

States in the next decade will be a civil or a warfare state. War arises in a circumstance of conflict in the absence of an appropriate instrument of political constraint. James Madison and Alexander Hamilton, in their commentary on the constitution of civil society in America, emphasized the necessity of an institutional arrangement which assured a capability to constrain individual behavior. Any attempt to constrain collectivities would lead to the emergence of hostile camps, and war. Madison, in *Federalist No. 20*, stated that "legislation for communities, as contradistinguished from individuals; as it is a solecism in theory; so in practice, it is subversive of the order and ends of civil polity, by substituting *violence* in the place of law, or the destructive *coercion* of the magistracy."[8] In a related vein, Madison wrote, "If one nation maintains constantly a disciplined army ready for the service of ambition or revenge, it obliges the most pacific nations, who may be within the reach of its enterprizes, to take corresponding precautions."[9] Sufficient attention to the constitutional arrangement of relations among communities could, in Madison's judgment, obviate the eventuality of war. It is the author's intention here to examine the relevance of Madison's analysis and his prescription to the organization of police in American cities.

What has been the contribution of the police in the drift of the American nation "toward two societies, one white, one black—separate and unequal" and, it might well be added, mutually hostile? The answer is controversial. Niederhoffer, a former New York City policeman, asserts, "The political fact is that police action was the immediate cause of the disastrous series of racial disturbances in Rochester, Philadelphia, Harlem, Hough, and Watts."[10] The Commission on Civil Disorders concluded, "The abrasive relationship between the police and the minority communities has been a major—and explosive—source of grievance, tension and disorder."[11] In his article "From Resentment to Confrontation: The Police, the Negroes, and the Outbreak of the Nineteen-Sixties Riots," Robert Fogelson advances the thesis that "With few exceptions . . . the nineteen-sixties riots were all precipitated by police actions."[12]

While the fact of police action "triggering" the disorders of the 1960's has been generally acknowledged, the inference that this may reflect adversely on police conduct has been resisted. Robert Fogelson has pointed out that police administrators especially have advanced the argument that in the riots "the Negroes vented their violence at patrolmen not as patrolmen but as representatives of white society; the police are the recipients rather than the source of the Negroes' resentment."[13] Administrators have insisted that unlike the past, now "the Negroes have no legitimate grievances against the police, and thus, no major departmental reforms are necessary."[14] An executive director of the

International Association of Chiefs of Police has responded to criticisms by saying:

> Never . . . have we been signalled [sic] out so mercilessly and so wrong-fully as the whipping boys by demonstrators for so-called sociological evolution and by out-and-out hoodlums who have abandoned the banner of civil rights to engage in senseless insurrection . . . Cloaking themselves in the mantle of civil rights, the rabble of society . . . have used so-called resentment against police to engage in savagery seldom witnessed in this country's history.[15]

There is little question that the Commission on Civil Disorders is correct when it states in its report that "it is wrong to define the problem solely as hostility to police. In many ways the policeman only symbolizes much deeper problems."[16] The political and theoretical implications of the argument that the police "represent" the white society are important and will be explored at a later point. The question of whether the grievances of Negroes against police are merely symbolic, or also substantial, needs consideration.

In "From Resentment to Confrontation: The Negroes, the Police, and the Nineteen-Sixties Riots," Robert Fogelson develops the thesis that police behavior is a separable, independent source of black resentment of the organization of society in America. He claims: "One of the salient lessons of the nineteen-sixties riots [is] that from beginning to the end of the riot the police were among the principal targets. Indeed it is impossible to conceive the riots erupting with the same frequency or assuming the same form were it not for the Negro's intense resentment of the police."[17] Fogelson supports his contention by noting the case of another symbol of public authority, the National Guard—which, except in the special case of Newark (where, he says, aggression by Guardsmen required self-defense) "most rioters treated Guardsmen with respect, or at any rate without sharp hostility."[18] Also supportive of Fogelson's thesis is the high percentage of disorders which were triggered by *routine* police action. As Walter J. Raine concluded in his survey of "The Perception of Police Brutality in South Central Los Angeles" for the Los Angeles Riot Study: "It is apparently no accident that the great majority of American riots since 1964 have been triggered by police arrest followed immediately by rumors of police brutality. For who in the Negro community would disbelieve such a rumor?"[19] As early as 1964, Helen B. Shaffer, in an editorial research report on "Negroes and the Police," observed:

A striking feature of the riots which occurred in Negro sections of a number of eastern cities during the latter part of the summer was their marked anti-police character. . . . . Authorities have long realized that a considerable segment of Negro slum dwellers is so hostile to the police that even those among them who are normally law-abiding may side with the miscreant of their own race rather than the arresting officer.[20]

The most impressive evidence that can be offered in defense of Fogelson's position is the catalogue of specific grievances expressed by urban Negroes against police, of which "brutality" is only the most notorious. In sum, there are, as Fogelson among others has shown, four basic reasons for the Negro reaction to the police, ranging from resentment to a hatred, which labels the police as "the enemy." These reasons are brutality, harassment, inadequate police protection, and a feeling of powerlessness to protect and remedy these grievances. The documentation of each of these reasons is extensive and cannot be reproduced here.[21]

Is there an alternative to the current potential for an escalation of urban violence in America? Or, is James Baldwin correct when he claims that "the only way to police a ghetto is to be oppressive?" Baldwin says of policemen in the ghetto:

Their very presence is an insult, and it would be even if they spent their entire day feeding gumdrops to children. They represent the force of the white world, and that world's criminal profit and ease, to keep the black man corralled up here, in his place. The badge, the gun in the holster, and the swinging club make vivid what would happen should his rebellion become overt. . . .[22]

While the ghetto may be oppressive by nature, the conclusion to be drawn from the evidence presented is that the police, as presently constituted, are a separable, independent source of some of the oppression of the black man in America. If ways to reform police can be found that reduce the prevalence of grievances, such reform offers the prospect of avoiding the grim future for urban America envisioned by the Commission on Civil Disorders and the Commission on the Causes and Prevention of Violence.[23]

There are few studies of police which do not discuss the question of reform. Academic studies of police, as Jameson Doig found, in "their conclusions tend to be pessimistic with reference to the prospect of significant change."[24] This tendency is largely attributable, I believe, to what Reiss and Bordua call "an organizational perspective."[25] Following Weber, they note that the emphasis has been on the internal structure of organizations. Analysis of police, they further note, requires a broadening of perspective to include the organization's "relations with the organized environment and its boundary transactions" and how these factors effect "internal differentiation and problems of integration, coordination, and control."[26] The central place of the organization as the unit of analysis in this perspective is reflected in the language of James D. Thompson:

We will argue that organizations do some of the basic things they do because they must—or else! ... The concepts of rationality brought to bear on organizations establish limits within which organizational action must take place. We need to explore the meanings of these concepts and how they impinge on organizations. Uncertainties pose major challenges to rationality, and we will argue that technologies and environments are basic sources of uncertainty for organizations. How these facts of organizational life lead organizations to design and structure themselves needs to be explored.[27]

This organizational perspective is undoubtedly useful in studying many kinds of organizations and some aspects of police behavior. It is my conclusion, however, that the organizational perspective is an inadequate framework for a discussion of police reform. Thompson's analysis implicitly assumes that organizations are constrained by the force of market-like competition and that each organization is effectively controlled by a hierarchical decision-making structure within the organization. Thompson notes in passing that some organizations do not meet these assumptions. For example, there are "domesticated" organizations that "are not compelled to attend to all their needs, society guaranteeing their existence."[28] Blau and Scott indicate the "domesticated" status of police organizations when they state "The city is not expected to close its police department ... because it fails to show a profit, but to operate it in the interest of the public even at a financial loss."[29] James Q. Wilson and other students of police have questioned the assumption of an effective hierarchy.[30] Wilson concludes that the police "administrator's ability to control the discretion of his subordinates is in many cases quite limited by the nature of the situation and the legal constraints that govern police behavior."[31] Sometimes, too, cliques within the department gain control.[32] Further, James Q. Wilson's study of "Police Morale, Reform and Citizen Respect: The Chicago Case" revealed that changes in the internal structure of the department wrought by Superintendent O. W. Wilson were less important in the formation of attitudes of policemen toward their work than the quality of the relationship between policemen and citizens in the community.[33] It would not be going beyond Wilson's analysis too far to say that police will not significantly change until citizen hostility is reduced, and citizen hostility will not subside unless the police change. Such is the pessimistic conclusion to which an "organizational perspective" leads.

An alternative perspective for a consideration of police reform is needed. It is useful to approach the organization of the provision of police service as a matter for public policy choosing between various structural arrangements. Instead of considering citizens and policy makers as "environment," it is useful to look at police from the perspective of citizens and policy makers. This perspective provides greater analytical leverage for dealing with the relationships between the citizenry and police. Instead of being limited to marginal adjustments in the internal structure of police organization and instead of trying to devise techniques or programs for coping with problems arising in the interaction between police and citizens, a departure from the organizational perspective raises possibilities for reforms not generally considered. It offers, more specifically, the prospect of reconstituting the political context in which police services are provided. The alternative perspective requires an exploration of the structural arrangements for the *governance* of police.

The American governmental experiment, Madison wrote two centuries ago, rests on "the capacity of mankind for self-government."[34] The acceptance of self-government as a basic premise of American political order helps to narrow questions of reform somewhat, to exclude for example certain authoritarian forms. As the nation's political history attests, however, many questions are not settled by consensus on self-government. A primary issue to be explored, and the one to be discussed here, is the proper loci of decision-making power for particular sets of policy decisions. The word "proper" immediately suggests value judgments; all reform—for that matter, all public policy—is predicated on value judgments. Yet it is possible, as Lasswell has argued, for political scientists to examine policies to determine their probable consequences.[35] Such examination shows that two major approaches to the governance of police administration have predictably different consequences.

The impact of different governmental structures on the output of administration is recognized both explicitly and implicitly in the reform orientation of the literature of political science in this country. Vincent Ostrom, in "Operational Federalism: Organization for the Provision of Public Services in the American Federal System," notes the importance of two models:

Scholarship in American political science during much of the twentieth century has been preoccupied with conceptions of representative democracy and political responsibility which owe more to Bagehot's conception of parliamentary government than to the doctrines of divided and limited rule inherent in the American political formulae. Bagehot's conception of parliamentary government was based upon a linear model of political authority as contrasted with an equilibrium model maintained by a system of checks and balances.[36]

The linear and equilibrium models differ primarily in their assessment of the point at which conflict in society should be resolved. In the linear model conflict over goals ("politics") is resolved into an unambiguous command, which is then simply "carried out" faithfully by administration. According to the equilibrium model, means are as debatable and important as ends; thus conflict and procedures for conflict resolution pervade the entire process. The linear view sees politics as a determination of *the* public interest; in the equilibrium view, politics is seen as a continuing process of balancing the diverse interests of a variety of publics. Thus Woodrow Wilson, a major exponent of the linear model, maintained that political issues should be resolved by an expression of the will of the majority in making public policy. Once made, the public will should be executed by an administrative staff of experts who would be free from the "meddlesome" influence of public opinion. Most particularly, "Although politics sets the task for administration, it should not be suffered to manipulate its offices."[37] Ostrom found that "Wilson's political community has one government and is dominated by a single center of power."[38] "The more power is divided," Wilson argued, "the more irresponsible it becomes."[39]

James Madison, as one of the principle architects of the "compound republic of America," might well agree with Wilson's observation about "irresponsibility." In fact, according to Madison, one of the virtues of the new constitution was that "a coalition of a majority of the whole society could seldom take place on any other principles than those of justice and the general good."[40] Madison believed that to have a political system which automatically responded to a majority faction was to run the grave risk of tyranny by the majority. The division of power, then, was intended to function precisely in the manner to which Woodrow Wilson later objected. Madison maintained,

Whilst all authority in it will be derived from and dependent on the society, the society itself will be broken into so many parts, interests, and classes of citizens, that the rights of individuals or of the minority, will be in little danger from interested combinations of the majority.[41]

The layers of government in the federal system as well as the separation of powers within each unit of government were designed to protect the freedom of individuals in the American republic and the "great variety of interests, parties, and sects which it embraces."[42] The federal structure and separated powers were an intentional contrivance to provide an overlap of jurisdictions or concurrence of regimes, to make all grant of authority partial in order to assure "a double security" to "the rights of the people." Citizens in the compound republic have access to a variety of decision-making structures.[43] Where there are alternatives there are checks and balances.

Alexis de Tocqueville, in his analysis of *Democracy in America,* observed that American "government" (the enactment of general laws) was concentrated at a high level, while the service of "local interests" ("administration") was left to functionaries in the townships and municipal bodies.[44] Vincent Ostrom observes:

Tocqueville found that, ". . . the executive power is disseminated into a multitude of hands." The people participate in the execution of their laws by their choice of administrative officials as well as in the making of their laws through the choice of legislators . . . Popular political control pervaded both the government and its administration.[45]

Woodrow Wilson sought administration conducted "with enlightenment, with equity, with speed, and without friction." To do this he believed it necessary to harness administration to the expression of "a single will." Furthermore, administration had to be "removed from the hurry and strife of politics."[46] Unlike Madison and Tocqueville, who saw advantages to the diversity and pervasiveness of politics found in American government, Woodrow Wilson lamented it as an obstacle to knowing "the public mind." "And where is this unphilosophical bulk of mankind more multifarious in its composition than the United States?"[47] Consequently, "In order to make any advance at all, we must instruct and persuade a multitudinous monarch called public opinion—a much less feasible undertaking than to influence a single monarch called a king."[48] "In trying to instruct our own public opinion, we are dealing with a pupil apt to think itself quite sufficiently instructed beforehand" and, thus not sufficiently "docile and acquiescent in learning what things it has *not* a right to think and speak about imperatively."[49]

Explicit in Tocqueville's analysis and implicit in Madison's political theory is a different conception of the role of citizens in a republican government. Tocqueville expresses what Ostrom calls "the basic postulate of self-government": "Everyone is the best and sole judge of his own private interest, and that society has no right to control a man's actions unless they are prejudicial to the common weal or unless the common weal demands his help."[50] Tocqueville spoke directly to the political theoretic tradition upon which Woodrow Wilson later replied:

That partisans of centralization in Europe are wont to maintain that the government can administer the affairs of each locality better than the citizens can do it for themselves . . . But I deny that it is so when the people are as enlightened, as awake to their interests, and as accustomed to reflect on them as the Americans are. I am persuaded, on the contrary, that in this case, the collective strength of the citizenry will always conduce more efficaciously to the public welfare than the authority of the government.[51]

Tocqueville's conclusion is that "whenever a central administration affects completely to supersede the persons most interested, I believe that it is either misled or desirous to mislead. However enlightened and skillful a central power may be, it cannot of itself embrace all of the details of the life of a great nation."[52] Centralization, according to Tocqueville, "provides skillfully for the details of the social police; represses small disorders and petty misdemeanors" and "perpetuates a drowsy regularity in the conduct of affairs which the heads of administration are wont to call good order and public tranquility." But "if once the cooperation of its citizens is necessary to the furtherance of its measures, the secret of its impotence is disclosed." Even in such moments the central power, accustomed to instructing the citizenry, says, "You shall act just as I please, as much as I please, in the direction I please . . . You are to take charge of the details without aspiring to guide the system; you are to work in darkness and afterwards you may judge work by its results." But Tocqueville claims, "These are not the conditions on which the alliance of the human will is to be obtained . . . The citizen had rather remain a passive spectator than a dependent actor in schemes with which he is unacquainted."[53]

The two models underlying the views of Woodrow Wilson, on the one hand, and Madison and Tocqueville on the other, have immediate relevance to the current American debate over the organization of governmental administration in general and police in particular in metropolitan areas. Wilsonian echoes are heard in the body of literature on urban politics and on police services (a literature that terms "pathological" the multiplicity of governments or police departments in the metropolis), and these echoes also ring clear in the proposals for "one government for one metropolitan area."[54] In another, smaller set of works on urban politics there is a critique of Wilson's model that draws upon the analytical framework of Madison and Tocqueville. In this second body of literature, a diversity of governmental arrangements is seen as an advantageous concomitant of a diverse ("multifarious") community.[55] Most of the literature on reform of police, however, is based on Wilsonian assumptions of administration. We turn now to consideration of the relevance of the concept of federalism in the analysis of police organization.

Political Reform of Police Organization

The American federal system, with its dispersion of governmental authority among many different decision structures, has sustained a relatively open system of public administration characterized by constrained rivalry among many different agencies functioning as relatively independent enterprises. The open rivalry among many of these agencies has kept alternative arrangements available for the provision of public services to most American communities. Perhaps the most serious institutional failure among public service agencies in the United States has occurred in the big cities which have the least diversity in their institutional arrangements for the provision of public services. Harlem, South Chicago, Watts are political non-entities served by the cities of New York, Chicago, and Los Angeles. Perhaps one solution to these problems would be to diversify the political sub-structure of the big city and permit various communities within the big city to gain an increased voice regarding the provision of public services for that community.[56]

Although proposals for police reform are common, the idea that solutions to many contemporary police problems might be found in decentralizing the structure of authority over police has received little serious attention. James Q. Wilson calls "community control of police" a political "slogan." While that may be an accurate charge, it is not grounds for dismissal of the case for dispersing authority over police.[57] The problem is, the *case* for dispersal has not yet been adequately made. While there have been advocates, nowhere has the case for a reduction in the scale of organization for some police service production in urban areas been based on a credible political theory. The political theory of the compound republic expounded by Madison and Hamilton in the *Federalist* and explicated by Tocqueville and Ostrom provides the base.

The most salient features of Madison's political theory were the provision of a variety of alternative and sometimes concurrent decision-making structures capable of accommodating diverse interests and, on the local level, a close elective bond between citizens and officials. These concepts can be applied to the organization of police service production in urban areas by disaggregating the services now produced primarily by a single structure, a police department, and placing some of those services under smaller jurisdictions where a reduced scale of operation is both necessary and feasible.[58] The jurisdictions would be governed by councils elected by the residents of the respective jurisdictions. The elected councils would be empowered to provide directly the localized police services, primarily the patrol function, or to contract for these services with external producers. They would retain, in either case, prerogatives with respect to general policies governing patrol and the consideration of grievances.

Dispersal of control over the patrol function to smaller, politically responsible jursidictions is the essential element of this proposal. While the patrol function is but one of many currently encompassed by city police departments, it is without doubt the biggest source of police-community conflict. The overwhelming preponderance of police-citizen contacts from which grievances arise involve patrolmen. Skolnick's study makes clear that police generally, and patrolmen in particular, have a pivotal position in what he calls "the system of justice without trial."[59] For a host of reasons, documented in Skolnick's and other studies, the action taken initially by policemen in charging persons with criminal behavior is crucial. A major factor is that "the typical method of conviction is by the accused plea of guilty, with no trial required." The use of the plea occurs in up to 80 percent of the state court cases. "Mostly therefore, the system of administering criminal justice in the United States is a system of justice without trial."[60] That much of the hostility against police is hostility toward patrolmen is also reflected in Skolnick's finding of an internal recruitment problem in the Westville Department: plainclothesmen rejected promotions and higher pay when to receive them meant return to the uniform which, despite braid or stripes, means "patrolman" to most citizens. Numerically, of course, patrolmen make up the largest part of the force. In Skolnick's Westville Department, for example, 73 percent have the rank of patrolman.[61] Consequently, a change in the political context in which patrolmen operate directly affects most producers of public police service. Indirectly, the remainder of the organization would be so reduced in size as to indicate a significantly different organization structure.[62] This would be true even if those police services most amenable to consolidation, such as communication, crime laboratory, records, and detention facilities, were organized on a metropolitan scale.

There are obviously some advantages to large-scale police services. The advent of automated data processing and electronic computers, with their vast capacity and high cost, suggests immediately the possibility of saving through consolidation. Localities also benefit from linking their facilities with those developed at the state and national levels. But to move in the direction of metropolitan government or an exclusively metropolitan police service without taking into consideration the internal pressures and interests among communities within the city will aggravate an already grave situation. As Cloward and Piven have argued quite persuasively, the movement toward metropolitan government at a time when

Negroes have become a large minority in many cities and a majority in several will be seen as a further attempt to disenfranchise that minority.[63] Power will have to be dispersed within the community before the possibility of consolidating on a selective, rational basis will be an acceptable direction in which to move, acceptable to a segment of urban society which has become crucial.

The advantages of community or neighborhood control over patrol services are many. Most important is the prospect it offers of regaining for police the legitimacy without which they can assume the nature of an occupying army. Robert Fogelson has made this point quite succinctly:

The United States is not an occupied territory; it is a policed society, a society in which police authority is severely limited and police action is essentially responsive. Accordingly, the fundamental basis of public order is not law enforcement—which is the ultimate sanction—but what Allan Silver aptly describes as the "moral-consensus" of the community. Put negatively, this means that the authorities cannot maintain law and order in the face of widespread indifference, not to mention out-and-out opposition, on the part of the populace. By denying Negroes due respect and presuming their criminality, the police are undermining the already unstable "moral consensus" in the ghetto; by practicing preventive patrolling in the ghetto they are treating these communities as occupied territories.[64]

A community council elected from the locality with authority over patrol services would predictably be more responsive to complaints from community residents. At the very least, it would be expected, by both citizens and patrolmen alike, to be more concerned. Furthermore, a locally elected council would be inclined to emphasize those aspects of law enforcement of greatest moment to the residents. In ghettos this would likely mean greater emphasis on providing citizen-invoked services and increased sensitivity to forms of law breaking currently not within the purview of patrolmen or merely ignored, such as violation of housing codes. The local community or neighborhood council would, it seems likely to assume, tap "the enormous concern for public safety among Negroes," mentioned by Fogelson,[65] where present authorities have been willing or unable to do so. There is the prospect, then, that through the proposed reform Negroes will gain a feeling of identification with the police effort directed to the public safety of their immediate neighborhood.

The proposal offers a partial solution to the critical problem of prejudiced policemen. Prejudice, it was noted earlier, is a poor substitute for judgment because it makes for inefficient and ineffective patrolling and because it generates waves of citizen hostility which undermine or destroy consensus-based law enforcement. At present urban police forces are predominantly white, a fact which contributes to the identification of police in black minds with white power. The Commission on Civil Disorders found that Negroes are substantially underrepresented on police forces in the country.[66] Nowhere is the percentage of nonwhites on the force equal to the percentage of nonwhites in the population of the city. Of twenty-six selected cities, including most of the largest in the country, the ratios of nonwhite in the population to nonwhite on the force were revealing (see Table 7.1). In many other cities not included in the study

TABLE 7.1. NONWHITE POLICE OFFICERS

Ratios of percentage of nonwhite in population to percentage nonwhite on the force	Frequency
1:1	0
1.5:1	2
2:1	2
3:1	7
4:1	3
5:1	3
6:1	4
7:1	0
8:1	4
9:1	0
10:1	1
Mean ratio: 4.6:1	26 (cities)

the ratio is as high as or higher than the mean ratio of 4.6:1 reflected in the Commission's findings. Walter J. Raine's report on the Watts riot emphasized the importance of the fact that "the policeman is usually white (over 96% in the City of Los Angeles and 87% white in Los Angeles County)." So impressed with this aspect of the police situation is Raine that his sole recommendation for reform is *"Let the police in the Negro ghetto be Negro."* While he acknowledges the "problems of organization, recruitment and political control" of such a force and is unable to venture solutions, he is convinced that they are not insurmountable.[67] As presently constituted, police find that it is as difficult to recruit Negroes to the force as it used to be for Negroes to get on it. Many Negroes today are unwilling to accept the stigma of association with "the enemy."[68] Local control might restore sufficient respect for the police so that many unemployed and underemployed Negroes would find police work acceptable. The advantages of familiarity with what is suspicious and what is ordinary and an awareness that Negroes do not all look alike in the ghetto are obvious. Since their contact with Negroes would not be limited to law enforcement situations, since the attitudes of citizens would be more favorable toward the institution itself, and since the patrolman's colleagues would be less likely to be mostly white, the tendency toward prejudice which James Q. Wilson and Jerome Skolnick found inherent in the task of policing a ghetto would be greatly reduced. Thus, organizational behavior which could not successfully be controlled by supervision or training or even the recruitment of educated whites, could be eliminated by making recruitment of Negroes practicable.

As the effectiveness of patrolling the ghetto is increased, as harassment, brutality, and the fear of harassment and brutality are reduced, as greater responsiveness to ghetto residents' demands for service is developed and more effective and credible grievance mechanisms provided —as these take place, the prospect of an upward spiraling of citizen confidence and cooperation with the police, leading to greater effectiveness and more confidence, becomes imaginable.

Some of the advantages of the reform would accrue to the nonpatrol aspects of police organization. First, after the most politically sensitive patrol service is placed under more localized jurisdiction, consolidation of some other services may not be found objectionable to citizens who presently oppose the dilution of their influence over police. Second, separating the patrol organization from investigation provides the prospects of more effective detective work. According to the Task Force on the police, the practice found in police departments throughout the country of requiring an apprenticeship as a patrolman before becoming a detective is a major obstacle to the recruitment of many capable individuals.[69] College educated persons such as those recruited by the F.B.I. who might find in detective work an appealing challenge are unwilling, apparently, to endure the three to five years as a patrolman, without guarantee of promotion, which most urban departments make a prerequisite for attainment of detective status. Also, within the patrol organization, outstanding performance in patrol would be rewarded by promotion or pay increases within the ranks related to patrol. The current practice is to reward the performance of a patrolman by removing him from the patrol duties in which he distinguished himself and making him a detective. Even by traditional organizational standards, the proposed reform is desirable.

The typical form of public police organization in big cities is under a citywide jurisdiction and encompasses a variety of police services, both "field" and "auxiliary." However, many metropolitan areas display other configurations of organization in the provision of police services. In the New York metropolitan area, for example, the city of New York provides a highly centralized model for the organization of police; Nassau County provides a quite different model.

While the arrangement in American metropolitan areas involving a number of police agencies has been widely criticized, these criticisms spring more from unexamined premises rather than careful evaluations of performances. In the President's Commission on Law Enforcement and the Administration of Justice *Task Force Report: The Police* is found "an analysis of the problems of local police administration and the potential of coordination or consolidation of services as an aid to the repression of crime." Instead of studying police performance to ascertain the advisability of consolidation, the *Report* begins by stating its underlying assumption

that the number of jurisdictions must be reduced in order to deal effectively with the need for more and better police ... Significant methods used in consolidating police jurisdictions will be described. It is a fair assumption that where these methods have been utilized, it was realized by the affected governmental jurisdiction that fragmented, decentralized policing was either uneconomical or ineffective. It will be assumed, also, that coordination or consolidation of selected police functions was not sufficient and that jurisdictional consolidation was the only answer.[70]

The *Report* also states, "The desire for local self-government no doubt accounts for the zealous development and protection of numerous local units—even when larger more cohesive units would seem to be a logical solution to metropolitan area problems."[71] Throughout the study "the desire for local self-government" is treated as an obstacle, in fact, *the* obstacle to bigger, thus better, police organizations. The "primary conclusions" of their study of coordination of police service, interestingly enough, are almost verbatim restatements of the *assumptions* set forth at the outset of their analysis.[72]

The "logic" which calls for jurisdictional consolidation is related to the same "organization and management principles" expressed in Woodrow Wilson's theory of administration. The Task Force says, "Available for the asking since the turn of the century has been a large and authoritative general body of guidance in public administration." Consequently, "There is little justification for American police forces not to be well organized."[73] This managerial logic corresponds to what Edmond Cahn calls "the imperial or official perspective." The official perspective "has been largely determined by the dominant interests of rulers, governors, and other officials."[74] Cahn notes, however, that "A free and open society calls on its official processors to perform their functions according to the perspective of consumers."[75] Skolnick, summing up Cahn's argument, states: "In the 'consumer' view, therefore, constraints on the decision-making powers of officials are given more importance than the requirements of the processing system and those who carry out its administration."[76] But in most studies of police, the Task Force *Report* included, reflecting the orientation of members of the police force, the emphasis is almost entirely on the needs and problems of administrators and policemen rather than those of consumers of police service.

The Task Force *Report,* ironically, discusses several institutional arrangements which articulate the consumer perspective, without noting that they are based upon a different logic. Their consideration of various forms of consolidation includes a discussion of the provision of police services by contract arrangements in Los Angeles County, California (the Lakewood Plan) and in Nassau County, New York. The basic feature of these plans is the retention of juridical responsibility for police service at the small unit level, with the production of police services by a county-wide agency optional, selective (in terms of services provided), and in the case of Lakewood, revocable. In both the Lakewood and Nassau arrangements, communities pay for whatever services they get. Some cities in Los Angeles County, for example, have their own patrol but call upon the sheriff for major problems. A pricing system has been developed there based on the cost of a single mobile police unit with one-man or two-man being a cost variable.[77]

These two plans reasonably approximate the "consumer perspective." In doing so, they reflect the logic of political organization developed by Madison and Tocqueville discussed above. James Q. Wilson's study of the Nassau County Police Department emphasizes the extent to which the department accommodates local preferences in order to "sell" its services. In Nassau the police practice what Wilson calls "the service style."[78] They use foot patrol extensively (because the people feel more secure) and maintain eight precinct stations where residents can have direct access to police command. The consumer perspective is expressed by one Nassau officer: "The wealthier people of Nassau know we are servants and they demand service. The kind of service they expect is prompt appearance and frequent, high visibility policemen on patrol."[79] Wilson notes that in contrast to other departments where the officer's first concern is maintaining self-respect, in the service style maintaining self-control is primary.[80]

The question is, can the "service style" be made available only to the wealthy? Can the ghetto dweller be visualized as a consumer, a discriminating one, who does "business" only where it is profitable to do so? The thrust of the proposal for reform is the idea that it is in the interest of both the producer and consumer of police service, especially patrol service, to function in a closer relationship. In this way and perhaps only in this way, will patrolmen know their "territory" well enough to be effective "salesmen" of police service and be respected enough to find willing customers. In this way, citizens will be in a position to demand recognition for their status as consumers of police service with councilors able to express their preferences, a necessary constraint on the power of police.

Proposals for reducing the scale of the jurisdiction under which police operate are not without their critics. James Q. Wilson has treated the subject at some length in his discussion of policy implications arising from his study of the *Varieties of Police Behavior*. It must be noted at the outset, however, that Wilson was not attacking the exact model presented here. From his discussion one would infer that to disperse authority over police to subcity units would necessarily entail *total dispersal*. He speaks of "suburbanizing" police in the city.[81] There is no suggestion whatever that he has considered the idea of concurrent regimes, involving selective disaggregation of authority with overlapping jurisdictions (the federal arrangement) as contrasted with the creation of a multiplicity of sovereign, autonomous police jurisdictions. Wilson fails to recognize that in the concurrent provision of police services the issue need not be one of centralization versus decentralization, that federal police, state police, city police, and community patrol services can exist side by side. Consequently, Wilson argues that a dispersal of authority over police is "balkanization." He asserts:

Where a community is deeply divided and emotionally aroused, the proper governmental policy is not to arm the disputants and let them settle matters among themselves; it is rather to raise the level at which decisions will be made to a point sufficiently high so that neither side can prevail by *force majeure* but low enough so that responsible authorities must still listen to both sides.[82]

Wilson is right that it is wrong to arm the disputants. But *they are already armed*, as Gary Wills describes in frightening detail in *The Second Civil War*.[83] The error of Wilson's argument is especially evident when we consider the fact that a major contributing factor in the conflict and emotional arousal is that a significant part of the arms of one of the disputants is in the hands of white police. Wilson argues that one reason for Negro complaints is that they are now "being brought under a single standard of justice."[84] While this proposition could be seriously contested, what it omits is more important. Commitment to a single standard of enforcement in police-initiated actions, combined with the failure of police to maintain a single standard of service on citizen requests for assistance, on top of the difficulties of a centralized police authority actually effectuating any consistent standard of enforcement in minority group neighborhoods promises an increased feeling in the ghetto of "Negro repression" rather than crime repression.

An important criticism which James Q. Wilson levels at the dispersal of authority over police is certain to concern others. He says that neighborhood control of the police will not work because the neighborhoods are in the *central* city. Central, according to Wilson, "means that many people from all over the metropolitan area use it for work, governing, recreation, and that, as a result, competing life styles and competing sets of community norms come into frequent and important contact."[85] There is pressure, he says, to maintain order at the highest level demanded by any group.

Some residents may not like having the police *try, for that is about all they can do,* to maintain order at a level demanded by the businessmen, shoppers, theater-goers, students, and public officials who use the central city, except for a person who comes to the city in search of disorder, prostitution, dirty-book stores, cheap bars, and the like.[86]

Wilson thus raises the important issue of whether different neighborhoods will demand substantially different standards. He assumes that this will be the case:

We have had some experience in this country with the notion that different neighborhoods should be allowed to have radically different levels of public order, and the results have not been altogether encouraging. The southern double standard of justice may have contributed to the difficulties we experience in our large cities. John Dollard in a classic account describes the high level of aggression among poor Negroes in a small southern town in the 1930's.[87]

Wilson goes on to quote Dollard's explanation that the Negro in the South was "outside the protection of white law" and that "So long as the law does not take over the protection of the Negro person he will have to do it himself by violent means."[88] And yet, Wilson draws the conclusion that Negro behavior under the circumstance of being *denied* any organized legitimate system of police provides a prediction of the behavior of Negroes when empowered to organize and maintain a public police force in their community.

In different neighborhoods, to cite a celebrated example, congregations of people on street corners on summer evenings may require relativistic interpretations. Just as there are some parking practices found in the suburbs that might cause havoc in the city, so too the policy toward children playing in the streets may vary with the availability of alternative recreational facilities. On the other hand, there are good reasons to believe that a majority in no neighborhood would favor police overlooking murders, rapes, robberies, and assaults, or even prostitution and heroin pushing. The question of the standard of police protection desired by Negroes does not need to be left, as James Q. Wilson leaves it, in the realm of conjecture. Studies done for the U.S. Commission on Civil Rights, the President's Commission on Law Enforcement and the Administration of Justice, and independent studies by Louis Harris, Michigan State University, and others have all returned the same finding: black citizens are only slightly less concerned with the problem of crime and violence than white citizens, and even those black citizens most hostile to current police practice acknowledge that the function of the police is essential.[89] The reason for their concern is obvious. A recent article notes: "Between 70 and 80 percent of major big-city crime is harbored in Negro or predominantly Negro precincts. Little is visited upon the whites."[90] The article quoted one Newark policeman who says: "The white woman out in the outer districts is the one who fears rape the most. But it is the black woman in the ghetto who gets raped."[91] While the distribution of rapes is correctly reported, the statement's more important suggestion is that policemen are less aware of the fears of the black woman. There is a danger that the police practices required to allay the fears of the white majority may reduce the ability of the police to lower the publicized rate of crime upon which the fear is based. Charles V. Hamilton, in a discussion of "The Silent Black Majority," claims:

These people are as concerned about "crime in the streets" as any middle-class person, and they want effective measures taken to combat it. But they ·want police protection, not police persecution, and because they believe that the incidence of the latter is greater than the former, they believe the present law-enforcement system must be viewed suspiciously, rather than optimistically.[92]

In sum, there appear to be good grounds for rejecting Wilson's assumption.

It might be argued that placing control of police in the hands of local community authorities responsive to local residents will result in Negro policemen violating the civil rights of whites. In answer, it should be noted that white citizens have recourse to the same legal instrumentalities as Negroes in protesting violations of their civil rights. It seems likely that if the white majority in America had to rely on the Civil Rights Commission and civil rights laws for its security that these instruments for protection of rights themselves would be strengthened to the advantage of all citizens.

Finally, James Q. Wilson argues that dispersal of authority in the central city resurrects the spectre of ward and precinct level corruption. While it would be possible to challenge the accuracy of the alleged connections between corruption and decentralization of authority over police, the argument is more vulnerable at another point. Its greatest weakness as an argument against the proposal presented here is that it omits the fact that there will be other police agencies in the field operating under wider auspices than the local patrol jurisdictions. Metropolitanwide detectives would have both the incentive and the means to detect local corruption. They could do so without tainting their own organization.

What Wilson in *Varieties of Police Behavior* proposes instead of dispersal of authority over police, is dispersal of authority within the police organization. He contends,

To decentralize an administrative apparatus is to give its component units greater freedom, within well defined general policies, to handle local situations in a measure appropriate to local conditions. Decentralization, properly understood *strengthens* local units; the dispersal of authority, by contrast, weakens them. Precinct commanders in a decentralized department would surrender to whatever constellation of political forces that neighborhood might produce.[93]

This proposal is contradictory at several points. After claiming for decentralization the "strength" of semi-autonomy, he says that the risk of corruption could be reduced "by insuring that the chief has absolute authority over his commanders, unchecked either by local politics, departmental cliques, or restrictive civil service regulations."[94] This is one of those curious constructions of the political scientific imagination which might be called a decentralized system with absolute authority at the center. Wilson argues for decentralization because it has the crucial virtue of improving the patrolman's ability to make reliable judgments by increasing his familiarity with the neighborhood. A good point. But Wilson would apply his decentralization only to what he terms the "order maintenance" function of police (settling arguments, sending drunks home, etc.) and not the law enforcement ("crime repression") function which has inspired such anathemas as aggressive preventative patrol and which has resulted in most charges of harassment and brutality. Under the plan for dispersal of authority over the patrol function, both order maintenance and law enforcement would benefit from familiarity with local circumstances.

It should be noted, too, that decentralization as proposed by James Q. Wilson would isolate the police even more from community control (presumably this is the source of strength of which Wilson speaks). Such isolation or insulation, when viewed in light of Wilson's suggestion that patrolmen and precinct commanders alike be rewarded for the extent to which they "keep the peace" in their precincts, has remarkable potential for becoming an oppressive system of satrapy. Because it fails to countenance the problem of the legitimacy of police organization, Wilson's proposal contains a critical flaw.

The proposal for dispersal of control function is based on the conclusion that the critical variable in police performance is the structure of the authority *over* police departments rather than the structure of authority *within* existing police departments. In view of this conclusion based on complaints against police, it is worth noting the observations of Gordon Misner and James Q. Wilson.

Misner: Generally speaking, the police of the nation have responded to the protest movements of the 1960's in precisely the way the political process has wanted—or directed them—to respond. The operating posture of the police generally reflects the posture of the political system itself.[95]

Wilson: The reason for a city's failure to exercise influence [over police policies] potentially at its disposal is that in most cases . . . such matters are not of general interest to the citizenry or a public official.[96]

Both statements reflect the finding reported by the Task Force that "the overwhelming majority of the public has a high opinion of the work of the police." (National opinion surveys which the Report summarizes indicates that no less than 80 percent of Americans think that the police do an excellent, good, or fair job.)[97] Further, Misner and Wilson suggest that *the political system is responsive to that majority.*

The majority in America, obviously, is neither black nor brown. Nonwhites, *regardless of income,* differ from the majority in their view of police operations. For reasons discussed at the outset of this analysis, nonwhites and Negroes especially, at a far higher rate than whites, see police as doing a poor job. In many cities where this issue has been studied, beliefs of police malpractice are held by more than 80 percent of the Negro population.[98] Misner, in claiming that the police reflect the will of the political system, and Wilson, in asserting that the public is not concerned about most policies and practices of the police, are in effect saying that our political system ignores the diversity of publics it comprises. In fact Misner and James Q. Wilson are unfortunately correct in saying that the present political structure tends to respond to one voice, to articulate a "single will." It may be true, but when applied to the police, that fact threatens the future order of urban communities in America. Those who believe the relative quiet of the present precludes this pessimistic assessment should recall that the riots of the 1960's came swiftly upon a genuinely surprised American majority.

WILLIAM HOWARD MOORE

8

THE KEFAUVER COMMITTEE AND
ORGANIZED CRIME

The field of law enforcement cherishes a number of enduring myths, among which one of the most popular is undoubtedly the idea that a national network of Italian criminals called the "Mafia" exists. William Howard Moore, after studying the workings of the Kefauver Crime Commission of 1950–51, demonstrates that the committee produced virtually no evidence for the existence of a national, ethnically based "Mafia." Nevertheless the committee concluded that a "nationwide crime syndicate known as [the] Mafia" existed and that it exercised "centralized direction and control" over various organized criminal activities. Moore indicates that members of the committee had doubts about these conclusions and that what evidence the committee did turn up could be explained in other ways. What was more important, however, was that "the Kefauver committee interpretations became the new conventional wisdom and in effect set the limits for later investigations and interpretations." The Kefauver committee did turn up a great deal of evidence which pointed to local corruption and the failure of local law enforcement agencies to deal with such activities as gambling and prostitution; the committee's recommendations for greater action at the state and local levels were consistent with that evidence. The consequences of the committee's findings, however, were much more serious. As Moore points out, "the Kefauver myths encouraged the public's tendency to think of crime, particularly organized crime, as a semimonopoly originating outside the social, political, and economic structure of American life." This had the effect of diverting public energies and funds from the real problems of organized crime.

In the past decade, as historians and social scientists have begun to explore the problem of organized crime in American society, an interesting literature on the so-called Mafia has developed. Most academic researchers have broken sharply with the interpretation of organized crime that has been advanced by government investigators and investigative reporters for over a generation. Essentially, the new scholarship stresses that organized crime has developed from political, legal, and economic factors internal to American life and was not a "foreign" importation; that the influence of Italian-Americans in organized crime has been exaggerated; and that the very word "Mafia" in the United States has undergone major shifts in meaning when used by sensational investigators and journalists. In short, while they acknowledge the existence of organized crime on a somewhat more decentralized basis than formerly believed, they have argued that the Mafia concept has little utility in defining or explaining the phenomenon.[1]

Indeed, most academic revisionists have concluded that use of the term has been detrimental. Some have maintained that the Mafia stereotype has harmed Italian-Americans or that it has led to government overzealousness and abuses of civil liberties. While there is no question that the Mafia image has worked some disadvantages upon Italian-Americans, at least one poll has tended to minimize the ethnic slur. In a broader sense, however, the term has unquestionably led to a great deal of confusion about the nature of organized crime itself, and it has consequently obstructed serious debate over alternative policies for dealing with it.[2]

The garbled definition of organized crime dates back to the Kefauver Crime Committee of 1950–51. Estes Kefauver, an ambitious young Tennessee senator, had hoped to convert a growing concern over an alleged postwar crime wave into a springboard for a national political campaign. His committee drew heavily from two originally distinct bodies of concern —a claim by the Federal Bureau of Narcotics that an Italian-American Mafia dominated the American underworld and a story by citizens' anticrime forces that Chicago gangsters had established a monopoly over illegal gambling in the United States. Both perspectives appealed to Kefauver's strongly held antimonopoly sentiments, and they would provide the essential structure for his investigation.[3]

By the time the Kefauver committee began its work, the Mafia legend had already had a rather tortured history in the United States. The word itself apparently surfaced in nineteenth-century Sicily and conveyed at least two somewhat related meanings. On the one hand it suggested a deep sense of cultural pride and independence and a pervasive suspicion of established governmental authority. The term was also used to describe a rather ill-defined series of criminal organizations that sometimes protected, sometimes exploited, the population of western Sicily. While the cultural *mafia* unquestionably accompanied the large scale Italian and Sicilian immigration at the turn of the century, there is no evidence that any extensive criminal organization was transported to the United States. Any immigrants who had been touched directly by a Mafia organization in the Old Country were likely to have been either victims or low-level strongmen; entrenched leaders were more likely to remain in Italy. The cultural isolation in the Italian colonies and the inadequate policing afforded immigrant areas, of course, reinforced traditional suspicions and intensified the Old World reliance on kinship and village loyalties for personal security. But, as in the Old Country, such ties did not always provide protection from personal vendettas or from Black Hand or Mafia extortion practiced by small, sometimes impromptu, gangs.[4]

While a variety of criminal activities existed in the colonies, the American press stereotyped the Italian as given to acts of smoldering passion, of family vendetta, and of a peculiar type of extortion involving threatening Black Hand letters. Slowly, however, the image shifted from one of peasant, almost anarchistic crime to suggestions of some broader ethnic conspiracy. Reporters professed to see signs of some pervasive Mafia or Black Hand organization in the circumstances surrounding the assassinations of New Orleans Police Superintendent David Hennessey in 1890 and of New York Police Lieutenant Joseph Petrosino in 1909. Hennessey had apparently become involved in a feud between two rival Sicilian stevedore firms, each of which had accused the other of involvement in a Mafia organization. At the time of his death, Petrosino was in Palermo gathering police intelligence on certain immigrants in New York. In part he was hoping to counter rumors of an extensive Black Hand or Mafia conspiracy in the United States, but his murder convinced some American newsmen that such an organization in fact existed.[5]

Ironically the new Italian stereotype had not matured in the 1920's when the celebrated bootlegging and beer wars in Chicago and elsewhere brought Italians within the mainstream of organized crime in America. Perhaps because the source of power was so obvious, the gun battles so consuming, and because gangs like Al Capone's operated across ethnic lines, the press directed relatively little public attention upon organized crime as an ethnic conspiracy.[6]

While we do not know the full implications of Prohibition on the underworld, the legal and technical aspects of liquor importation, manufacture, and delivery unquestionably called forth managerial skills and stimulated contacts and understandings between underworld groups in various cities. The gasoline engine and telephone made rapid transportation and communication possible. Within the Italian underworld, kinship and business ties brought together leaders from Chicago, New York, and other cities. The "cannon mob" convention in Cleveland in 1928, the multi-ethnic Atlantic City meeting in 1929, and other gatherings certainly involved interests in several northern and eastern cities, although the precise purposes remain unknown.[7]

In the 1930's and 1940's investment opportunities in gambling and real estate, particularly in resort areas such as Florida, New Orleans, and Nevada, continued to bring some underworld figures together. Despite the charges and implications by newspapermen and law enforcement officials that these contacts were structured, no one presented evidence either that a single person or ethnic group directed or controlled organized crime on more than a regional or metropolitan basis. The prevailing pattern appeared to be decentralization, with city and sometimes regional agreements among underworld figures themselves and with politicians, with local politicians having the ultimate veto power and responding to local demands more than to some broader ethnic conspiracy.[8]

With the skills and political contacts developed during Prohibition, however, Italians certainly did play a more decisive role in the rackets than they had previously. Some became gambling entrepreneurs just as expansion and rationalization restructured that illegal activity. While recent studies have suggested that Jewish figures exercised more power than Italians, the coincidence of increasing rationalization and the appearance of Italians in decision-making roles in Chicago and elsewhere unquestionably lent a certain credence to allegations that a sinister ethnic conspiracy was taking shape.[9]

The charges that an Italian Mafia organization dominated most racketeering in the United States really sprang from the Federal Bureau of Narcotics in the late 1930's. By the late 1940's Bureau Commissioner Harry J. Anslinger and his agents were arguing that certain Italians and Italian-Americans, knit together by a mysterious organization, controlled the international narcotics traffic and were deeply involved in other rackets in this country, a claim Anslinger dramatized with a celebrated list of 800 "master-criminals" from the bureau's files. The Narcotics Bureau had apparently drifted into this argument in part because of the frequent contact, both before and after the war, between Anslinger's agents and the Italian police, many of whom remembered Mussolini's anti-Mafia campaign. Because of these contacts and because some—perhaps even a disproportionate number—of Italian-Americans were involved in the narcotics traffic, Anslinger's secret files may have suggested to myopic eyes the kind of ethnic conspiracy he claimed to have discovered. In any event, Anslinger made a great deal of his discovery after the war—linking the controversial pardon of Charles ("Lucky") Luciano in 1946 to an alleged expansion in the narcotics business and seeking additional funds for his agency to combat the Mafia menace.[10]

At the same time Anslinger was advancing his theories of a Mafia monopoly, various citizens' crime commissions were busy fanning the fears of a national gambling cartel. Alarmed by increased public gambling and the demands for wider legalization, business and civic leaders listened respectfully to charges that sinister underworld figures were spearheading the progambling efforts, systematically corrupting local law enforcement, and trying to "infiltrate" legitimate business. Virgil W. Peterson of the Chicago Crime Commission in particular warned citizens' groups around the country that an alleged "Capone syndicate" in Chicago had seized control of Continental Press, a wire service specializing in last-minute horse-racing information supposedly vital to bookmakers around the country. Through its ability to cut off or supply information and through the influence of its alleged "fronts" in various cities, the "Capone syndicate" was able to "muscle in" on lucrative gambling operations in Miami, New Orleans, St. Louis, Kansas City, Los Angeles, San Francisco, and several other cities. While Peterson, a former F.B.I. agent, cited an impressive array of interlocking contacts, he did not prove that most of the alleged "fronts" were in fact "fronts"; there was much to suggest that many were essentially independent operators and in any event were largely responsive to local and state police control. Nor did he establish that his alleged "Capone syndicate" really controlled Continental, although it did have control over a Chicago subdistributor and could apparently exercise some influence over who received the service elsewhere. Peterson did demonstrate quite clearly that there were interstate gambling operations and sometimes personal and business ties between underworld figures involved in these activities.[11]

Peterson's emphasis on an alleged "Capone syndicate" and the wire service paralleled the build-up of New York gambler Frank Costello as "Prime Minister of the Underworld" by politicians and journalists. Unquestionably Costello had exercised significant influence on Tammany Hall in the early 1940's, and he had brought a number of Italian politicians into power with him. Given the chorus of denunciations by District Attorney Frank Hogan, Mayors Fiorello LaGuardia and William O'Dwyer, as well as other politicians and law enforcement persons, it is altogether likely that Costello's political power was already slipping by the late 1940's. Nonetheless even Peterson acknowledged Costello as the single most powerful underworld figure in America.[12]

In the excitement of the gambling and Mafia debates, journalists confused the quite separate theories of Virgil Peterson and Harry Anslinger. Peterson had spoken of local and regional gambling syndicates linked by personal contacts and the necessity of obtaining the wire service. Anslinger suggested a more sweeping conspiracy dominated by Italian gangsters. By merging the two, newspapermen maximized the supposed centralization of the underworld and gambling operations, using each man's evidence to support the other's conclusions. Hearst reporters Jack Lait and Lee Mortimer were probably the worst offenders in their best-selling *Chicago Confidential* (1950), in which they describe the election of Frank Costello and Charles Fischetti, a Chicago cousin of Al Capone, as President and Vice President of the Unione Siciliana, a term they used interchangeably with the Mafia. A totally untrustworthy cynic, Mortimer linked his Mafia creation not only to a booming narcotics traffic and interstate gambling, but also to international communism and an alleged homosexual takeover of big-city nightclubs.[13]

Both the monopolistic aspects of the Mafia and wire service allegations as well as the general publicity value of an investigation appealed to Kefauver and the committee staff. Even before he joined the committee, Chief Investigator Harold G. Robinson enumerated for Chief Counsel Rudolph Halley the supposed membership of the Mafia "Grand Council"—a listing that coincided with that of Lait and Mortimer. At the same time, the senators began to consider modeling their investigation after the Temporary National Economic Committee's study of the concentration of national wealth in the late 1930's. Virgil Peterson specifically suggested an antitrust suit against Continental, which he claimed had a "100% monopoly on the interstate dissemination of racing news information."[14]

While Halley begged off from any immediate recommendation on Continental, the committee did focus most of its energies on the Peterson wire service thesis—on demonstrating how the alleged Capone syndicate controlled Continental on a national basis.[15] In city after city, the senators sought to show how the Capone syndicate used its wire service monopoly to discriminate among local gambling operations, to extort revenue from them, and then systematically to corrupt the law enforcement machinery. Once having obtained control of local law enforcement, the syndicate could then, it was reasoned, exercise some influence over the types of gambling and racketeering not dependent upon the wire service as such. While the committee painted this picture of the evidence, the facts actually developed suggest a great deal of autonomy by local racing wire distributors, gamblers, and law enforcement officials.

First, the committee failed to establish in several cases that local "front" men were as closely allied to Continental as it suggested. For example, an important Kansas City gambler, Tony Gizzo, formerly of Chicago, freely admitted to knowing certain Chicago underworld figures as individuals, but denied knowing any as a representative of Continental Press. He admitted only a nodding acquaintance with gangsters outside of Chicago. And even if the supposed Capone syndicate did control an indispensable service for the larger horserooms across the country, ultimate power as to whether gambling operations would be permitted at all rested with local law enforcement and political officials. In Miami, for example, the critical factor in the "Capone syndicate's" movement into a local bookmaking arrangement appeared to be influence with the state and local police. In Jefferson Parish near New Orleans, Sheriff Frank J. ("King") Clancy was indeed "king," and Phil Kastel, alleged partner of Costello, approached Clancy to obtain permission to operate the swank Beverly Club. Clancy agreed on the condition that the Beverly employ local people. In Kansas City, according to the thesis the committee accepted, gambler-politician Charles Binaggio had been assassinated because he failed to demonstrate sufficient influence over Governor Forrest Smith and local police commissioners. The net effect of the wire service story appeared to have been the exaggeration of interregional contacts and associations and a tendency to overlook the actual local control of underworld activity.[16]

If Peterson's arguments suggested elements of monopoly, the Anslinger Mafia thesis implied a more closely knit ethnic conspiracy. Even if the Kefauver committee had had the inclination to explore the historic weaknesses in the Narcotics Bureau position, it lacked the time and expertise. Anslinger himself testified early before the committee, presented the senators his confidential "master list" of 800 criminals, and reinforced the interest of Chief Counsel Halley in the dramatic note "the Mafia" would provide the investigation. Journalists, following the committee into fourteen major cities around the country continued to raise questions concerning "the Mafia," and neither the antigambling forces nor Italian-American organizations voiced any real reservations to use of the term.

If those searching for the Mafia had no significant opposition, they also had no evidence worthy of the word. In public testimony, both Anslinger and his field agents retreated into vague generalizations on the Mafia theory. Agent Claude Follmer informed the committee that he had "heard" that the slain Charles Binaggio was "a member of the Mafia," that to his "best information" there were from twenty-five to thirty members in Kansas City, that the local head man was "supposed" to be one James Balestrere, and that there was "supposed" to be an international head in Palermo through whom chiefs in other countries were named. Despite "some contention," Follmer's "understanding" was that the American head was either Vincent Mangano or Joseph Profaci. The structure of this organization consisted of a dominant "inner circle" and a less influential "outer circle." Follmer also played the senators a taped conversation in which a suspect laughingly referred to "the Mafia," a reference that apparently impressed Kefauver. Yet from the tape it is unclear whether or not the remark was part of a joke, and in any event it indicates that the phenomenon was loose and dependent on the whims of local law enforcement.[17]

Going beyond the Narcotics Bureau, Halley tried to extract admissions about the Mafia organization from reluctant witnesses, who in general denied knowing anything about such an organization or associated it with Black Hand extortion of the pre–World War I days. When Gizzo and others admitted that they knew persons whom the press had labeled as Mafia members, the committee concluded that it constituted evidence of a Mafia; when other alleged *mafiosi* denied membership or knowledge of such an organization, the committee thought it indicated an effort to conceal the presence of the secret society. In effect, as Gordon Hawkins has pointed out, no matter what the witness said, the committee construed it as evidence for the existence of the Mafia and its pervasive influence in the underworld. The committee was much impressed in Chicago by the testimony of Philip D'Andrea, one-time Capone bodyguard, convicted extortionist, and former head of Unione Siciliana, the Italian-American fraternal society that had supposedly been dominated by Capone. D'Andrea observed that because the fear of the Mafia was discussed in the homes of those born in Sicily and Italy, it would be "unusual" for anyone of that background to deny having heard of the Mafia. Senator Kefauver attempted to use this statement to demonstrate that other witnesses had lied about their knowledge of the Mafia society. He essentially ignored the broader context of D'Andrea's testimony—that the Mafia was equivalent to the widely feared Black Hand extortion, that D'Andrea knew no individuals as members of the Mafia, and that the "organization" appeared to be decentralized and declining.[18]

During its California hearings, the committee heard two supposed "Mafia experts" from the San Francisco police department—Inspectors Frank Ahern and Thomas Cahill. In rambling, frequently off-the-record, testimony the police inspectors provided details about the 1947 murder of a Chicago underworld figure, Nick DeJohn. Impressed by Ahern and Cahill's apparent knowledge of the secret organization, the committee immediately appointed the men as its "Special Mafia Squad," put them in contact with the Narcotics Bureau, and asked them to coordinate the various leads on the organization from across the country. No clear definition of the Mafia issued from either the "Special Mafia Squad" or committee field investigators, who submitted reports to Halley that simply equated the secret organization with earlier Black Hand activities and with Italian criminals in general. Obviously frustrated, Chief Investigator Robinson tried to cultivate some sources on his own, but none developed the concrete information he desired.[19]

Probably the Tampa hearings, more than any others, revealed the tenuous nature of the committee's Mafia arguments. There veteran law enforcement official M. C. Beasley averred that a Mafia organization was behind a recent series of gangland murders in the Tampa area. The committee reproduced in its report portions of Beasley's testimony claiming that the Mafia existed and exercised influence through local politicians. It ignored, on the other hand, testimony appearing on the same page in which Senator Lester Hunt tried to determine which political figures protected the alleged organization. Beasley stalled and then admitted:

Well, maybe it is not the Mafia influence so much as it is the gamblers, we will say, because I can't say that the Mafia has direct influence on any politician.[20]

While several local officeholders claimed to be outraged that they had not had the opportunity to respond to Beasley's charges of corruption, Tampa attorney Cody Fowler, president of the American Bar Association, condemned the general tone of the hearings. Neither links to interstate crime nor to the Mafia had really been developed, Fowler maintained. "I have been practicing law in Tampa for twenty-five years. I am acquainted with hundreds of Italians, and I have never even heard the word 'Mafia' mentioned." While the committee claimed to have received additional confidential information convincing it of the existence of the Mafia structure and influence, its distorted use of material presented in public hearings and a subsequent search of its own files makes any such claim highly questionable.[21]

Both the committee members and the staff recognized the real limitations of their evidence on the Mafia. Kefauver wobbled in his public statements. He told a Tennessee audience in early November of 1950 that while evidence was very scanty, the committee did have "indications that there is some supersecret organization which gives protection to its members." Three months later he confessed to New Orleans reporters that "we've had difficulty in determining just what the Mafia is." Investigator Henry Patrick Kiley cautioned the senator against overstating the Mafia theme in the committee conclusions. Noting that about an equal number of Irish, Jewish, and Italian figures were being sought by the committee, he opposed giving "all the oak leaf clusters" to Italians.[22]

Despite the internal reservations, committee members recognized the widespread interest of the media in a Mafia statement, and since there was no serious objection to use of the term, they drifted toward an endorsement of Anslinger's position. They concluded that a "[n]ationwide crime syndicate known as Mafia" existed, that it had ties with the international traffic in narcotics, and that it exercised "centralized direction and control" over other, more profitable, rackets in the United States. This Mafia supposedly provided the "cement" that bound together various crime syndicates throughout the country, including the large Costello-Adonis-Lansky group on the East Coast and the powerful "Capone syndicate" in Chicago. Essentially the committee had combined the moderate Peterson analysis with the extremist Anslinger thesis and, like numerous sensational reporters before it, had used the evidence of one to support the position of the other. It had, in effect, selectively garbled the evidence to suggest the maximum possible concentration in the underworld. Although conceding that it had encountered difficulty in accumulating "reliable data" on the Mafia, it had nonetheless placed its prestige behind the proposition that there indeed existed this "elusive, shadowy, and sinister organization."[23]

Among the committee members, staff, and friends, nagging doubts about the Mafia conclusions remained. An exhausted Rudolph Halley remarked to a *Collier's* reporter that the committee "might have learned the truth" about the Mafia if it had had more time and a larger staff. Counsel Rufus King, who had joined the committee to help draft legislation, thought its Mafia statements were "romantic myth." Senator Kefauver himself told a "Meet the Press" panel that the Mafia appeared to be more a way of life than an organization. The same year when he spoke to the American Bar Association on "The Menace of Organized Crime," he did not mention the Mafia. And in Chicago, Virgil Peterson, who had worked closely with the committee in its study, was baffled at the report's emphasis on the Mafia. A quarter of a century later, he still remained skeptical that a Mafia dominated organized crime in the United States.[24]

Through its field hearings, the committee had gathered a significant amount of evidence pointing to widespread corruption at the local and state levels. Even when it revealed interstate investments and contacts, as it frequently did, the Kefauver committee discovered again and again that local politicians and law enforcement officials were generally the final arbiters of who operated within their jurisdictions. Indeed the burden of the committee's recommendations—limited federal action, renewed local vigilance, and structural reform in statewide law enforcement—remained consistent with its own evidence. The dramatic tone of the committee, its antimonopolistic stance, its preoccupation with interstate associations and particularly ethnic conspiracies, however, overshadowed its more constructive work. It left the impression that organized crime itself was the product of a sinister conspiracy by a small group of Italian-Americans, and it diverted its own and the public's attention from consideration of broad policy alternatives, such as legalized and regulated public gambling.[25]

At the same time, the supposedly definitive statements of the Kefauver committee—and the enormous public following its televised hearings attracted—blunted any contrary view that might have emerged from the academic community. On the basis of sociological work published by 1950 on juvenile delinquency, ethnic subcultures, and white-collar crime, one might have extrapolated that organized crime had much broader sociological roots than the senators suggested. One could have argued that certain ethnic minorities were exposed to America's competitive, capitalistic goals but were denied realistic opportunities to achieve them in legitimate society; that members of these groups, in disproportionate numbers, were consequently willing to run the risks of apprehension in delivering essentially black market goods and services to the broader society; and that the political corruption involved was a natural consequence of cultural conflicts, illicit profits, and a confusing, fragmented law enforcement structure.[26] It was probably inevitable, however, that the committee would view organized crime not from a sociological but from a law enforcement perspective—from the point of view of determining how best to enforce existing state laws and public policy against gambling, prostitution, the narcotics traffic, and other forms of vice. Certainly the personal dispositions of the senators and staff, the political and legislative exigencies of the committee system, the traditional reliance on pressure groups, and the absence of significant press, academic, or professional criticism encouraged that approach.

The flurry of anticrime activities following the Kefauver committee's reports subsided by the mid-1950's, but the popular images of organized crime it had helped foster did not. Popular writers, motion picture and television producers, and scholars and legal experts continued to speculate and enlarge on the committee's conclusions. The Kefauver committee interpretations became the new conventional wisdom and in effect set the limits for later investigations and interpretations, notably those of the McClellan committees and President Johnson's Commission on Law Enforcement and the Administration of Justice. Out of the study of the celebrated Apalachin meeting in 1957 and the testimony of Joseph Valachi in 1963 there emerged a slightly more elaborate version of the basic Kefauver perspective—that organized crime in the United States was dominated by a secret Italian criminal organization, this time one of about five thousand members grouped in twenty-four "families," topped by a "Commission" and called La Cosa Nostra.[27] While available scholarly studies suggest that the ethnic element in organized crime has probably undergone some change since the early 1950's, the evidence to support the McClellan conclusions on La Cosa Nostra is surprisingly thin.[28] Insights provided by Daniel Bell, Joseph Albini, Gordon Hawkins, Dwight Smith, and reporter Hank Messick suggest that the same fixed preconceptions that the Kefauver committee helped shape dominated these later studies.[29]

The Kefauver committee had not, of course, created the Mafia myth, for a certain vague, shifting stereotype of Italian crime had existed in the United States for over half a century. What the committee did was to sharpen the definition, to publicize the image, and to place its own prestige behind the Mafia interpretation. And it did this not because of the evidence, but in spite of the evidence. Given its wide public following, the committee's conclusions were accepted by the public and modified only in matters of detail by the later McClellan studies. The Kefauver myths encouraged the public tendency to think of crime, particularly organized crime, as a semimonopoly originating outside the social, political, and economic structure of American life; it distorted the degree of centralization within the underworld; and it diverted study from alternative public policies for dealing with the problem. Its final, confusing legacy would shape American policy toward organized crime for at least a full generation.

JOHN A. CONLEY

9

CRIMINAL JUSTICE HISTORY AS A FIELD OF RESEARCH
A Review of Literature, 1960-1975

It is appropriate to conclude with a survey of other research in the general field of criminal justice history. John Conley provides convincing evidence for the need for additional work in the history of criminal justice. He notes first that the literature produced in the past decade is "ahistorical in structure, content, and perspective." This, for students and scholars in the field of criminal justice, is a serious deficiency because historical research can establish a sense of balance in the field "by contributing to our understanding of the long-range implications of reform, by investigating the origin of current problems, and by studying criminal justice issues over time." Despite the limitations of recent scholarship, Conley provides a useful critical guide through the major literature on the history of various aspects of the American criminal justice system. He points out a number of gaps in our present knowledge and identifies the works making major contributions to our understanding of the American criminal justice system.

The President's Crime Commission report, in discussing the need for more research, claimed that the "revolution in scientific discovery has largely bypassed the problem of crime and crime control."[1] There was little disagreement with that statement, and educators became excited about the possibility of large sums of federal dollars being funneled into the academic and research institutions. But the results have not been

From *Journal of Criminal Justice* (Spring, 1977), pp. 13–28.

satisfactory; research expenditures have been minimal when compared to total dollars spent on grants for technology, hardware, and operations of the criminal justice process.[2] Others can determine the value of the overall research effort (or lack of it). This paper will focus on criminal justice history as one area in need of research by outlining the problem, critiquing selected recent literature, and suggesting areas in need of further study.

The criminal justice literature produced in the past decade is ahistorical in structure, content, and perspective. The textbooks published during the past five years as introductions to "criminal justice" are completely lacking in historical depth. For example, of fifteen such textbooks,[3] eleven had fewer than twenty pages devoted to history and five of these had no historical material or analysis.[4] The bulk of the historical discussion, when present, concentrated on two areas—criminological theories of crime causation and police development.

The four texts that had a concentration of historical analysis included a traditional criminology publication and three anthologies. The criminology text had an excellent summary discussion of the history of criminological theory and the evolution of correctional practice.[5] Richard Quinney[6] (1969) had four standard-length articles that detailed the historical roots of law and order in colonial society, vagrancy laws, prohibition, sexual psychopath laws, and the marihuana tax act. His 1974 publication had ten separate articles devoted to historical analysis of various aspects of crime and justice. He covered the development of criminological theory, the evolution of the concepts of legal order and criminal law, the development of the police and the penitentiary, and the history of racism, riots, and juvenile delinquency.[7] The book by Richter Moore, Thomas Marks, and Robert Barrow had three articles that covered the theoretical development of punishment, police history, and the development of juvenile courts.[8]

The obvious conclusion to be drawn from this survey is that unless faculty members are providing historical material in their lectures as a supplement to the basic texts or unless the undergraduate programs offer specific courses dealing with the history of criminal justice, the students graduating from these programs are getting a narrow, contemporary view of criminal justice. The two documents that outline the course offerings in criminal justice programs nationally do not give support to the notion that criminal justice history is an important ingredient of these programs.[9] There is no source to determine the amount of history provided through lectures, but it is safe to assume that little more than cursory exposure is the norm.

There are other indicators that support the contention that history is not a priority in criminal justice education and research. The author of a recent book published for the purpose of encouraging more applied research in criminal justice said that "what matters is how future generations will judge our contribution in solving major social problems."[10] Obviously the author appreciated the role of history, yet his book did not have any model for or thrust toward historical analysis.

A review of the research aids used by scholars (and, if hopes are realized, by students) did not produce evidence to support an assumption that historical research had been done, but, because of the newness of the field of criminal justice, the research had not yet evolved into full-scale books. Of six recently published bibliographies checked by the writer, not one had a general category for history or topical listings of historical research.[11]

One index is systematically organized to facilitate learning of the historical development of concepts, terms, theories, and research, but it failed to have a general category devoted to history. The abstracts proved generally to have the same void, with only *Crime and Delinquency Abstracts* (vols. 4–8) designed to include categories for "historical," "histories," and "history."

This lack of reference to historical research does not mean that absolutely no work of this nature has been completed in the area of criminal justice. There are historical studies listed in these resource guides, but the citations are hidden within topical and subtopical areas. The lack of specific categories does, however, indicate that the volume of historical work is minimal and therefore does not warrant a separate listing. Obviously scholars and teachers within criminal justice and within other disciplines that study criminal justice have not devoted much effort to researching the history of the field or to training their students to conduct such research. The reasons for not conducting historical research in criminal justice are many, and although they explain why we have such limited output, they do not excuse the various disciplines from failing to fill that gap in our knowledge.

Legal historians have ignored the field of criminal justice because of the nature of their professional training. Legal historians learned their trade and approached their studies from a constitutional perspective and, as a result, doctoral dissertations and subsequent research focused on the federal Supreme Court and appellate courts.[12] From an evolutionary perspective historians naturally looked to these courts for broad patterns of legal development, but this myopia also resulted in a distorted picture of law and its role in society. The concentrated study of appellate courts produced research on technical and philosophical aspects of the law, but ignored the day-to-day operations of the legal system. Few legal historians heard the call from such scholars as Roscoe Pound and Jerome Hall for more research on the relationship between law and its operation in society.[13]

A practical consideration that reinforced the pattern of studying only appellate courts was the availability and access to documentary sources. The ease with which historians can secure records from the federal government and the sophisticated organization of these records is far superior to that found at the state and local levels. It is much easier to conduct research in large, well-organized libraries than it is to rummage through the scattered files of a clerk of a lower court or the unorganized records of an urban police department.

Finally, the diverse cultural heritage of the United States served as a barrier to any synthesis of criminal law or criminal justice history. The fifty states with their legacy of Dutch, British, French, Spanish, and Indian legal systems provided what appeared to be insuperable obstacles to a coherent and intelligent investigation of the origin of criminal law, patterns of judicial administration, and the growth of institutions of enforcement. But some scholars have found that these problems are not insurmountable and, in fact, they provide a richness to the research effort.[14] Before we evaluate the state of the art of American criminal justice research, we should discuss briefly recent developments in English scholarship and its importance to our body of knowledge.

English scholars have not ignored their criminal justice heritage. There is an abundant supply of rich, scholarly research on the development of law in England, and that interest is seen in the criminal law field as well.[15] This deep concern for history, which is so characteristic of the English, has extended into the areas of crime and crime control institutions to a far greater degree than is true for the United States. The classic example is the four-volume work *History of Criminal Law*, by Sir Leon Radzinowicz,[16] which depicted the evolution of criminal law principles and the origin and development of institutions of crime control such as the office of justice of the peace, the constable, and the urban police force. Who in the United States can equal the level of scholarship and productivity of Charles Reith, the father of English police history? His series, *The Police Idea* (1938), *British Police and the Democratic Ideal* (1943), *The Blind Eye of History* (1952), and *A New Study of Police History* (1956),[17] provided a cornerstone for any serious attempt to understand the development of Anglo-American policing. A recent publication by Thomas Critchley, *A History of Police in England and Wales, 900–1966* (1967),[18] is not written in the same grand style of the interpretive narrative of Reith, but it is packed with new facts because

Critchley located records not available when William Lee wrote *History of Police in England*.[19] Indeed the Critchley book and recent American publications on urban policing raise enough new questions about the inevitability of the modern police model and its role in crime reduction to warrant a new investigation into the history of English policing. Reith conducted his research during the turbulent period of World War II and he wrote from a very conservative ideology that placed a heavy emphasis on order. A fresh look at these and other police issues is long overdue.

More research is needed on the differences and similarities of the authority of the English and American police forces in the nineteenth century.[20] We need to know more about the philosophical foundation and the functional aspects related to the issue of controlling police authority. Did we misinterpret or modify the concept of popular control during the transplantation of the English police model to America?[21] Did we transplant that model? Criminal justice scholars need to focus more attention on these questions if we are to better understand the extent of our debt to England and other countries that influenced the settlement of the New World.

Other English scholars have begun to re-evaluate earlier conclusions about crime and disorder throughout England's history. J. J. Tobias's *Crime and Industrial Society in the Nineteenth Century* (1968) and *Nineteenth Century Crime in England: Prevention and Punishment* (1972)[22] challenged the lingering belief that crime rose as a result of unmanageable urban growth. The first book did not meet quantitative expectations, however, because Tobias covered too broad a time period and avoided using extant statistics to support his conclusions. The second work is a collection of nineteenth-century documents from public and private sources that has brief introductory essays and a useful bibliography. This book is an excellent reference work for upper level and graduate students working in the area. For medieval crime, John Bellamy's *Crime and Public Order in England in the Later Middle Ages* (1973)[23] is the first look at this topic since L. O. Pike wrote *A History of Crime in England* (1873–1876).[24] Bellamy used legal records (court indictments, sentencing reports, appeals) and concluded that crime was not abnormal and was committed by all classes and that the sudden rise in criminal activity was linked to broader social and economic changes during this transitional period away from feudalism. The book failed to support these interpretations, however, with any systematic use of the court records. Joel Samaha's *Law and Order in Historical Perspective: The Case of Elizabethan Essex* (1974)[25] is a study of one city based on extant court records. Samaha challenged some traditional interpretations by claiming that most felons were lone offenders and that the constable was more conscientious and efficient than we had been led to believe.

These areas need much more study, and American scholars should use these research approaches on the earlier periods of United States history. Particular attention should be given to the daily lives of the people through the application of sociological and psychological theories and concepts that help explain individual and group actions.[26]

American criminologists have not kept pace with their European counterparts in developing a commitment to historical research. Sellin,[27] Barnes,[28] and Teeters[29] did have a deep interest in historical analysis of crime and punishment, but succeeding generations have not followed their lead. This failure to follow the course shaped by early American criminologists is ironic because it was their influence on the school of sociological jurisprudence that gave impetus to and recognition of criminal justice history as a respectable academic field of study.[30] Yet the United States has not produced a Leon Radzinowicz or a Charles Reith.

A significant amount of the history found in criminological literature concentrates on theory development or penology. Recent publications have emphasized this tradition of criminological thought. Stephen Schaefer outlined the development of law and criminological theories.[31] He discussed the various intellectual foundations of the utilitarians, constitutionalists, utopians, Marxists, and early and modern criminologists. The weakness of the book lies in Schaefer's failure to link the legal and criminological themes to contemporary society and to illustrate their relationship. Sawyer Sylvester compiled a collection of essays by some of the leaders of modern criminology into one brief but valuable book.[32] He included such figures as Beccaria, Mayhew, Tarde, Bonger, and Sellin; and he provided a brief biographical introduction that placed the individuals in their proper position within the stream of intellectual history. Both books are valuable contributions to criminological thought, but are not histories of criminal justice. One overall weakness of the literature on early criminologists is that everyone is neatly packaged into a particular school with no discussion of the questions that plagued these scholars.

The second largest area of interest to criminologists has been the field of penology, now called "corrections." Through their interest in punishment, criminologists have studied the offender in prison and the various philosophies of and approaches to punishment. George Killenger and Paul Cromwell, Jr.,[33] have published a solid collection of standard approaches to the topic. The historical study of penal institutions, however, has not received any significant attention since the turn of the century when McKelvey[34] and Lewis[35] researched their classic works. Recent scholarship does not appear to be aiming in that direction. Only six dissertations on the history of state penal systems have been written by young scholars in the past decade.[36] Of these, only [one] has been published.[37] [The author, M. T. Carleton], studied the brutal conditions and political administrations of the Louisiana penal system and analyzed various reform attempts. The analyzation of reform attempts is crucial to our understanding of the failure and successes of penal reform movements and their applicability to today's problems. There is little research on the various reform movements in the penal area. Questions of how, when, where, and why remain unexplored.

A recent attempt to place the origin of correctional institutions within the social context of the times is David Rothman's book, *The Discovery of the Asylum.*[38] The author claims that Americans saw their traditional society and values disintegrating under the pressure of immigration and industrialization, and they reverted to institutionalization as a model for social order. This thesis, however, is too simplistic to explain such complex phenomena as the impact of immigration, individualism, emerging capitalism, class conflict, and personal freedom on the stability of society. Rothman does not use the extensive manuscripts of various social reformers of the period, and he conveniently ignores any opposition that developed over these correctional issues. Furthermore, it is questionable whether jails, mental hospitals, almshouses, and penitentiaries represent more than variations of a single class. His conclusion that the United States invented the penitentiary is also not without error. We did build new and larger facilities, but the legal and philosophical theory for such institutions can be found in Blackstone's writings.

Much more detailed research about the evolution of state and local penal systems is needed before we have a clear picture of the role of these institutions in the development of criminal justice and social control.[39] The origin and development of local and territorial jails is a fertile field of research that has been completely ignored. An analysis of the changing social and demographic characteristics of the inmates and the types of crimes for which they were convicted would tell us much about the shifting patterns of sentencing, labelling of outgroups, and the reaction of these groups to changing social conditions. Finally, we need extensive historical research on the rank-and-file employees of state penal systems to determine their personal attitudes, social characteristics, and job conditions. There is a great scholarly potential in these areas, and the knowledge generated would add to our understanding of the social and legal strains in United States penal history.

As a historian of and a teacher in the field of criminal justice, I am constantly amazed by the lack of historical research on criminal justice agencies in the urban community. The urban history literature that has been so plentiful during the past three decades rarely mentions the urban courts, police, or jails and the roles of the officials who had responsibility for their functions. Surely these agencies and officials were not mere appendages to the intense development of these communities and to the social, political, and economic issues that shaped their development. Four new books[40] shed some light on this area and illustrate the value of research on local crime control agencies. The most recent, a case study, is, unfortunately, the most disappointing. *Horse to Helicopter*[41] is an uncritical, descriptive survey of the history of the Atlanta police department that ignores conceptual themes and lacks an analytical scheme. The book is not without value, however, because it is the first history of a southern, urban police department to be written in decades, and it does provide basic information and issues that should be investigated through further research. For a field that has so little research on police history and because most of that research focused on the eastern cities, *Horse to Helicopter* is a welcome change, for it explores new ground and should serve as encouragement to future scholars interested in this area.

Richardson's *Urban Police in the United States*[42] is the first attempt to write a synthesis of police history in the United States. The first four chapters are a deft survey of the English heritage during the colonial period and the development of policing to the early twentieth century; but Richardson relied solely on standard secondary publications that, in this author's opinion, are in need of major revision. The balance of the book attempts to link the historical antecedents of current police issues such as alcohol, technology, drugs, riots, and community relations. This is an admirable goal and, in fact, is the thrust of this paper; but Richardson failed to conduct any significantly new research, and the reader is left with the idea that the book was hurriedly written to fill an obvious void in the literature used by criminal justice college programs. It is unfortunate that Richardson did not meet the standards set in his earlier study of *The New York Police*,[43] in which he linked police development to the contemporary problems of the emerging urban society and the conflicts between various political factions and ideologies. This is an excellent case history and is equal to the detailed account of the Boston police by Roger Lane.[44] Lane provides us with clear descriptions of daily functions of the police and how they changed over time. The best parts of the book show how the police began as a service to private citizens and slowly moved to a public service as the administrative reward systems of government were established on an equal, if tenuous, footing with private methods.

These case studies point to the potential richness of research on police history and to the obvious need for more case studies from other cities— north, south, east, and west. Other universal issues that need investigation center around questions of whose law and whose order prevailed, what similarities and dissimilarities of police development existed between cities and among regions, and how the rank and file viewed their problems and their jobs during this critical period.

Recent research,[45] which documented the differences in law enforcement styles and patterns of operations and organizational structures, raised serious questions about the efficacy of current approaches to standardization, community control, and general reform. Case studies of the historical development of these police departments and their traditional functions will help in the evaluation of current change models.

Another area that cries out for research is the relationship of urban police departments to the power structure.[46] A systematic analysis of the linkages of police officials and the rank and file to the political and economic leadership,[47] as well as an investigation of the bonds between the police and lower socioeconomic groups[48] will help shed light on the simplistic and false dichotomy between corruption and reform and between oppressor and oppressed that permeates the literature.

Much research is yet to be completed on police involvement in the industrial labor movement of the late nineteenth and early twentieth centuries.[49] Adequate histories of the various local police fraternal associations and national groups such as the International Association of Chiefs of Police would be invaluable to our understanding of the police field in general and its political power in particular.

Another area of neglect is the federal role in law enforcement. There has not been a history of the federalization of crime and the expanding role of federal agencies in local law enforcement.[50] A major study of the United States Department of Justice has not been conducted since the late 1930s.[51]

Finally, the criminal justice field is in dire need of analytical biographies of its past leaders. Recent studies of August Vollmer and O. W. Wilson are steps in that direction.[52] A biography of William H. Parker is probably forthcoming, but surely we have more people throughout criminal justice history who have contributed to the growth and development of the field. To date we have few role models for ourselves or the future generations of professionals. This void contributes to the fuzziness of the outer boundaries of law enforcement "professionalism." In short, we have no tradition.

Before leaving the police area a note should be given to encourage more research on state police systems and other state law enforcement agencies. An uncritical portrayal of the origin of the Pennsylvania State Police by Katherine Mayo, *Justice to All*,[53] bordered on fiction and presented simplistic notions of the role of this agency during the early twentieth century labor disputes. A more scholarly and objective study of a state police is Leo J. Coakley's *Jersey Troopers: A Fifty-Year History of the New Jersey State Police*.[54] But neither work is satisfactory for our understanding of the complex role of state law enforcement agencies and the historical parameters of that role.

One of the most abused areas of historical research is that dealing with law and order on the western frontier. Most of the history written on this period reflects an antiquarian romanticism in which a gun-slinging sheriff or marshal restores law and order through the infamous shoot-out in the dusty street of the town. Criminal justice scholars interested in this area should begin with Ramon Adams's bibliography, *Six Guns and Saddle Leather*, which provides the researcher with annotations on books and pamphlets on western outlaws. In his *Burrs under the Saddle*,[55] Adams corrects errors in historical scholarship found in more than four hundred selected titles on western law and order. In this work Adams fails to distinguish between the antiquarian and the professional scholars, but the book is an excellent reference for leads and issues relating to crime on the western frontier.

Much more work is needed in this area and the criminal justice scholar should pay heed to recent works that have raised new questions or used new methods of research. Glenn Shirley's *Law West of Fort Smith*[56] is a classic study of the crime problem and the role of the federal courts in bringing order to the territories. Judge Isaac Parker is given credit for filling the legal void, but Shirley does not paint the infamous judge larger than life—he is studied within the social and political climate of the time. Phillip Jordan focuses on the nature of the statutes, their enforcement, and the compliance level of the citizenry in his *Frontier Law and Order: Ten Essays*.[57] The book is a collection of independent articles written by the author and as a result there is a loss of theme, but he does raise significant questions that need further research. For example, he concludes that law and order issues were not different on the frontier from what they were in eastern cities. Frank Prassel, in *The Western Peace Officer: The Legacy of Law and Order*,[58] argues the same point, but raises a more significant issue. He studied many types of peace officers, from sheriffs and marshals to private police and Indian law officers, to pony soldiers and the military; he concludes that urban growth, not frontier tradition, accounted for the crime problems.

This homogenizing of crime and social control issues is questionable, but until serious scholars research more towns, cities, and states of the frontier period and publish their findings on the extent of crime, the reaction of the communities, the mechanism and strategies for enforcement, and the impact of the conflict between the Indian and white man's cultures, we will have little understanding of the current crime problems whose roots lie deep in the frontier experiences.[59] Eugene Hollon's study of violence[60] is a beginning. Hollon challenged the myth that most frontier violence was the one-to-one duel that pitted the law officer against the outlaw, and he documented that much of the violence was directed toward unarmed or outgunned minorities such as the Chinese, Indians, Mexicans, and Mormons. Research comparing law and order issues of eastern, midwestern, and western cities at approximately equal periods in their development would do much to shed light on whether law and order needs and strategies were different on the frontier from what they were in the eastern cities. Robert Dykstra's[61] study of frontier Kansas towns is an excellent model that explored the impact of internal conflict on community development.

Juvenile delinquency has yet to surface as a sophisticated field of its own. Its theoretical development leans heavily on the general theories of deviance and as a result we have not had a heavy interest in either its theoretical or institutional history.[62] There is a growing literature on the juvenile court, however, and we may be in for a period of repetitious studies. One study[63] centered on the court movement at its origin in Chicago and concentrated on the cultural heritage of the reformers whose class values influenced their definition of delinquency and their solutions to the "new" problem. This is an adequately researched book by a criminologist who used a theoretical approach to study a social phenomenon in history. Platt later stated that his book focused too heavily on the middle-class reformers and failed to link the child-saving movement both to other reforms of the same period and to the ideological base that supported these reforms.[64] In spite of these shortcomings, the book is a valuable and critical contribution to the history of juvenile justice.

We will not have a satisfactory understanding of the history of juvenile delinquency until we see more research on the daily operations of the many institutions that developed in response to the problem. Recent attempts cover the period between 1825–1940 and are well-researched books.[65] The authors failed, however, to develop any conceptual interpretations for understanding delinquency, and they resisted outlining issues for further research. Criminal justice scholars interested in juvenile delinquency will have to balance the views of the reformers and practitioners with studies on the impact of the institutional and treatment models on the target population, i.e., the children. In that sense, juvenile delinquency should be studied within the larger social group of children and youth and their changing status. Documentary sources that link the legal, social, public, and private elements of this topical area are now available for reference as a starting point.[66]

Local courts have not received much attention from legal historians. The traditional focus on the appeals courts and the difficulty in locating court records at the local level have hindered the investigation of these courts. Historians, until recently, failed to recognize the importance of local courts to the maintenance of order in society, yet the vast majority of people looked to these courts for solutions to interpersonal disputes, crime, as well as political and social issues. During the formative years of the states, the local magistrates not only controlled the direction of order and growth in local communities, but they also served simultaneously as leaders of political parties and as members of the legislatures.[67] There is much to be learned about the forces that shaped our legal system by studying these local courts. To encourage this research, bibliographies of research in progress have been compiled[68] and should be consulted by researchers.

Many colonial court records have been painstakingly collected by historians and published as monographs or in series for research purposes.[69] Many of these early court records are on microfilm and are available to researchers through interlibrary loan.[70] These collections are either verbatim or edited transcriptions of the original court proceedings. Some scholars have written invaluable, lengthy essays introducing the material and placing the court and its personnel into the historical context of the times. There is a wealth of information about crime, punishment, order, social conflict, and the daily operation of the courts in these records of early court proceedings. Unfortunately, these criminal justice issues have not been explored by legal historians, criminologists, or those in criminal justice.

In addition to understanding the operations of the courts, we need to know more about the evolution of our local judicial systems. Although the colonial courts have received more attention recently, there is little historical research on the courts of the nineteenth and early twentieth centuries. Robert M. Ireland's study of the county court in Kentucky[71] is an excellent model that could be replicated in other states. Ireland focuses on the social and political characteristics of the judges and explores the changes in the procedure and structure of the courts during the early nineteenth century. His research looked at county courts statewide, however, and did not explore in detail the court operations of any particular county. Detailed studies of the sentencing patterns, the selection and tenure of judges, the differences between the formal and real power of courts, the social and political forces behind jurisdictional disputes, and the interaction between the courts and other components of the criminal justice process are sorely needed if we as a society are to understand the historical forces behind the problems of criminal justice today. A recent historical survey of an urban judicial system illustrated the richness of issues available to criminal justice scholars.[72] What impact did the social and political forces of change have on the structure, jurisdiction, and decisions of local courts? What role did these courts play in controlling urban disorder and class conflict? How and why did the lay citizenry come to play less and less of a role in local criminal justice matters? These are only a few of the issues that need to be researched by criminal justice scholars.

Through the innovative use of court records researchers can compensate for the lack of crime statistics during the formative years of the country. One study noted that the effectiveness of the criminal process in eighteenth-century New York was less than adequate.[73] The author concluded that, because only one-fifth of the cases were resolved in the courts, the courts and the police were weak. Another study used the number of indictments and convictions as a measure of a community's response to crime.[74]

Roger Lane used court records in his study of crime in nineteenth-century Massachusetts and concluded that crimes of personal violence decreased, but property crimes increased during the period of rapid urbanization.[75] A recent study of two county courts on the West Coast found that civil litigation changed from dispute settlement to routine administrative work over an eighty-year period with no differences in the type of work between the rural and urban courts.[76]

All these conclusions are location specific and tentative because we have not had enough replication of these studies elsewhere in the country. Many master's theses and doctoral dissertations can be written by investigating the early operations of local and county courts.

This paper attempted to point the way toward new areas of research by expanding our research horizon. The literature cited and discussed indicates a slowly growing interest in criminal justice history. A prestigious national journal devoted its January 1976 issue to thirteen historical articles on crime and justice that were written by a respected group of authors from many fields.[77] The special editor and the journal should be commended for their effort, but one wonders if this interest will continue and begin to shape its own unique approach to historical research, or will it be short lived and simply feed the current bicentennial fever? The answer will depend on criminal justice teachers and professionals, because if they do not see history as an important part of the education of new generations of students, then history will not be researched.

If criminal justice is to survive as a viable and contributing field of study then it must use its unique interest to address current problems. Research will (or should) play an expanded role in this problem-solving effort particularly in the applied and evaluative spheres. But there should be a balance to the research effort so that we do not lose sight of the evolutionary thrust of criminal justice change and the larger issues related to crime control in a democratic society. Historical research can provide this balance by contributing to our understanding of the long-range implications of reform, by investigating the origin of current problems, and by studying criminal justice issues over time.

Criminal justice history would provide us with tradition; it would develop a framework with outer boundaries. Other scholars, practitioners, and the general public could use that framework to evaluate current levels of crime and crime control activity and future attempts at change. Criminal justice history, in essence, would provide society with a method of blending or integrating the story of "why" with the techniques of "how."[78]

Two recent thought-provoking articles looked to the future and raised questions about how our society will respond to crime and issues by the year 2000.[79] But how can the professionals in criminal justice or society in general respond to such questions when our perspective is limited to the 1960s? The question of how we respond to crime and justice in the future may be irrelevant if we do not know why.

NOTES

1: The Development of American Criminal Law

1. Marcello T. Maestro, *Voltaire and Beccaria as Reformers of Criminal Law* (1942), pp. 51–72.
2. On the statute in general, see Edwin R. Keedy, "History of the Pennsylvania Statute Creating Degrees of Murder," 97 *Univ. Pa. L. Rev.* 759 (1949).
3. See, in general, David B. Davis, "The Movement to Abolish Capital Punishment in America, 1787–1861," 63 *Am. Hist. Rev.* 23 (1957).
4. *Memorial to the Legislature*, N.Y. Senate Documents, Vol. 4, 1842, Doc. No. 97, pp. 21–39.
5. Laws Maine 1837, ch. 292.
6. Jack K. Williams, *Vogues in Villainy: Crime and Retribution in Ante-Bellum South Carolina* (1959), p. 100. In general, there were more capital crimes in the South than in the North. Some of the difference is accounted for by the special, severe laws relating to slaves and free Negroes.
7. Williams, op. cit., p. 38.
8. Md. const. 1851, art. 10, sec. 5. It was a common provision that juries were judges of fact and law in "prosecutions or indictments for libel," for example, N.J. const. 1844, art. 1, sec. 5.
9. See Francis Wharton, *A Treatise on the Criminal Law of the United States* (4th ed., 1957), pp. 1115–25.
10. Williams, op. cit., p. 39.
11. *State* v. *Bennet*, 3 Brevard (S. Car.) 515 (1815).
12. Jerome Hall, *Theft, Law, and Society* (2nd ed., 1952), p. 140.
13. Roger Lane, *Policing the City: Boston, 1822–1885* (1967), p. 34.
14. Jack Williams, "Crime and Punishment in Alabama 1819–1840," 6 Ala. R. 1427 (1953).
15. 1 Greenl. (Me.) 226 (1821).
16. *State* v. *Williams*, 2 Overton (Tenn.) 108 (1808).
17. 7 Cranch 32 (1812).
18. *People* v. *Heely*, New York Judicial Repository, 277 (1819).
19. 4 Blackstone, *Commentaries*, 90.
20. J. Willard Hurst, "Treason in the United States," 58 *Harv. L. Rev.* 226 (1944); see also Bradley Chapin, *The American Law of Treason, Revolutionary and Early National Origins* (1964).

21. Hurst, op. cit., p. 256.
22. U.S. Const., Art. 3, sec. 3.
23. See, in general, James Morton Smith, *Freedom's Fetters: the Alien and Sedition Laws and American Civil Liberties* (1956).
24. William E. Nelson, *The Americanization of the Common Law during the Revolutionary Era: A Study of Legal Change in Massachusetts, 1760-1830*, pp. 344-57.
25. The story of Howe and Hummel has been entertainingly recounted by Richard Rovere, in *The Magnificent Shysters* (1947).
26. Rovere, op. cit., p. 34.
27. N.Y. Penal Code 1881, secs. 2, 675.
28. 8 Ind. 494 (1856).
29. Edward L. Kimball, "Criminal Cases in a State Appellate Court: Wisconsin 1839-1959," 9 *Am. J. Leg. Hist.* 95, 99-100 (1965).
30. Herbert Asbury, *The Gangs of New York* (1928), pp. 235-37.
31. See Joe B. Frantz, "The Frontier Tradition: An Invitation to Violence," and Richard Maxwell Brown, "The American Vigilante Tradition," in Hugh D. Graham and Ted R. Gurr, eds., *Violence in America: Historical and Comparative Perspectives* (1969), pp. 127 ff, 154 ff.
32. Thomas J. Dimsdale, *The Vigilantes of Montana* (new edition, 1953), p. 13.
33. Richard Maxwell Brown, op. cit., p. 175.
34. Quoted in Richard M. Brown, op. cit., p. 183.
35. Hubert H. Bancroft, *Popular Tribunals* (1887), Vol. I, pp. 10, 11, 16.
36. John W. Caughey, *Their Majesties the Mob* (1960), pp. 6-7.
37. Laws Wis. 1861, ch. 222.
38. Laws Pa. 1869, ch. 991.
39. Richard M. Brown, op. cit., pp. 190-91.
40. J. P. Shalloo, *Private Police, with Special Reference to Pennsylvania* (1933), pp. 60, 62, 88.
41. Roscoe Pound, *Criminal Justice in America* (1945), p. 16.
42. Laws Ind. 1891, ch. 33, 39, 146, 150.
43. Laws N.Y. 188, ch. 330.
44. Livingston Hall, "The Substantive Law of Crimes, 1887-1936," 50 *Harv. L. Rev.* 616, 633 (1937).
45. See Joseph Gusfield, *Symbolic Crusade, Status Politics and the American Temperance Movement* (1963).
46. Roger Lane, "Urbanization and Criminal Violence in the 19th Century: Massachusetts as a Test Case," in Hugh D. Graham and Ted R. Gurr, eds., *Violence in America: Historical and Comparative Perspectives* (1969), p. 468.
47. Interestingly, the same study by Lane which suggests a decline in arrests for *major* arrests in Massachusetts suggests an equally striking increase in arrests for *minor* offenses, mainly drunkenness. This confirms the notion of a diminished tolerance for what is defined as antisocial behavior.
48. The examples above are drawn from Thomas M. McDade, *The Annals of Murder, A Bibliography of Books and Pamphlets on American Murders from Colonial Times to 1900* (1961), pp. 35-37, 87, 311-16.
49. M'Naghten's case, 10 Cl. & F. 200 (1843).
50. *State v. Felter*, 25 Iowa 67, 82 (1868).
51. On contemporary tests of insanity see, in general, Joel P. Bishop, *Commentaries on the Criminal Law* (6th ed., 1877), Vol. I, pp. 213-29.
52. John P. Reid, *Chief Justice, The Judicial World of Charles Doe* (1967), pp. 114-21; *State v. Pike*, 49 N.H. 399, 442 (1869).
53. The story of this trial has been beautifully recreated in Charles Rosenberg's *Trial of the Assassin Guiteau* (1968).
54. Livingston Hall, "The Substantive Law of Crimes—1887-1936," 50 *Harv. L. Rev.* 616, 642 (1937).

55. N.Y. Penal code, 1881, sec. 549.
56. "Wilful" was a troublesome word, however; and the requirement of "wilful" violation, common in statutes, certainly meant that the defendant could not be punished for *reasonable* mistakes of law. See Hall, op. cit., p. 646.
57. Hall, op. cit., p. 647.
58. *Commonwealth* v. *Pulaski County Agricultural & Mechanical Ass'n.*, 92 Ky. 197, 17 S.W. 442 (1891).
59. See *State* v. *Beach*, 147 Ind. 74, 46 N.E. 145 (1897).
60. William C. Osborn, "Liquor Statutes in the United States," 2 *Harv. L. Rev.* 125, 126 (1888). Stats. N.H. 1878, ch. 109, secs. 24, 25; Iowa Code 1873, sec. 1542.

2: Poverty, Pauperism, and Social Order

1. R. H. Wiebe, *The Search for Order: 1877-1920* (1967).
2. On colonial urbanism, the classic works remain C. Bridenbaugh, *Cities in the Wilderness: The First Century of Urban Life in America, 1625-1742* (1938) and Bridenbaugh, *Cities in Revolt: Urban Life in America, 1743-1776* (1955). Studies which suggest nineteenth-century changes include: R. Berthoff, "The American Social Order: A Conservative Hypothesis," 65 *American Historical Review* 495 (1960); R. Berthoff, *An Unsettled People: Social Order and Disorder in American History* (1971), pp. 125-298; D. Rothman, *The Discovery of the Asylum: Social Order and Disorder in the New Republic* (1971); R. A. Mohl, *Poverty in New York, 1783-1825* (1971); M. B. Katz, *The Irony of Early School Reform: Educational Innovation in Mid-Nineteenth Century Massachusetts* (1968); F. Somkin, *Unquiet Eagle: Memory and Desire in the Idea of American Freedom, 1815-1860* (1967).
3. D. T. Gilchrist, ed., *The Growth of Seaport Cities, 1790-1825* (1967), pp. 38-46; G. R. Taylor, "American Urban Growth Preceding the Railway Age," 27 *Journal of Economic History* 309 (1967).
4. R. Ernst, *Immigrant Life in New York City, 1825-1863* (1949), pp. 48-60; G. Osofsky, "The Enduring Ghetto," 55 *Journal of American History* 243 (1968); J. E. Ford et al., *Slums and Housing: With Special Reference to New York City,* 2 vols. (1936), 1, pp. 72-121; S. B. Warner, Jr., *The Private City: Philadelphia in Three Periods of Its Growth* (1968), pp. 50-56.
5. K. H. Claghorn, "The Foreign Immigrant in New York City," 15 *United States Industrial Commission Reports* 464 (1901); Gilchrist, ed., *Growth of the Seaport Cities,* pp. 32-33; O. Handlin, *Boston's Immigrants: A Study in Acculturation* (1968), p. 243; *The [Eighth] Annual Report of the Boston City Missionary Society* (1849), p. 12. See also R. A. Billington, *The Protestant Crusade, 1800-1860: A Study of the Origins of American Nativism* (1938).
6. J. Henretta, "Economic Development and Social Structure in Colonial Boston," 22 *William and Mary Quarterly* 75 (1965); J. T. Main, *The Social Structure of Revolutionary America* (1965); D. T. Miller, "Immigration and Social Stratification in Pre–Civil War New York," 49 *New York History* 157 (1968). On limited mobility in the later nineteenth century, see S. Thernstrom, *Poverty and Progress: Social Mobility in a Nineteenth Century City* (1964).
7. *Christian Herald and Seaman's Magazine* 8 (June 16, 1821) 71, and 9 (Feb. 1, 1823) 553; S. Thernstrom, "The Case of Boston," 79 *Proceedings of the Massachusetts Historical Society* 114 (1967); Account Book of Cash Distributions to the Poor, 1809–1816, entries for Jan. 11, 20, 30, 1810, volume 0383, Alms House Records, New York City Municipal Archives and Records Center; B. Still, *Mirror for Gotham* (1956), pp. 114-115; K. Roberts and A. M. Roberts, trans. and eds., *Moreau de St. Mery's American Journey, 1793-1798* (1947), p. 165. See also S. Thernstrom and P. R. Knights, "Men in Motion: Some Data and Speculations about Urban Population Mobility in Nineteenth-Century America," 1 *Journal of Interdisciplinary History* 7 (1970).

8. Warner, *The Private City*, pp. 5–8; S. I. Pomerantz, *New York: An American City, 1783–1803* (1965), pp. 194–199; D. Montgomery, "The Working Classes of the Pre-Industrial American City, 1780–1830," 9 *Labor History* 3 (1968); P. S. Foner, *History of the Labor Movement in the United States*, 4 vols. (1947–1967), 1, pp. 97–142; E. Pessen, *Most Uncommon Jacksonians: The Radical Leaders of the Early Labor Movement* (1967); W. Hugins, *Jacksonian Democracy and the Working Class: A Study of the New York Workingmen's Movement, 1829–1837* (1960).

9. On business and economic changes, see T. C. Cochran, "Business Organization and the Development of an Industrial Discipline," in H. F. Williamson, ed., *The Growth of the American Economy* (1946), pp. 303–318; G. R. Taylor, *The Transportation Revolution, 1815–1860* (1951), pp. 10–14, 207–243. On expectant capitalists, see B. Hammond, *Banks and Politics in America from the Revolution to the Civil War* (1957), pp. 326–368; R. Hofstadter, "Andrew Jackson and the Rise of Liberal Capitalism," *The American Political Tradition* (1948), pp. 45–67; M. A. Lebowitz, "The Jacksonians: Paradox Lost?" in B. J. Bernstein, ed., *Towards a New Past: Dissenting Essays in American History* (1968), pp. 65–89. On changes in politics, see M. D. Peterson, ed., *Democracy, Liberty, and Property: The State Constitutional Conventions of the 1820's* (1966); Warner, *The Private City*, pp. 79–98. Suggestive on the impact of both economic and political changes is M. Meyers, *The Jacksonian Persuasion: Politics and Belief* (1957).

10. A. Nevins and M. H. Thomas, eds., *The Diary of George Templeton Strong*, 4 vols. (1952), 1, p. 110; W. Dalton, *Travels in the United States and Part of Upper Canada* (1821), p. 5. On the inadequacies of municipal government in the early nineteenth century, the following are useful: N. Blake, *Water for the Cities* (1956); J. Duffy, *A History of Public Health in New York City, 1625–1866* (1968); J. B. Blake, *Public Health in the Town of Boston, 1630–1822* (1959); C. E. Rosenberg, *The Cholera Years* (1962); J. F. Richardson, *The New York Police: Colonial Times to 1901* (1970), pp. 3–50; R. Lane, *Policing the City: Boston, 1822–1885* (1967), pp. 1–58; S. F. Ginsberg, "Above the Law: Volunteer Firemen in New York City, 1836–1837," 50 *New York History* 165 (1969); L. H. Larsen, "Nineteenth-Century Street Sanitation: A Study of Filth and Frustration," 52 *Wisconsin Magazine of History* 239 (1969); Warner, *The Private City*, pp. 99–123.

11. These points are elaborated in L. K. Kerber, *Federalist in Dissent: Imagery and Ideology in Jeffersonian America* (1970), pp. 173–215; D. B. Davis, "Some Themes of Counter-Subversion: An Analysis of Anti-Masonic, Anti-Catholic, and Anti-Mormon Literature," 47 *Mississippi Valley Historical Review* 205 (1960); D. B. Davis, *Homicide in American Fiction, 1798–1860* (1957); L. Richards, *"Gentlemen of Property and Standing": Anti-Abolition Mobs in Jacksonian America* (1970); Warner, *The Private City*, pp. 125–157; Somkin, *Unquiet Eagle;* Rothman, *Discovery of the Asylum*. The violent dimension of American history can also be sampled in R. Hofstadter and M. Wallace, eds., *American Violence: A Documentary History* (1970).

12. The British writer who most clearly distinguished between poverty and pauperism was P. Colquhoun. See P. Colquhoun, *A Treatise on Indigence* (1806), pp. 7–9; O. Sherwin, "An Eighteenth Century Beveridge Planner," 52 *American Historical Review* 281 (1947); R. Pieris, "The Contributions of Patrick Colquhoun to Social Theory and Social Philosophy," 12 *University of Ceylon Review*, 129 (1954). Colquhoun's ideas were influential in the United States. See, for example, *Report to the Managers of the Society for the Prevention of Pauperism in New York: By Their Committee on Idleness and Sources of Employment* (1819), pp. 4–5. Useful for placing American welfare ideas and attitudes in the perspective of British thought and practice are S. Mencher, *Poor Law to Poverty Program: Economic Security Policy in Britain and the United States* (1967) and J. R. Poynter, *Society and Pauperism: English Ideas on Poor Relief, 1795–1834* (1969).

13. On these general points, see B. J. Klebaner, "Poverty and Its Belief in American Thought, 1815–61," 38 *Social Service Review* 382 (1963); R. H. Bremner, "The

Rediscovery of Pauperism," in Council on Social Work Education, *Current Issues in Social Work Education Seen in Historical Perspective* (1962), pp. 10-19. Typical statements of the moralistic attitude toward pauperism may be found in J. Tuckerman, *Eleventh Semiannual Report, as a Minister at Large in Boston* (1833) and W. Douglas, *Annual Report of the Providence Female Domestic Missionary Society* (1843).

14. *Independent Journal* (Feb. 18, 1784); De Witt Clinton to Members of the Assembly from the City and County of New York, Jan. 23, 1805, De Witt Clinton Papers, Columbia University Library; *Minutes of the Common Council of the City of New York, 1784-1831,* 21 vols. (1917-1930), 8, p. 204; Thomas Eddy to De Witt Clinton, Feb. 15, 1817, Clinton Papers; *New-York Evening Post,* March 12, 1817.

15. *Commercial Advertiser* (New York), (Nov. 1, 1798); *Daily Advertiser* (New York), (Sept. 6, 1798).

16. For analysis of the transition from benevolence to moralism in social welfare attitudes, see Mohl, *Poverty in New York,* pp. 159-170.

17. W. O. Bourne, *History of the Public School Society of the City of New York* (1970), p. 90; New York Society for the Prevention of Pauperism, *Documents Relative to Savings Banks, Intemperance, and Lotteries* (1819), p. 21. See also J. Tuckerman, *A Sermon Preached on Sunday Evening, Nov. 2, 1834, at the Ordination of Charles F. Barnard and Frederick T. Gray, as Ministers at Large in Boston* (1834), p. 37; T. Thwing, *An Address Delivered before the Association of Delegates from the Benevolent Societies of Boston, at Their Meeting October 10, 1843* (1843), p. 14.

18. R. A. Mohl, "Humanitarianism in the Preindustrial City: The New York Society for the Prevention of Pauperism, 1817-1823," 57 *Journal of American History* 576 (1970); B. D. Coll, "The Baltimore Society for the Prevention of Pauperism, 1820-1822," 61 *American Historical Review* 77 (1955); J. T. Scharf and T. Westcott, *History of Philadelphia, 1609-1884,* 3 vols. (1884), 1, p. 589; B. M. and S. K. Selekman, "Mathew Carey," 19 *Harvard Business Review* 340 (1941); C. I. Foster, "The Urban Missionary Movement, 1814-1837," 75 *Pennsylvania Magazine of History and Biography* 53 (1951); N. I. Huggins, *Protestants Against Poverty: Boston's Charities, 1870-1900* (1971), pp. 26, 30.

19. L. Beecher, *A Reformation of Morals Practicable and Indispensable. A Sermon Delivered at New-Haven on the Evening of October 27, 1812* (1814), p. 18; L. Beecher, "Prosperity and Importance of Efforts to Evangelize the Nation," 3 *The National Preacher* 154 (March, 1829); Somkin, *Unquiet Eagle,* p. 34. On the social uses of such organizations, the following are useful and suggestive: R. E. Pumphrey, "Compassion and Protection: Dual Motivations in Social Welfare," 33 *Social Service Review* 21 (1959); C. S. Griffin, "Religious Benevolence as Social Control, 1815-1860," 44 *Mississippi Valley Historical Review* 423 (1957); M. J. Heale, "Humanitarianism in the Early Republic: The Moral Reformers of New York, 1776-1825," 2 *Journal of American Studies,* 161 (1968); C. S. Griffin, *Their Brothers' Keepers: Moral Stewardship in the United States, 1800-1865* (1960); C. I. Foster, *An Errand of Mercy: The Evangelical United Front, 1790-1837* (1960).

20. *Daily Advertiser* (New York), (Oct. 27, 1789); C. C. Andrews, *The History of the New-York African Free Schools* (1830), p. 47; Bourne, *Public School Society,* p. 7; *Eleventh Annual Report of the Boston Children's Friend Society* (1844), p. 7; *Report on a Farm School* (n.p., n.d.), p. 8.

21. 1 *American Sunday School Teachers' Magazine* 60 (1824); *Third Annual Report of the Boston Society for the Moral and Religious Instruction of the Poor* (1819), p. 11; T. Raffles, *The Sunday School Teacher's Monitor, together with Hints for Self-Examination, Addressed to Persons of Various Classes, in Connection with Sunday Schools* (1817), p. 2; *Commercial Advertiser* (New York), (May 8, 1816); 1 *The Evangelical Guardian* 4588 (1818); *Seventh Annual Report of the Board of Managers of the Boston Sabbath School Union* (1836), p. 5.

22. Bourne, *Public School Society*, p. xx. This point is also emphasized in Katz, *Irony of Early School Reform*.

23. *The First Report of the New-York Bible Society* (1820), p. 16; *The Second and Third Annual Reports of the Bible Society of Virginia* (1816), p. 14; *The Third Annual Report of the Managers of the Marine Bible Society of New-York* (1819), p. 8; *The Eighth Report of the Bible Society of Philadelphia* (1816), p. 16; *Christian Herald* (New York), 9 (April 5, 1823), p. 690.

24. *The Fifth Annual Report of the New-York Religious Tract Society* (1817), pp. 45, 47; *The Thirteenth Annual Report of the New-York Religious Tract Society* (1825), p. 5. See also *Fifth Annual Report of the Executive Committee of the New England Tract Society, May 26, 1819* (1819), p. 8.

25. R. S. Storrs, *Man's Duty, in Relation to the Lord's Work. A Semi-Centennial Discourse, Delivered before the Massachusetts Home Missionary Society, in Boston, May 29, 1849* (1849), p. 24; W. M. Engles, *The Patriot's Plea for Domestic Missions* (1833), p. 4. For typical city missionary activities, see *Proceedings of the First Anniversary of the New-York Evangelical Missionary Society of Young Men* (1817); *[First] Report of the Boston Society for the Moral and Religious Instruction of the Poor* (1817); *First Annual Report of the Board of Directors of the Boston Seaman's Friend Society* (1829); *The [First] Annual Report of the Boston City Missionary Society, for the Year 1841* (1842).

26. Report of Committee of Charity on Petition of the Trustees of the African Church, December 8, 1817, Box 3175, City Clerk Documents, New York City Municipal Archives and Records Center; G. Spring, *An Appeal to the Citizens of New-York, in Behalf of the Christian Sabbath* (1823), p. 16.

27. See, for example, A. Gunn, *A Sermon, on the Prevailing Vice of Intemperate Drinking* (1813); *Journal of the Assembly of the State of New York*, 47th session (1824), Part II, Appendix B, p. 44; *First Annual Report of the New York City Temperance Society* (1830); L. M. Sargent, *An Address Delivered Before the Seaman's Bethel Temperance Society* (1833). See also J. R. Gusfield, *Symbolic Crusade: Status Politics and the American Temperance Movement* (1963).

28. *Ordinances, Rules and Bye-Laws, for the Government of the Alms-House, and House of Employment, of the City of New-York, June 16, 1784* (1785), broadside, in New-York Historical Society; *Plan of the Society for the Promotion of Industry; with the First Report of the Board of Managers* (1816); *Explanation of the Views of the Society for Employing the Poor; with the Constitution and Bye-Laws* (1820); Common Council of the City of New York, *Report of Special Committee on Pauperism, May 31, 1830* (n.p., n.d.), pp. 9–10.

29. New York Society for the Prevention of Pauperism, *Documents Relative to Savings Banks, Intemperance, and Lotteries*, pp. 3–16; *Commercial Advertiser* (New York), (Feb. 15, 1820); *New-York Evening Post* (May 7, 1821); *Plan of the Boston Fuel Savings Institution* (1821).

30. *Commercial Advertiser* (New York), (July 15, 1815); *Third Annual Report of the Boston Female Moral Reform Society* (1838).

31. See, for example, 5 *Juvenile Reformer, and Sabbath School Instructor* (Portland, Me.), 2 (May 27, 1835), 5 (June 3, 1835), 10 (June 10, 1835), 23 (July 1, 1835), 162 (March 2, 1836), 164 (March 2, 1836). Some evidence suggests that such zealous moral reformers did not have full public support, especially in publicizing things like prostitution and masturbation. Within the space of two months in 1836, Daniel C. Colesworthy, the young editor of the *Juvenile Reformer*, was beaten up twice in the streets of Portland, his press was temporarily stopped by the courts, and he was suspended from his Sunday school teaching position. The Colesworthy case suggests that the public backed moral reforms which promised restoration of order and stability, but opposed radical causes which violated middle-class propriety or threatened socially upsetting effects. Similar journals which touched raw public nerves in the 1830's were the *Advocate of Moral Reform* (New

York) and the *Friend of Virtue* (Boston). For similar problems faced by abolitionists, see Richards, *"Gentlemen of Property and Standing."*
32. F. F. Piven and R. A. Cloward, "The Relief of Welfare," 8 *Transaction* 31
(1971). See also their new book, *Regulating the Poor: The Functions of Public
Welfare* (1971).

3: Prisons in Early Nineteenth-Century America

1. B. Rush, *An Inquiry into the Effect of Public Punishments upon Criminals
and upon Society* (1787), pp. 3–4.
2. Ibid., pp. 10–11.
3. O. F. Lewis, *The Development of American Prisons and Prison Customs,
1776-1845* (1967), p. 13; B. McKelvey, *American Prisons: A Study in American
Social History Prior to 1915* (1968), p. 5; J. M. Hawes, *Children in Urban Society:
Juvenile Delinquency in Nineteenth-Century America* (1971), p. 23.
4. "Memorials of the Society for Alleviating the Miseries of Public Prisons,"
quoted in N. K. Teeters, *They Were in Prison: A History of the Pennsylvania Prison
Society, 1787-1937* (1937), pp. 3, 447–448.
5. Lewis, p. 9; P. Klein, *Prison Methods in New York State: A Contribution
to the Study of the Theory and Practice of Correctional Institutions* (1920), p. 25.
6. McKelvey, pp. 5–6; Lewis, pp. 25–26.
7. Lewis, pp. 25–30.
8. McKelvey, p. 7; Klein, p. 37; H. E. Barnes, "The Origins of Prison Reform
in New York State," 2 *New York State Historical Association Quarterly Journal*
93 (April, 1921).
9. A. A. Ekirch, Jr., "Thomas Eddy and the Beginnings of Prison Reform in New
York," 24 *New York History* 376 (July, 1943).
10. S. V. James, *A People among Peoples: Quaker Benevolence in Eighteenth-
Century America* (1963), p. 101.
11. Quoted in Lewis, p. 81.
12. Lewis, pp. 80–84.
13. G. de Beaumont and A. de Tocqueville, *On the Penitentiary System in the
United States and Its Application in France*, ed. T. Sellin (1964), p. 44; "Memorials,"
quoted in Teeters, pp. 458–462; Lewis, pp. 118–122.
14. McKelvey, p. 9; W. Jenks, "Memoir of Rev. Louis Dwight," *Reports of the
Prison Discipline Society, Boston*, Vol. 1 (1855), pp. 11–29.
15. Lewis, p. 122; Prison Discipline Society, Boston, *First Annual Report, June 2,
1826* in *Reports of the Prison Discipline Society, Boston*, Vol. 1 (1855), pp. 6, 36.
Hereafter the Prison Discipline Society will be cited as P.D.S. with the dates of reports given only.
16. McKelvey, pp. 122–123.
17. Lewis, pp. 229–233.
18. Beaumont and Tocqueville, p. 76.
19. Ibid., pp. 84, 103–104.
20. Ibid., pp. 91, 162.
21. W. Crawford, *Report on the Penitentiaries of the United States* (1834), pp.
11–14.
22. Ibid., pp. 17, 19.
23. Beaumont and Tocqueville, p. 84; Crawford, p. 14; S. G. Howe, *Report of a
Minority of the Special Committee of the Boston Prison Discipline Society, May 27,
1845* (1846), p. v.
24. Howe, pp. 11, 78, passim.
25. Ibid., p. 78.
26. McKelvey, p. 10.

27. P.D.S. 1830, pp. 19–20; Beaumont and Tocqueville, pp. 90–91; P.D.S. 1832, p. 74.
28. P.D.S. 1833, p. 81.
29. Ibid., p. 87. Italics in original.
30. P.D.S. 1834, p. 57.
31. Beaumont and Tocqueville, p. 89.
32. "Penitentiary System of the United States," 20 *Christian Examiner* 389 (July, 1836).
33. D. L. Dix, *Remarks on Prisons and Prison Discipline* (1845), p. 73.
34. P. Miller, *The Life of the Mind in America. From the Revolution to the Civil War* (1965), p. 33.

4: The Triumph of Benevolence

1. See, for example, The President's Commission on Law Enforcement and Administration of Justice, *Juvenile Delinquency and Youth Crime* (1967), pp. 2–4.
2. C. L. Chute, "The Juvenile Court in Retrospect," 13 *Federal Probation* 7 (September, 1949); Harrison A. Dobbs, "In Defense of Juvenile Court," ibid., p. 29.
3. C. L. Chute, "Fifty Years of the Juvenile Court," *National Probation and Parole Association Yearbook* (1949), p. 1.
4. G. H. Mead, "The Psychology of Punitive Justice," 23 *American Journal of Sociology* 577 (March, 1918); A. Aichhorn, "The Juvenile Court: Is It a Solution?" in *Delinquency and Child Guidance: Selected Papers* (1964), pp. 55–79.
5. M. Levine and A. Levine, *A Social History of Helping Services: Clinic, Court, School, and Community* (1970), p. 156.
6. G. O. W. Mueller, *History of American Criminal Law Scholarship* (1962), p. 113.
7. See, for example, H. H. Lou, *Juvenile Courts in the United States* (1927); N. K. Teeters and J. O. Reinmann, *The Challenge of Delinquency* (1950); and O. Nyquist, *Juvenile Justice* (1960).
8. R. S. Pickett, *House of Refuge: Origins of Juvenile Reform in New York State, 1815–1857* (1969), p. 188.
9. See, for example, A. M. Schlesinger, *The American as Reformer* (1950).
10. See, for example, R. Hofstadter, *The Age of Reform* (1955), and J. R. Gusfield, *Symbolic Crusade: Status, Politics and the American Temperance Movement* (1963).
11. For discussions of earlier reform movements, see Pickett, loc. cit., and S. J. Fox, "Juvenile Justice Reform: An Historical Perspective," 22 *Stanford Law Review* 1187 (June, 1970).
12. The child-saving movement was broad and diverse, including reformers interested in child welfare, education, reformatories, labor, and other related issues. This paper is limited primarily to child savers involved in antidelinquency reforms and should not be interpreted as characterizing the child-saving movement in general.
13. W. P. Letchworth, "Children of the State," National Conference of Charities and Correction, *Proceedings* (1886), p. 138.
14. R. W. Hill, "The Children of Shinbone Alley," National Conference of Charities and Correction, *Proceedings* (1887), p. 231.
15. W. A. Williams, *The Contours of American History* (1966), especially pp. 345–412.
16. Pickett, op. cit., pp. 50–55.
17. Committee on the History of Child-Saving Work, "History of Child-Saving in the United States," National Conference on Charities and Correction *Proceedings* (1893), p. 5.
18. C. L. Brace, *The Dangerous Classes of New York and Twenty Years' Work among Them* (1880), pp. 282–83.

19. Committee on the History of Child-Saving Work, op. cit., pp. 70–73.
20. Ibid., pp. 80–81.
21. Ibid., p. 270.
22. For more about these child savers, see A. Platt, *The Child Savers: The Invention of Delinquency* (1969), pp. 75–100.
23. L. C. Wade, *Graham Taylor: Pioneer for Social Justice, 1851-1938* (1964), p. 59.
24. G. W. Domhoff, *The Higher Circles: The Governing Class in America* (1970), p. 48, and Platt, op. cit., pp. 92–98.
25. "The transformation in penal systems cannot be explained only from changing needs of the war against crime, although this struggle does play a part. Every system of production tends to discover punishments which correspond to its productive relationships. It is thus necessary to investigate the origin and fate of penal systems, the use or avoidance of specific punishments, and the intensity of penal practices as they are determined by social forces, above all by economic and then fiscal forces." G. Rusche and O. Kirchheimer, *Punishment and Social Structure* (1968), p. 5.
26. See, for example, G. Kolko, *The Triumph of Conservatism: A Reinterpretation of American History, 1900-1916* (1967); J. Weinstein, *The Corporate Ideal in the Liberal State, 1900-1918* (1969); S. Haber, *Efficiency and Uplife: Scientific Management in the Progressive Era, 1800-1920* (1964); and R. H. Wiebe, *Businessmen and Reform: A Study of the Progressive Movement* (1962).
27. Kolko, op. cit., p. 282.
28. Weinstein, op. cit., pp. ix, xi.
29. J. P. Felt, *Hostages of Fortune: Child Labor Reform in New York State* (1965), p. 45.
30. Brace, op. cit., p. 352.
31. D. K. Cohen and Marvin Lazerson, "Education and the Corporate Order," 8 *Socialist Revolution* 50 (March–April, 1972). See also M. B. Katz, *The Irony of Early School Reform: Educational Innovation in Mid-Nineteenth Century Massachusetts* (1968), and Lawrence A. Cremin, *The Transformation of the School: Progressivism in American Education, 1876-1957* (1961).
32. It should be emphasized that child-saving reforms were predominantly supported by more privileged sectors of the feminist movement, especially those who had an interest in developing professional careers in education, social work, or probation. In recent years, radical feminists have emphasized that "we must include the oppression of children in any program for feminist revolution or we will be subject to the same failing of which we have so often accused men: of not having gone deep enough in our analysis, of having missed an important substratum of oppression merely because it didn't directly concern us." S. Firestone, *The Dialectic of Sex: The Case for Feminist Revolution* (1971), p. 104.
33. R. Sunley, "Early Nineteenth Century American Literature on Child-Rearing," in M. Mead and M. Wolfenstein (eds.), *Childhood in Contemporary Cultures* (1955), p. 152; see also O. G. Brim, *Education for Child-Rearing* (1965), pp. 321–49.
34. For an extended discussion of this issue, see Platt, loc. cit., and C. Lasch, *The New Radicalism in America, 1889-1963: The Intellectual as a Social Type* (1965), pp. 3–68.
35. T. Parsons and R. F. Bales, *Family, Socialization and Interaction Process* (1955), pp. 3–33.
36. C. T. Leonard, "Family Homes for Pauper and Dependent Children," Annual Conference of Charities, *Proceedings* (1879), p. 175.
37. Williams, op. cit., p. 356.
38. Committee on the History of Child-Saving Work, op. cit., p. 3.
39. See, generally, J. Higham, *Strangers in the Land: Patterns of American Nativism, 1860-1925* (1965).

40. Brace, op. cit., pp. 30, 49; B. K. Pierce, *A Half Century with Juvenile Delinquents* (1969 repr. of 1869 ed.), p. 253.
41. N. Allen, "Prevention of Crime and Pauperism," Annual Conference of Charities, *Proceedings* (1878), pp. 111–24.
42. J. A. Riis, *How the Other Half Lives* (1957 repr. of 1890 ed.), p. 134.
43. Brace, op. cit., pp. 27, 29.
44. See, for example, Lombroso's comments in the Introduction to A. MacDonald, *Criminology* (1893).
45. Allen, loc. cit.
46. H. D. Wey, "A Plea for Physical Training of Youthful Criminals," National Prison Association, *Proceedings* (1888), pp. 181–93. For further discussion of this issue, see Platt, op. cit., pp. 18–28 and A. E. Fink, *Causes of Crime: Biological Theories in the United States, 1800–1915* (1962).
47. R. L. Dugdale, *The Jukes: A Study in Crime, Pauperism, Disease, and Heredity* (1877).
48. S. B. Cooper, "The Kindergarten as Child-Saving Work," National Conference of Charities and Correction, *Proceedings* (1883), pp. 130–38.
49. I. N. Kerlin, "The Moral Imbecile," National Conference of Charities and Correction, *Proceedings* (1890), pp. 244–50.
50. Williams, op. cit., p. 354.
51. Fink, op. cit., p. 247.
52. See, for example, Illinois Board of State Commissioners of Public Charities, *Second Biennial Report* (1873), pp. 195–96.
53. P. Caldwell, "The Duty of the State to Delinquent Children," National Conference of Charities and Correction, *Proceedings* (1898), pp. 404–10.
54. E. R. L. Gould, "The Statistical Study of Hereditary Criminality," National Conference of Charities and Correction, *Proceedings* (1905), pp. 134–43.
55. C. H. Cooley, "'Nature' v. 'Nurture' in the Making of Social Careers," National Conference of Charities and Correction, *Proceedings* (1896), pp. 399–405.
56. Committee on the History of Child-Saving Work, op. cit., p. 90.
57. E. C. Wines, *The State of Prisons and of Child-Saving Institutions in the Civilized World* (1880).
58. H. P. Bates, "Digest of Statutes Relating to Juvenile Courts and Probation Systems," 13 *Charities* 329 (January, 1905).
59. J. F. Handler, "The Juvenile Court and the Adversary System: Problems of Function and Form," *Wisconsin Law Review* 7 (1965).
60. G. L. Schramm, "The Juvenile Court Idea," 13 *Federal Probation* 21 (September, 1949).
61. M. G. Paulsen, "Fairness to the Juvenile Offender," 41 *Minnesota Law Review* 547 (1957).
62. J. W. Mack, "The Chancery Procedure in the Juvenile Court," in J. Addams (ed.), *The Child, the Clinic and the Court* (1925), p. 315.
63. M. Van Waters, "The Socialization of Juvenile Court Procedure," 21 *Journal of Criminal Law and Criminology* 61 (1922).
64. H. H. Baker, "Procedure of the Boston Juvenile Court," 23 *Survey* 646 (February, 1910).
65. Illinois Board of State Commissioners of Public Charities, *Sixth Biennial Report* (1880), p. 104.
66. F. H. Wines, "Reformation as an End in Prison Discipline," National Conference of Charities and Correction, *Proceedings* (1888), p. 198.
67. J. F. Handler, op. cit., p. 9.
68. J. F. Handler and M. K. Rosenheim, "Privacy and Welfare: Public Assistance and Juvenile Justice," 31 *Law and Contemporary Problems* 377 (1966).
69. From a report by Enoch Wines and Theodore Dwight to the New York legislature in 1867, quoted by M. Grunhut, *Penal Reform* (1948), p. 90.

70. P. Caldwell, "The Reform School Problem," National Conference of Charities and Correction, *Proceedings* (1886), pp. 71–76.

71. Letchworth, op. cit., p. 152.

72. Committee on the History of Child-Saving Work, op. cit., p. 20.

73. See Platt, op. cit., pp. 55–66.

74. Katz, op. cit., p. 187.

75. Rusche and Kirchheimer, op. cit., pp. 131–32.

76. American Friends Service Committee, op. cit., p. 28.

77. Z. R. Brockway, *Fifty Years of Prison Service* (1912), p. 393.

78. Ibid., pp. 310, 421.

79. Ibid., pp. 389–408.

80. Ibid.

81. Peirce, op. cit., p. 312.

82. E. Wines, op. cit., p. 81.

83. On informal cooperation in the criminal courts, see J. H. Skolnick, "Social Control in the Adversary System," 11 *Journal of Conflict Resolution* 52 (March, 1967).

84. Committee on the History of Child-Saving Work, op. cit., p. 20.

85. Ibid., p. 237.

86. Ibid., p. 251.

87. Rusche and Kirchheimer, op. cit., pp. 155–56.

88. Ibid., p. 76. For a similar point, see American Friends Service Committee, op. cit., p. 33.

89. See, generally, F. Musgrove, *Youth and the Social Order* (1964).

90. P. Aries, *Centuries of Childhood: A Social History of Family Life* (1965).

91. Williams, op. cit., p. 382.

92. On benevolence and repression in foreign policy, see F. Greene, *The Enemy: What Every American Should Know about Imperialism* (1971). For examples of domestic repression, see W. Preston, Jr., *Aliens and Dissenters: Federal Suppression of Radicals, 1903–1933* (1966), and J. ten Broek, E. N. Barnhart, and F. W. Matson, *Prejudice, War and the Constitution* (1968).

93. Andre Gorz, *Strategy for Labor: A Radical Proposal* (1964), p. 8.

94. Platt, op. cit., p. 148.

95. See, for example, A. Shaffer, "The Cincinnati Social Unit Experiment: 1917–19," 45 *Social Service Review* 159 (June, 1971), and E. Burgess, J. D. Lohman, and C. R. Shaw, "The Chicago Area Project," *Yearbook of the National Probation Association* (1937), 21–23.

96. This issue is treated more fully in A. Platt, "Saving and Controlling Delinquent Youth: A Critique," 5 *Issues in Criminology* 1 (Winter, 1970).

97. The facts and figures cited in the following discussion are taken from The President's Commission on Law Enforcement and Administration of Justice, *Juvenile Delinquency and Youth Crime* (1967), and H. James, *Children in Trouble* (1969), pp. 162–71.

98. See, for example, H. D. McKay, "Report on the Criminal Careers of Male Delinquents in Chicago," in *Juvenile Delinquency and Youth Crime*, op. cit., pp. 107–13.

99. The following discussion is adapted from a paper prepared for J. H. Skolnick (Director), *The Politics of Protest* (1969), pp. 162–71.

100. National Advisory Commission on Civil Disorders, *Report* (1968), p. 21.

101. See, for example, R. M. Fogelson and R. B. Hill, "Who Riots? A Study of Participation in the 1967 Riots," in *Supplemental Studies for the National Advisory Commission on Civil Disorders* (1968), pp. 221–48.

102. R. Komisaruk and C. Pearson, "Children of the Detroit Riots," 44 *Journal of Urban Law* 599 (Spring and Summer, 1968).

103. W. H. Grier and P. M. Cobbs, *Black Rage* (1968), p. 211.

104. See, generally, Platt, "Saving and Controlling Delinquent Youth: A Critique," loc. cit.
105. *In re Gault,* 387 U.S. 1, 41, (1967).
106. President's Commission on Law Enforcement and Administration of Justice, *The Challenge of Crime in a Free Society* (1967), p. 87, and *Juvenile Delinquency and Youth Crime,* pp. 31, 33.
107. *New York Times* (May 16, 1967), p. 1.
108. A. Platt and R. Friedman, "The Limits of Advocacy: Occupational Hazards in Juvenile Court," 116 *Pennsylvania Law Review* 1156 (1968), and A. Platt, H. Schechter and P. Tiffany, "In Defense of Youth: A Case Study of the Public Defender in Juvenile Court," 43 *Indiana Law Journal* 619 (1968).
109. G. Marwell, "Adolescent Powerlessness and Delinquent Behavior," 14 *Social Problems* 35 (Summer, 1966).
110. E. Lemert, "Juvenile Justice—Quest and Reality," 4 *Transaction* 32 (1967).
111. *Chicago Tribune* (November 8, 1968), p. 4.
112. R. Momboisse, *Riot and Civil Emergency Guide for City and County Officials* (1968), p. 11.

5: Complainants and Kids

1. A. Reiss, *The Police and the Public* (1971).
2. I. Piliavin and S. Briar, "Police Encounters with Juveniles," 70 *American Journal of Sociology* 206 (1967); W. LaFave, *Arrest: The Decision to Take a Suspect into Custody* (1965); C. Werthman and I. Piliavin, "Gang Members and the Police," in D. Bordua, ed., *The Police: Six Sociological Essays* (1967).
3. J. Skolnick, *Justice Without Trial* (1966); B. Jackson, "Exiles from the American Dream: The Junkie and the Cop," 219 *Atlantic Monthly* 44 (January 1967); A. Stinchcombe, "Institutions of Privacy in the Determination of Police Administrative Practice," 69 *American Journal of Sociology* 150 (1963).
4. E. Bittner, "The Police on Skid Row," 32 *American Sociological Review* 63 (1970).
5. Y. Cohn, "Criteria for the Probation Officer's Recommendations to the Juvenile Court Judge," 9 *Crime and Delinquency* 262 (1963); N. Goldman, *The Differential Selection of Juvenile Offenders for Court Appearance* (1963); R. Terry, "The Screening of Juvenile Offenders: A Study in the Societal Reaction to Deviant Behavior," unpublished Ph.D. dissertation, University of Wisconsin (1965).
6. D. Black and A. Reiss, "Police Control of Juveniles," 35 *American Sociological Review* 63 (1970); J. Webster, "Police Task and Time Study," 58 *Journal of Criminal Law, Criminology and Police Science* (1970); Reiss, op. cit.
7. J. Conklin, *The Impact of Crime* (1975), p. 15.
8. Black and Reiss, op. cit.
9. M. Cain, *Society and the Policeman's Role* (1973), p. 238.
10. Black and Reiss, op. cit.
11. N. Denzin, "Rules of Conduct and the Study of Deviant Behavior: Some Notes on the Social Relationship," in G. J. McCall, et al, *Social Relationships* (1971), pp. 62–94.
12. LaFave, op. cit.
13. S. Wheeler, "Criminal Statistics: A Reformulation of the Problem," 58 *Journal of Criminal Law, Criminology and Police Science* 317 (1967).
14. M. Banton, *The Policeman in the Community* (1964); J. Clark, "Isolation of the Police: A Comparison of the British and American Situations," 56 *Journal of Criminal Law, Criminology and Police Science* 307 (1965); R. Stark, *Police Riots* (1972).

15. See J. Q. Wilson, *Varieties of Police Behavior* (1970).
16. A. Porterfield, *Youth in Trouble* (1946), p. 15.

6: The Rise and Fall of the Policewomen's Movement

1. P. Bloch and D. Anderson, *Policewomen on Patrol: Final Report* (1974).
2. C. Owings, *Women Police* (1925).
3. Los Angeles Police Department, *Annual Report* (1915), pp. 34, 59.
4. Owings, pp. 101–106.
5. National Prison Association, *Proceedings* (1886), pp. 301–306, Owings, pp. 97–99.
6. Owings, pp. 101–102, 131–132.
7. S. Marshall, "Development of the Policewoman's Movement in Cleveland, Ohio," 11 *Journal of Social Hygiene* (1925).
8. Ibid., pp. 199–200.
9. Ibid., pp. 201–209.
10. Owings, pp. 124–129.
11. E. A. Beveridge, "Establishing Policewomen in Baltimore in 1912," 42 *Proceedings of National Conference of Charities and Corrections* (1915).
12. M. E. Hamilton, *The Policewoman: Her Service and Ideals* (1924), p. 4.
13. Ibid., pp. 11, 33.
14. The literature to date on the history of the police and the professionalization movement emphasizes the ideology of crime fighting and managerial efficiency (see for example Gene and Elaine Carte's *Police Reform in the United States: The Era of August Vollmer* [1975]). This author's research, however, suggests that this ideology did not completely triumph until the 1930's. The pre–World War I period in particular offered a number of different interpretations of the police role, although all fell within the parameters of the broader ideology of progressivism.
15. Carte (see note 14).
16. Hamilton, p. 5.
17. A. S. Wells, "The Policewomen's Movement, Present Status and Future Needs," 43 *Proceedings of the National Conference of Charities and Corrections* (1916), p. 548.
18. E. Hutzel and M. MacGregor, *The Policewoman's Handbook* (1933), p. 11.
19. Hamilton, p. 170.
20. International Association of Policewomen, *Bulletin* (1925), p. 13; U.S. Federal Security Agency, National Advisory Police Committee on Social Protection, *Techniques of Law Enforcement in the Use of Policewomen* (1945), p. 5.
21. Ibid., p. 65.
22. Hamilton, pp. 179–180.
23. A. S. Wells, "Remarks," *Proceedings of the International Association of Chiefs of Police* (1914), pp. 129–130.
24. A. S. Wells (1916), p. 549.
25. International Association of Policewomen, *Bulletin* (1927), p. 9.
26. Women Peace Officers Association of California, *Proceedings* (1939), pp. 8–13.
27. Hamilton, pp. 57–64.
28. Ibid., p. 64.
29. H. Additon, "The Functions of Policewomen," 10 *Journal of Social Hygiene* (1924), p. 325.
30. C. M. Williams, *The Organization and Practices of Policewomen's Divisions in the United States* (1946).

31. U.S. Federal Security Agency.
32. *Philadelphia Policewomen* (April-August, 1949), p. 1.
33. International City Management Association, *Municipal Police Administration,* 7th ed. (1971), p. 153.
34. O. W. Wilson, *Police Administration* 2d ed. (1963), p. 334.
35. Owings, p. 197.
36. C. Milton, *Women in Policing* (1972).
37. The best critique of the current movement to use policewomen on patrol is in *The Iron Fist and the Velvet Glove* (Center for Research on Criminal Justice, 1975: 60–62).

7: Reforming the Police

1. See T. A. Knopf, "Sniping . . . A New Pattern of Violence," in *Law and Order: Police Encounters,* M. Lipsky, ed. (1970), pp. 103–124.
2. I. L. Horowitz, "The Military Elites," in *Elites in Latin America,* S. Lipset and A. Solari, eds. (1967), p. 183.
3. See J. H. Skolnick, *Justice without Trial* (1966), chapter 3.
4. For example, see "Killing Cops: Signs of a Nationwide Plot," in 69 *U.S. News* 61 (October 19, 1970); or "The 'War against the Police,'" in 69 *U.S. News* 82 (October 26, 1970).
5. According to A. Niederhoffer in *Behind the Shield: The Police in Urban Society* ([1967], p. 1), "the rubric *police organization* obviously includes far more than police departments. The provisions of police service can be conceptualized as a multifaceted industry which includes, in the public sphere, the sheriff's department, state police, F.B.I., Secret Service, Treasury and narcotics agents, to name some. In addition there are private agencies such as patrol and detective services, store guards, and so on." See V. Ostrom and E. Ostrom, "A Behavioral Approach to the Study of Intergovernmental Relations," 359 *The Annals,* 140. Although the existence of all these forces public and private, affect and reflect the quality of police service in an area, they are not the central focus of this study for one primary reason: only the police departments in the cities have inspired such intense hatred in so many persons as to constitute a major national social problem.
6. See W. C. Skouson, *The Communist Attack on U.S. Police* (1966). This book was popular reading among Indiana policemen in the summer of 1969.
7. *Varieties of Police Behavior* (1968), p. 3.
8. *The Federalist,* J. E. Cooke, ed. (1961), p. 129; see also V. Ostrom, *The Political Theory of a Compound Republic: A Reconstruction of the Logical Foundations of American Democracy as Presented in The Federalist* (1971).
9. *The Federalist,* p. 262.
10. Niederhoffer, p. 1.
11. *Report of the National Advisory Commission on Civil Disorders* (1963), pp. 17 and 299.
12. See Fogelson, "From Resentment to Confrontation . . ." 83 *Political Science Quarterly* 217 (June 1968).
13. Fogelson, p. 220.
14. Ibid., p. 221.
15. Statement of Quin Tamm, Executive Director of the IACP, quoted to H. B. Shaffer, "Negroes and the Police," in *Editorial Research Reports* (September 21, 1964), p. 692.
16. *Report of the National Advisory Commission on Civil Disorders,* p. 299.
17. Fogelson, pp. 219–220.

18. Ibid., p. 222.
19. W. J. Raine, *Los Angeles Riot Study: The Perception of Police Brutality in South Central Los Angeles* (1966), p. 27.
20. Shaffer, p. 683.
21. Task Force on the Police, President's Commission on Law Enforcement and the Administration of Justice, *Task Force Report: The Police* (1967); see also Fogelson.
22. Quote in Skolnick, p. 49.
23. See the "Summary of Report" of the *Report of the National Advisory Commission on Civil Disorders*, pp. 1–29.
24. J. W. Doig, "The Police in a Democratic Society: Police Problems, Proposals, and Strategies for Change," 28 *Public Administration Review* 393 (Fall 1968).
25. A. J. Reiss, Jr., and D. J. Bordua, "Environment and Organization: A Perspective on Police," in D. J. Bordua, ed., *The Police: Six Sociological Essays* (1967), pp. 25–55.
26. Reiss and Bordua, p. 25.
27. J. D. Thompson, *Organizations in Action* (1967), p. 1. The language of James Q. Wilson's analysis in *Varieties* is remarkably reminiscent of Thompson's.
28. Ibid., p. 30.
29. P. Blau and W. Scott, *Formal Organizations* (1962), p. 43.
30. See J. Q. Wilson, *Varieties of Police Behavior*, p. 227. For a general discussion of the possibility of maintaining hierarchical control in large bureaucracies, see G. Tullock, *The Politics of Bureaucracy* (1965).
31. J. Q. Wilson, p. 227.
32. See W. Serrin, "God Help Our City," in *The Atlantic Monthly* (March, 1969), p. 116. The article quotes a Michigan Civil Rights Commission official who says, "When you get right down to who runs the department, I'd say the DPOA [Detroit Police Officers Association] runs it."
33. J. Q. Wilson, "Police Morale, Reform, and Citizen Respect," in D. J. Bordua, *The Police: Six Sociological Essays* (1967), pp. 137–162.
34. *The Federalist*, J. E. Cooke, ed. (1961).
35. See D. Lerner and H. D. Lasswell, eds., *The Policy Sciences; Recent Developments in Scope and Method* (1951).
36. V. Ostrom, "Operational Federalism: Organization for the Provision of Public Services in the American Federal System" 6 *Public Choice* 1 (Spring 1969).
37. W. Wilson, "The Study of Administration," in P. Woll, ed., *Public Administration and Policy* (1966), p. 29.
38. V. Ostrom, "The Politics of Administration" (Bloomington, Ind., unpublished manuscript), p. 15.
39. W. Wilson, p. 4.
40. Madison, p. 357, in *The Federalist*.
41. Ibid., p. 351.
42. See V. Ostrom, *The Political Theory of the Compound Republic* (1971), chapter 6, "The Federal Principle: A Theory of Concurrent Regimes."
43. For an exploration of Madison's theory, see V. Ostrom, *The Political Theory of a Compound Republic*.
44. A. de Tocqueville, *Democracy in America*, P. Bradley, ed. (1945), Vol. 1, pp. 89–90.
45. Ostrom, "The Politics of Administration," p. 12.
46. W. Wilson, p. 28.
47. Ibid.
48. Ibid., p. 26.
49. Ibid., p. 34.
50. Tocqueville, Vol. 1, p. 67. See also Ostrom, "The Politics of Administration," p. 11.

51. Tocqueville, p. 93.
52. Ibid.
53. Ibid., p. 94.
54. For one of the best illustrations of this approach, see the recommendations of "A Statement on National Policy" by the Research and Policy Committee of the Committees for Economic Developments on *Modernizing Local Government* (1966). See especially Summary of Recommendation, p. 17:

1. The number of local governments in the United States, now about 80,000, should be reduced at least 80 percent.
2. The number of overlapping layers of local government should be severely curtailed.

55. See V. Ostrom, C. M. Tiebout, and R. Warren, "The Organization of Government in Metropolitan Areas: A Theoretical Inquiry," 55 *American Political Science Review* 831 (December, 1961); also V. Ostrom, "The Politics of Administration" (Bloomington, Ind., mimeo) for a discussion of models of the relationship between politics and administration.
56. Ostrom, "Operational Federalism," p. 14. For a proposal of a "federation of neighborhood police forces" without any explicit treatment of relevant political theory, see A. I. Waskow, "Community Control of the Police," in 7 *Transaction* 4 (December, 1969).
57. J. Q. Wilson, "What Makes a Better Policeman," in *The Atlantic Monthly* (March, 1969), p. 135.
58. See W. Z. Hirsch, "The Supply of Urban Public Services," in H. S. Perloff and L. Wingo, Jr., eds., *Issues in Urban Economics* (1968), pp. 477–525. Hirsch summarizes a number of studies of police service provision, all of which had the same conclusion: "No significant economics of scale were found" (p. 505). See also E. Ostrom, "The Effect of Institutional Arrangements in Citizen Evaluation of Urban Police Performance" (Bloomington, Ind., unpublished manuscript, Table 1, p. 17).
59. Skolnick, *Justice without Trial.*
60. Ibid., p. 13.
61. Ibid., p. 266.
62. See W. H. Starbuck, "Organizational Growth and Development," in J. G. March, *Handbook of Organizations* (1965), pp. 451–534. See also Tullock, *The Politics of Bureaucracy,* for consideration of size as a variable in organizational behavior.
63. F. F. Piven and R. A. Cloward, "Black Control of the Cities: Heading It Off by Metropolitan Government," in *The New Republic* (September 30, 1968).
64. Fogelson, pp. 232–233.
65. Ibid., p. 237.
66. *Report of the National Advisory Commission on Civil Disorders,* p. 321.
67. Raine, pp. 3–28.
68. "Recruitment of Negroes as Policemen Falls Off," in Louisville *Courier-Journal,* January 25, 1971, p. 1.
69. *Task Force Report: The Police for The President's Commission on Law Enforcement and the Administration of Justice,* (Washington: U.S. Government Printing Office, 1967), p. 124.
70. Ibid., p. 70.
71. Ibid., p. 68.
72. Ibid., p. 72.
73. Ibid., p. 46.
74. Quoted in Skolnick, p. 240.
75. E. Cahn, "Law in the Consumer Perspective," 112 *University of Pennsylvania Law Review* 1 (November, 1963).
76. Skolnick, p. 240.

77. *Task Force Report: The Police*, pp. 98-109. For a comprehensive analysis of the "Lakewood Plan," see R. Q. Warren, *Governments in Metropolitan Regions: A Reappraisal of Fractionated Political Organization* (1966).
78. See "The Service Style," in J. Q. Wilson, *Varieties of Police Behavior*, pp. 200-226.
79. Ibid., pp. 204-206.
80. Ibid., p. 206.
81. Ibid., pp. 286-290.
82. Ibid., p. 290.
83. G. Wills, *The Second Civil War: Arming for Armegeddon* (1968).
84. J. Q. Wilson, *Varieties*, p. 298.
85. Ibid., p. 288.
86. Ibid., p. 233; emphasis added.
87. Ibid., p. 297.
88. Ibid., p. 298.
89. See Fogelson, pp. 233-235; also, *Report of the Task Force: The Police*, pp. 147-149.
90. J. Barbour, "Crime Stalks the Ghetto Streets, and the Negro Suffers," in the Louisville *Courier-Journal* (July 26, 1970), p. B-11.
91. Ibid.
92. C. V. Hamilton, "The Silent Black Majority," in the *New York Times Magazine* (May 10, 1970), p. 42.
93. J. Q. Wilson, *Varieties*, p. 290.
94. Ibid., p. 291.
95. G. Misner, "The Response of Police Agencies," in *Protest in the Sixties* 382 *The Annals*.
96. J. Q. Wilson, *Varieties*, p. 228.
97. *Task Force Report: The Police*, p. 145.
98. See Fogelson, pp. 217-247; see also *Report of the National Advisory Commission on Civil Disorders*, pp. 299-312.

8: The Kefauver Committee and Organized Crime

1. See in particular J. L. Albini, *The American Mafia: Genesis of a Legend* (1971); F. A. J. Ianni, *A Family Business: Kinship and Social Control in Organized Crime* (1972); H. Nelli, *The Business of Crime: Italians and Syndicate Crime in the United States* (1976); and D. C. Smith, Jr., *The Mafia Mystique* (1975). This article is largely based on materials published in W. H. Moore, *The Kefauver Committee and the Politics of Crime, 1950-1952* (1974). Additional manuscript work reflected in this study was completed in the summer of 1977 with the financial assistance of the National Endowment for the Humanities.
2. Ianni, *Family Business*, p. 192; Smith, *Mafia Mystique*, pp. 325-326, 330-331; "War on Organized Crime Faltering—Federal Strike Force Not Getting the Job Done," *Report to the Congress by the Comptroller General* (1977), pp. i, 8-9. A 1971 Louis Harris poll revealed that while about 80 percent of Americans believed there was a Mafia organization involved in organized crime in the United States, most did not think it was necessarily dominated by Italian-Americans. Chicago *Tribune*, May 17, 1971.
3. Moore, *Kefauver Committee*, pp. 44-49, 85-87, 115.
4. G. Tyler, ed., *Organized Crime in America: A Book of Readings* (1962), pp. 323-336, 344-347; Albini, *American Mafia*, pp. 167-173; Nelli, *Business of Crime*, pp. 3-23; Ianni, *Family Business*, pp. 17-47.

5. Albini, *American Mafia*, p. 175; Smith, *Mafia Mystique*, pp. 27–61; Nelli, *The Italians in Chicago, 1880–1930: A Study in Ethnic Mobility* (1970), pp. 126–146; G. C. Speranza, "Petrosino and the Black Hand," *The Survey* (April 1909), pp. 11–14; "The Black Hand Scourge," *Cosmopolitan Magazine* (June 1909), pp. 31–41; G. E. Pozzeta, "Another Look at the Petrosino Affair," 1 *Italian Americana* 86 (1974).

6. Smith, *Mafia Mystique*, pp. 86–89. Important members of the Capone gang were Jack ("Greasy Thumb") Guzik, a Jew, and Murray ("The Camel") Humphreys, of Welsh descent. Historian Mark Haller has estimated that twice as many leading bootleggers were Jewish as were of Italian extraction. Haller, "Bootleggers and American Gambling, 1920–1950," Commission on the Review of the National Policy toward Gambling, *Gambling in America*, appendix 1 (1977), pp. 102–143.

7. Ibid., pp. 115–116; *Cleveland Plain Dealer*, December 6, 1928; Nelli, *Business of Crime*, pp. 214–216.

8. Moore, *Kefauver Committee*, pp. 21–24.

9. Haller, "Bootleggers and American Gambling," pp. 109–114, 133; Nelli, *The Business of Crime*, pp. 219–253.

10. Moore, *Kefauver Committee*, pp. 21–22, 31–32, 115. Some commentators have suggested that Anslinger developed the Mafia scare in the 1930's as a counter to the publicity J. Edgar Hoover had created for the F.B.I. through his crackdown on midwestern bank robbers and auto thieves. R. King, *The Drug Hang-Up* (1972), p. 115; S. J. Ungar, *FBI* (1976), p. 422.

11. Peterson testimony, *Hearings before the Special Committee to Investigate Organized Crime in Interstate Commerce*, 81st Cong., 2nd sess. (1950), pt. 2, pp. 127, 159, 160, 162, 170–172, 175–187, 135–155; Moore, *Kefauver Committee*, pp. 34–41, 91–96, 97–98, 100–102, 110–113.

12. H. Asbury, "America's Number One Mystery Man," *Collier's* (April 12, 1947), pp. 16–17, 26–33 and (April 19, 1947), pp. 333–344; *Newsweek* (November 21, 1949), p. 31; *Time* (October 17, 1949), p. 27; J. A. Bell, "Frank Costello: Statesman of the Underworld," *The American Mercury* (August, 1950), pp. 131–137. See also L. Katz, *Uncle Frank: The Biography of Frank Costello* (1973), pp. 109–130.

13. J. Lait and L. Mortimer, *Chicago Confidential* (1950), pp. 181–182, 176; Lait and Mortimer, *U.S.A. Confidential* (1952), pp. 29, 44–46.

14. Lait and Mortimer, *Chicago Confidential*, pp. 176–178; Memorandum from Robinson to Halley, May 9, 1950; undated, "Suggested Program for Initial Committee Investigations," box 41, and Peterson to Kefauver, July 25, 1950, box 128, Kefauver Committee Records, Record Group 46, National Archives, Washington, D.C. The committee never completely resolved questions about the role of certain radio stations in disseminating horse-racing information. See Wayne Coy to Kefauver, July 18, 1950, box 46, Memorandum from Robinson to Halley, November 30, 1950, box 40, and the "Liberty Mutuel Broadcasting Co." file, box 96, Kefauver Committee Records.

15. Halley to Peterson, July 27, 1950, box 21, Kefauver Committee Records; Moore, *Kefauver Committee*, pp. 87–113.

16. Gizzo testimony, *Crime Hearings*, pt. 4-A, pp. 285–305; *Third Interim Report* of the Special Committee to Investigate Organized Crime in Interstate Commerce, 82nd Cong., 1st sess. (1951), pp. 34–36, 88, 40–41. Sheriff Clancy insisted that he, and "no syndicate" or "Mafia," ran things in Jefferson Parish. When possible violence seemed to be developing among competing slot machine operators, Clancy claimed he called them in and had it stopped "at once." *New Orleans Item*, October 12, 1950.

17. Follmer testimony, *Crime Hearings*, pt. 4-A, pp. 418–423, pt. 4, pp. 81–100. The tone of the Follmer dictaphone conversation among two Kansas City underlings

was critical of the power and money of the more prestigious gang figures such as Paul ("The Waiter") Ricca and the extravagant "protection" charged by various local officials. Ibid., pp. 86–87.

18. Gizzo testimony, ibid., pt. 4-A, pp. 492, 504, 508–510, 513, 521, 288–289, 295–296, 299–300, 127–129; G. Hawkins, "God and the Mafia," 14 *The Public Interest* 26 (Winter 1969); D'Andrea testimony, *Crime Hearings,* pt. 5, pp. 346–372. Despite the qualifications in D'Andrea's testimony, the *Knoxville News-Sentinel* claimed that he "sang" about the Mafia before the committee; *Knoxville News-Sentinel,* October 8, 1950.

19. Ahern and Cahill testimony, *Crime Hearings,* pt. 10, pp. 494–503. Memorandum from John Burling to W. D. Amis, January 18, 1951, box 136. Memorandum from Halley to Kefauver, November 30, 1950, and Memorandum from Burling to Halley, January 25, 1951, box 23; Memorandum from George A. Fickeissen to Halley and Robinson, December 11, 1950, box 137; Robinson to Sheriff C. V. Kern, December 18, 1950, box 149; all in Kefauver Committee Records.

20. Beasley testimony, *Crime Hearings,* pt. 1-A, pp. 167–186, 86–87.

21. Moore, *Kefauver Committee,* pp. 129–130; Unlabeled, undated newsclipping, box 134, Kefauver Committee Records.

22. *Providence Journal,* November 2, 1950; *New Orleans States,* January 25, 1951; Kiley to Kefauver, n.d., crime box 37, Estes Kefauver Papers, University of Tennessee, Knoxville.

23. *Third Interim Report,* pp. 149–150.

24. L. Velie, "Rudolph Halley—How He Nailed America's Racketeers," *Collier's* (May 19, 1951), p. 82; Rufus King, "The Control of Organized Crime in America," 4 *Stanford Law Review* 52n4 (December, 1951); "Meet the Press," April 1, 1951, viewing print in Motion Picture Division, Library of Congress; *Congressional Record,* September 25, 1951, pp. A5840–5842; Virgil W. Peterson, interview at home, Riverside, Illinois, July 22, 1970; Peterson to author, October 7, 1974.

25. Technically, the committee was prohibited by the Senate from making recommendations for changes in the state gambling laws, but Kefauver felt no compunction against recommending that states *not change* their antigambling positions. Supposedly the committee reached this conclusion after a superficial two-day hearing in Nevada, but the senators long before had accepted Peterson's antilegalization arguments. In fact, among the approximately 1,000 witnesses, not one appeared for the purpose of advocating legalization.

26. F. M. Thrasher, *The Gang: A Study of 1,313 Gangs in Chicago* (1927); W. F. Whyte, *Street Corner Society: The Social Structure of an Italian Slum* (1943); E. H. Sutherland, *White Collar Crime* (1949).

27. Moore, *Kefauver Committee,* p. 134; *The Challenge of Crime in a Free Society: A Report by the President's Commission on Law Enforcement and the Administration of Justice* (1969), pp. 448–456.

28. F. A. J. Ianni, *Black Mafia: Ethnic Succession in Organized Crime* (1974), pp. 11–22; Nelli, *Business of Crime,* pp. 264–265; Hawkins, "God and the Mafia," pp. 32–51.

29. D. Bell, "The Myth of the Cosa Nostra," *The New Leaders* (December 23, 1963), pp. 12–15; Albini, *American Mafia,* pp 221–261; Hawkins, "God and the Mafia," pp. 32–51; Smith, *Mafia Mystique,* pp. 152–188; H. Messick, *John Edgar Hoover* (1972), pp. 188–205.

9: Criminal Justice History as a Field of Research

1. President's Commission on Law Enforcement and Administration of Justice, *The Challenge of Crime in a Free Society* (1967), p. 273.

2. U.S. Department of Justice, *LEAA 1973* (1973), Vol. 2, p. 106; U.S. Department of Justice, *Sixth Annual Report of LEAA* (1974), Vol. 4, pp. 208–215.

3. T. F. Adams, *Introduction to the Administration of Justice: An Overview of the Justice System and Its Components* (1975); N. C. Chamelin, V. Fox, and P. M. Whisenand, *Introduction to Criminal Justice* (1975); G. F. Cole, ed., *Criminal Justice: Law and Politics* (1972) and *The American System of Criminal Justice* (1975); G. T. Felkenes, *The Criminal Justice System: Its Functions and Personnel* (1973); E. H. Johnson, *Crime, Correction, and Society* (1974); J. Kaplan, *Criminal Justice: Introductory Cases and Materials* (1973); H. B. Kerper, *Introduction to the Criminal Justice System* (1972); R. H. Moore, T. Marks, and R. V. Barrow, eds., *Readings in Criminal Justice* (1976); H. W. More, Jr., and R. Chang, eds., *Contemporary Criminal Justice* (1974); D. J. Newman, *Introduction to Criminal Justice* (1975); R. Quinney, ed., *Crime and Justice in Society* (1969) and *Criminal Justice in America: A Critical Understanding* (1974); J. N. Swaton and L. Morgan, *Administration of Justice* (1975); H. J. Vetter and C. E. Simonsen, *Criminal Justice in America: The System, the Process, the People* (1976).
4. Cole (1972), Kerper, More and Chang, Newman, and Vetter and Simonsen. Johnson, pp. 169–204, 397–418.
5. Johnson, pp. 169–204, 397–418.
6. Quinney (1969).
7. Ibid., pp. 33–105, and Quinney (1974), pp. 2–126, 152–169, 263–274, 299–322, 340–389.
8. More, Marks, and Burrow, pp. 42–52, 81–93, 357–372.
9. C. C. Howard, comp., *Criminal Justice Undergraduate Programs Catalog* (1975); R. W. Kobetz, *Law Enforcement and Criminal Justice Education: Directory, 1975-1976* (1975).
10. E. Viano, ed., *Criminal Justice Research* (1975).
11. H. K. Becker and G. T. Felkenes, *Law Enforcement: A Selected Bibliography* (1974); D. L. C. C. Tompkins, comp., *Court Organization and Administration: A Bibliography* (1973), and *The Prison and the Prisoner* (1972); M. E. Wolfgang, R. M. Figlio, and T. P. Thornberry, *Criminology Index: Research and Theory in Criminology in the United States, 1945-1972* (1975).
12. L. M. Friedman, *A History of American Law* (1973); M. J. Horowitz, "The Conservative Tradition in the Writing of American Legal History," 17 *Journal of Legal History* 275 (1973).
13. R. Pound, *An Introduction to the Philosophy of Law* (1922), *Outline of Lectures on Jurisprudence* (1928), *Criminal Justice in America* (1930), *Social Control Through Law* (1942); J. Hall, *Living Law of Democratic Society* (1949), *Theft, Law, and Society* (1952), *Foundations of Jurisprudence* (1973).
14. J. Goebel, Jr., and R. T. Naughton, *Law Enforcement in Colonial New York: A Study in Criminal Procedure, 1664-1776* (1970 repr. of 1944 ed.); "King's Law and Local Custom in Seventeenth Century New England," 31 *Columbia Law Review* 417 (1931).
15. W. S. Holdsworth, *A History of English Law*, 14 vols. (1922–1952); L. Radzinowicz, *A History of English Criminal Law and Its Administration from 1750*, 4 vols. (1948–1968); J. F. Stephen, *A History of the Criminal Law of England*, 3 vols. (1883).
16. Radzinowicz (1948–1968).
17. C. Reith, *The Police Idea: Its History and Evolution in England in the Eighteenth Century and After* (1938), *British Police and the Democratic Ideal* (1942), *Blind Eye of History: A Study of the Origins of the Present Police Era* (1952), *A New Study of Police History* (1956).
18. T. A. Critchley, *A History of Police in England and Wales, 900-1966* (1967).
19. W. Lee, *History of Police in England* (1970 repr. of 1901 ed.).
20. W. R. Miller, "Police Authority in London and New York City, 1830–1870," 8 *Journal of Social History* 81 (1975).
21. J. F. Richardson, *The New York Police: Colonial Times to 1901* (1970), pp. 16–17.

22.   J. J. Tobias, *Crime and Industrial Society in the Nineteenth Century* (1968), *Nineteenth-Century Crime in England: Prevention and Punishment* (1972).
23.   J. Bellamy, *Crime and Public Order in England in the Later Middle Ages* (1973).
24.   L. O. Pike, *History of Crime in England, Illustrating the Changes of the Laws in the Progress of Civilization*, 2 vols. (1968).
25.   J. Samaha, *Law and Order in Historical Perspective: The Case of Elizabethan Essex* (1974).
26.   B. Abel Smith and R. Stevens, *Lawyers and the Courts: A Sociological Study of the English Legal System, 1750-1965* (1967); J. Demos, *A Little Commonwealth: Family Life in Plymouth Colony* (1970); K. T. Erikson, *Wayward Puritans: A Study in the Sociology of Deviance* (1969); M. J. Horan, "Political Economy and Sociological Theory as Influences upon Judicial Policy Making: The Civil Rights Case of 1883," 16 *Journal of Legal History* 71 (1972).
27.   J. T. Sellin, *Pioneering in Penology: Houses of Correction in the Sixteenth and Seventeenth Century* (1944).
28.   H. E. Barnes, *Repression of Crime: Studies in Historical Penology* (1969 repr. of 1926 ed.), *The Story of Punishment: A Record of Man's Inhumanity to Man* (1972 repr. of 1930 ed.), *A History of the Penal, Reformatory, and Correctional Institutions of the State of New Jersey: Analytical and Documentary* (1974 repr. of 1918 ed.).
29.   N. K. Teeters, *The Cradle of the Penitentiary: The Walnut Street Jail at Philadelphia, 1773-1835* (1955), and J. D. Shearer, *Prison at Philadelphia: Cherry Hill; The Separate System of Penal Discipline: 1829-1913* (1957).
30.   G. O. Mueller, *Crime, Law, and the Scholars: A History of Scholarship in American Criminal Law* (1969).
31.   S. Schafer, *Theories in Criminology: Past and Present Philosophies of the Crime Problem* (1969).
32.   S. F. Sylvester, comp., *The Heritage of Modern Criminology* (1972).
33.   G. G. Killinger and P. F. Cromwell, Jr., *Penology: The Evolution of Corrections in America* (1973).
34.   B. McKelvey, *American Prisons: A Study in American Social History Prior to 1915* (1936).
35.   O. F. Lewis, *The Development of American Prisons and Prison Customs* (1967 repr. of 1922 ed.).
36.   J. L. Carey, "A History of the Indiana Penitentiary System, 1821-1933," unpublished Ph.D. dissertation, Ball State University (1966); M. T. Carleton, "The Political History of the Louisiana State Penitentiary, 1835-1968," unpublished Ph.D. dissertation, Louisiana State University (1971); H. Crow, "A Political History of the Texas Penal System, 1829-1951," unpublished Ph.D. dissertation, University of Texas (1964); R. S. Janowitz, "Corrections in New York State Institutions, 1945-1968 and Vocational Rehabilitation, a Synthesis," unpublished Ph.D. dissertation, New York University (1972); T. O. Murton, "The Alaska Penal and Correctional Institutions in Transition, 1952-1967," unpublished Ph.D. dissertation, University of California at Berkeley (1968); G. Thomason, "The History of Penal Institutions in the Rocky Mountain West, 1846-1900," unpublished Ph.D. dissertation, University of Colorado (1965).
37.   M. T. Carleton, *Politics and Punishment: The History of the Louisiana State Penal System* (1971).
38.   D. J. Rothman, *The Discovery of the Asylum: Social Order and Disorder in the New Republic* (1971).
39.   See, for example, D. Lewis, *From Newgate to Dannemora: The Rise of the Penitentiary in New York, 1796-1848* (1965).
40.   W. J. Mathias and S. Anderson, *From Horse to Helicopter: First Century of the Atlanta Police Department* (1973); R. Lane, *Policing the City: Boston,*

1822-1885 (1967); J. F. Richardson, *The New York Police: Colonial Times to 1901* (1970), and *Urban Police in the United States* (1974).
41. Mathias and Anderson (1973).
42. J. F. Richardson, *Urban Police in the United States* (1974).
43. J. F. Richardson, *The New York Police: Colonial Times to 1901* (1970).
44. Lane, 1967.
45. J. Q. Wilson, *Varieties of Police Behavior: The Management of Law and Order in Eight Communities* (1969).
46. T. N. Ferdinand, "Politics, the Police and Arresting Policies in Salem, Massachusetts since the Civil War," 19 *Social Problems* 572 (1972); M. H. Haller, "Urban Crime and Criminal Justice," 17 *Journal of American History* 619 (1970), and "Historical Roots of Behavior: Chicago, 1890–1925," 10 *Law and Society Review* 303 (1976); C. D. Robinson, "The Mayor and the Police: The Political Role of the Police in Society," in G. L. Morse, ed., *Political Forces in History* (1975).
47. S. L. Harring and L. M. McMullin, "The Buffalo Police, 1872–1900: Labor Unrest, Political Power, and the Creation of the Police Institution," 4 *Crime and Social Justice* 5 (1975).
48. A. Silver, "The Demand for Order in Civil Society: A Review of Some Themes in the History of Urban Crime, Police, and Riots," in D. Bordua, ed., *The Police: Six Sociological Essays* (1967).
49. J. S. Auerbach, "The LaFollette Committee and the C.I.O.," 48 *Wisconsin Magazine of History* 1 (1965); S. Fine, *Sit Down: The General Motors Strike of 1936–37* (1969).
50. A small beginning is found in G. Kaplan, "Reflections on the Nationalization of Crime, 1964–68," *Law and the Social Order* (1973).
51. H. Cummings and C. McFarland, *Federal Justice: Chapters in the History of Justice and the Federal Executive* (1937).
52. G. E. Carte and E. A. Carte, *Police Reform in the United States: The Era of August Vollmer* (1975); William J. Bopp, *O. W.: O. W. Wilson and the Search for a Police Profession* (1977).
53. K. Mayo, *Justice to All: The Story of the Pennsylvania State Police* (1971 repr. of 1917 ed.).
54. L. J. Coakley, *Jersey Troopers: A Fifty-Year History of the New Jersey State Police* (1971).
55. R. F. Adams, *Burrs under the Saddle: A Second Look at Books and Histories of the West* (1964), and *Six-Guns and Saddle Leather: A Bibliography of Books and Pamphlets on Western Outlaws and Gunmen* (1969).
56. G. Shirley, *Law West of Fort Smith: A History of Frontier Justice in the Indian Territory, 1834–1896* (1957).
57. P. D. Jordan, *Frontier Law and Order: Ten Essays* (1971).
58. F. R. Prassel, *The Western Peace Officer: The Legacy of Law and Order* (1972).
59. E. G. Brown, "Frontier Justice: Wayne County, 1796–1836," 16 *American Journal of Legal History* 126 (1972); D. P. Kommers, "Law and Justice in Pre-Territorial Wisconsin," 8 *Journal of Legal History* 20 (1964).
60. W. E. Hollon, *Frontier Violence: Another Look* (1974).
61. R. R. Dykstra, *The Cattle Towns* (1968).
62. F. L. Faust and P. Brantingham, ed., *Juvenile Justice Philosophy: Readings, Cases and Comments* (1974).
63. A. Platt, *The Child Savers: The Invention of Delinquency* (1969).
64. E. Currie, "Dialogue with Anthony Platt," 8 *Issues in Criminology* 19 (1973).
65. R. M. Mennel, *Thorns and Thistles: Juvenile Delinquents in the United States, 1825–1940* (1973); J. M. Hawes, *Children in Urban Society: Juvenile Delinquency in the Nineteenth Century* (1971).
66. R. H. Bremmer, *Children and Youth in America: A Documentary History*, 3 vols. (1971–1974).

67.   R. M. Ireland, "The Place of the Justice of the Peace in the Legislative and Party System of Kentucky, 1792–1850," 13 *Journal of Legal History* 202 (1969).
68.   H. F. Ball, "Research in Progress in Legal History" 18 *Journal of Legal History* 332 (1974); D. B. Nunis, Jr., comp., "Historical Studies in United States Legal History, 1950–1959: A Bibliography of Articles Published in Scholarly Non-Law Journals," 7 *Journal of Legal History* (1963).
69.   S. M. Ames, *County Court Records of Accomack-Northampton, Virginia, 1640–1645* (1973); J. H. Smith, ed., *Colonial Justice in Western Massachusetts: The Pynchon Court Records* (1961); J. H. Smith and P. A. Crawl, eds., *Court Records of Prince Georges County, Maryland, 1696–1699* (1964).
70.   D. H. Flaherty, "A Select Guide to the Manuscript Court Records of Colonial Virginia," 19 *Journal of Legal History* 112 (1975), and "A Select Guide to the Manuscript Records of Colonial New England," 11 *Journal of Legal History* 107 (1967); W. Jeffery, "Early New England Court Records,"1 *Journal of Legal History* 119 (1957); M. G. Kammen, "Colonial Court Records and the Study of Early American History: A Bibliographic Review," 70 *American Historical Review* 732 (1965).
71.   R. M. Ireland, *The County Courts in Antebellum Kentucky* (1972).
72.   E. C. Surrency, "The Evolution of an Urban Judicial System: The Philadelphia Story, 1683–1968," 18 *Journal of Legal History* 95 (1974). See also E. C. Surrency, "The Courts in the American Colonies," 11 *Journal of Legal History* 253 (1967).
73.   D. Greenberg, "The Effectiveness of Law Enforcement in Eighteenth-Century New York," 19 *Journal of Legal History* 173 (1975).
74.   J. K. Williams, *Vogues in Villainy: Crime and Retribution in Antebellum South Carolina* (1959).
75.   R. Lane, "Crime and Criminal Statistics in Nineteenth-Century Massachusetts," 2 *Journal of Social History* 156 (1968).
76.   L. M. Friedman and R. V. Percival, "A Tale of Two Courts: Litigation in Alameda and San Benito Counties," 10 *Law and Society Review* 267 (1976).
77.   G. R. Newman, ed., "Crime and Justice in America, 1776–1976," 432 *Annals of the American Academy of Political and Social Sciences* (1976).
78.   H. S. Hughes, *History as Art and Science: Twin Vistas of the Past* (1964), pp. 1–21, 86; J. Higham, L. Krieger, and F. Gilbert, *History: The Development of Historical Studies in the United States* (1965), pp. 145–232.
79.   L. T. Wilkins, "Crime and Criminal Justice at the Turn of the Century," in R. Moore, Jr., T. Marks, and R. V. Barrow, eds., *Readings in Criminal Justice* (1976); V. Clear and S. Clear, "Horizons in the Criminal Justice System," ibid.